PRINCESS ALEXANDRA

Helen Cathcart

SAPERE
BOOKS

PRINCESS ALEXANDRA

Published by Sapere Books.

20 Windermere Drive, Leeds, England, LS17 7UZ,
United Kingdom

saperebooks.com

ISBN: 978-1-80055-517-4.

TABLE OF CONTENTS

PRELUDE   7
1: THE ABDICATION BABY   8
2: "MARA MAMA"   37
3: A WARTIME CHILDHOOD   58
TOCCATA   79
4: GROWING PAINS   80
5: THE TEENAGE PRINCESS   103
6: A PRINCESS IN KENSINGTON   131
FUGUE   151
7: THE NURSE, THE COLONEL AND THE
TRAVELLER   152
8: THE WHIRLPOOL OF THE HEART   182
9: ANGUS   201
10: MRS. ANGUS OGILVY   230
11: THE BALANCED LEDGERS   245
ACKNOWLEDGEMENTS   259
A NOTE TO THE READER   261

PRELUDE

"The term may be said to imply no formal restrictions."
— *Grove's Dictionary of Music*

1: THE ABDICATION BABY

I

Over much of Britain it had been the sunniest December on record, in spite of the fog and drizzle that had darkened the setting and circumstance of the Abdication. The months of sustained and intense public excitement had ended and the departure of Edward VIII had assuaged "the shock and strain of it all", to use the words that the new King George VI confided to his assistant private secretary, Sir Godfrey Thomas. Fourteen days later all was calm and, in the pale frosty sunlight of Christmas morning, an itinerant musician played a penny whistle in Belgrave Square.

A period touch clings to the remembrance of that shabby figure and his forlorn choice of instrument. There were beggars innumerable in the London of 1936, with more than a million-and-a-half unemployed, painfully clambering from the gulf of economic depression. Attracted by the line of parked cars outside No. 3, opposite the great plane trees in the north-east corner of the Square, the ragged performer optimistically addressed his hopes to the group of waiting photographers and pressmen. And so, at 11.30 a.m. on December 25th, 1936, the reporters seized the sugary though realistic fact that Princess Alexandra of Kent was born to the distant fluting of a Christmas carol.

Yet, in truth, street sounds were far-off and muted in the lush second-floor bedroom where three doctors and two nurses royally attended the mother. The new baby came to the light of Christmas morning, it would seem, in an elegant bed of Directoire style, beneath a canopy hung with silk of peach and tea-green stripes. But now the handsome room was prepared for effort and advent rather than rest, the atmosphere was aseptic rather than rich, and the cushioned *chaise-longue* had been pushed aside for the surgeon's trolley.

One of the nurses afterwards wryly recollected the panels of mirror-glass that walled a broad alcove almost from floor to ceiling, presenting the illusion of a stage, its depths disconcertingly reflecting every move she and her colleagues made. She had never before seen it all done with mirrors and, though absorbed at the time, she thought of herself later as being like a dancer in a ballet of nativity. Perhaps it would not be amiss to deepen the fantasy by peopling that looking-glass world with less positive images, with an impalpable company of czars and empresses, kings and queens, grand dukes and princes, awaiting this Christmas child, a princess of their blood.

Genetically the new baby compounded the chromosomes of the Empress Catherine and Queen Victoria, the genes of Romanoffs and Hanoverians, intermixed with Saxe-Coburg-Gotha and Mecklenburg-Schwerin, and blended with the Danish house of Schleswig-Holstein-Sonderburg-Glucksberg-Beck and with the dynasties of Saxony and Teck and Windsor. Through her mother, the new Princess was only seven generations removed from Catherine the Great of Russia and thus descended from the impetuous Emperor Paul I. Through her father, she stemmed four generations from her great-great-grandmother Queen Victoria, the obstinate and dutiful, and through six generations from King George III. Her paternal grandfather was, of course, King George V, the sunset of whose death had occurred at Sandringham eleven months before she was born.

It was in April, 1936, that Princess Marina, the Duchess of Kent, confided to her eldest sister, Olga, in Belgrade, her hopes of having another baby. Her other child, her baby son, Prince Edward, was then six months old. Back in London, it amused the elegant young mother — then in her thirtieth year — to keep her secret from the public. In May, her duties included an indefatigable deck-by-deck tour of the liner *Queen Mary* before the ship sailed on the maiden voyage. In June, the adoring and inquisitive public knew nothing of Marina's health except that she had endured an unpleasant session with the dentist. In July, consideration for the Duchess may have dictated the somewhat strange protocol of King Edward VIII's garden parties at which the royal ladies gathered under the silken Durbar canopy and remained somewhat aloof and secret from the general company. The expectant mother's summer holiday with Princess Olga and her husband, Prince Paul, at their mountain villa in Yugoslavia further triumphantly postponed discovery; but Queen Mary felt that there should be at least a four-months retirement and in the autumn, after leaving Balmoral, the secret was out. "Her Royal Highness The Duchess of Kent has cancelled her forthcoming engagements," it was announced, "and she will not be undertaking any further functions…"

As it happened, an exception had to be made for the macabre and unnecessary funeral of her grandmama, Queen Olga of the Hellenes, who had been dead ten years, and of her aunt and uncle, King Constantine and his Queen Sophia, who had been defunct for thirteen and six years respectively. Dying in exile, during the temporary effacement of the Greek monarchy, their bodies had been ledged in a mausoleum in Florence, where they might have peacefully remained. King Constantine's son, Marina's cousin George II, was however restored to the throne of Greece in 1935, and thereupon he oddly decided within a year to inflict a full state funeral on his rejoicing people by bringing his parents and grandmother home for reburial. These obsequies, so hollow and overdue, were echoed in London, where Princess Marina attended a memorial service at the Greek Orthodox Church in Bayswater only four weeks in fact before her baby arrived. In Athens, another Princess Alexandra — later Alexandra, Queen of Yugoslavia — noted that at the prelude of the ceremonies "aunts, uncles, cousins and all one's kith and kin arrived to drive through streets decked with flags and lined by cheering people". A few days later "the dark drapes of mourning" were erected. At the "final funeral service" another youthful member of the family, then a fifteen-year-old Gordonstoun schoolboy, was so overcome by a blend of food poisoning and nerves at his first State appearance that of necessity he used his top hat as an improvised sick bowl. This quick-witted cousin was the schoolboy Prince Philip, whose father, Prince Andrew, had stood as Guard of Honour with Marina's father, Prince Nicholas, at the triple bier.

Again, at all the cheerful family parties incongruously centred around these obsequies, Prince Philip had conspicuously asked questions about all his royal relations, as if discovering his own importance in the Greek succession for the first time. Prince and Princess Nicholas of Greece then hurried to join their daughter in London in the ferment of the Abdication, and no doubt heard the final irrevocable broadcast of Prince Edward of Windsor as the ex-monarch (now as the Duke of Windsor) was announced at the microphone. The abdicated King had dwelt on his brother's "one matchless blessing enjoyed by so many of you and not bestowed on me — a happy home with his wife and children". Although he was referring to the new King George VI, the nation inevitably thought also of his younger brother, the handsome Prince George, Duke of Kent.

As Christmas approached and the Royal Family re-formed its ranks and prepared for the traditional family holiday at Sandringham, the Duke and Duchess of Kent considered it prudent to remain at their town house in Belgrave Square, although the baby was not anticipated until the New Year. It would be a quiet Christmas, with the expectant mother's parents and only two or three close friends. The Duke was due however to make a broadcast to the Empire for the centenary of South Australia at nine a.m. on December 28th, and on Christmas Eve Post Office engineers invaded the house with cables and equipment. The intrusion perhaps disturbed the meticulous Duchess, anxious for the perfection of her Christmas arrangements. Her physician from St. Bart's, Dr. A. E. Gow, was summoned with the first light of dawn on Christmas Day, and he in turn called the gynaecologist, Mr. (later Sir) William Gilliatt, and the anaesthetist, Mr. H. A. Richards. Meanwhile, it was the harassed father's secretary, Mr. John Lowther, rather than the Duke of Kent himself, who remembered to telephone the Home Secretary, Sir John Simon, for what was considered the constitutional necessity of his presence in the house for a royal birth. Sir John hurried up from his home at Walton-on-the-Hill without having his breakfast. At all events this was more convenient than the birth of Prince Edward of Kent, fifteen months earlier, when he had been summoned from his bed shortly after midnight and forced to dress, travel and sit up through the small hours.

When the Home Secretary reached Belgrave Square at ten a.m., there was still no news. Prince and Princess Nicholas waited nervously in the quiet of the small sitting-room. The reporters were asked into the marble-paved hall for a Christmas drink. In the same way, while awaiting the birth of his son, the previous year, the Duke had served the waiting pressmen coffee and had nervously confessed, with an upward nod of his head, "I can't stand much more of this!" This time, her white-starched aplomb demonstrating that nursery discipline was never to be broken, Nanny Smith wheeled out the little Prince for his morning pram ride; and the kerbside musician obligingly earned a nurse's shilling with a penny whistle rendering of "Good King Wenceslas". The reporters all grew concerned with the probability of getting home in time for their Christmas dinners and with the impetuosity that has heightened her popularity ever since, Princess Alexandra obliged them. At about 11.30, doors opened and closed upstairs and a woman's voice called down the stairwell, "It's a girl".

The birth was an easy one, as the doctors had anticipated for a mother with her second baby, a six-and-a-half pound daughter. At Sandringham, a message was passed to the new King and Queen while they were still in church. The news spread like wildfire and when the Royal Family appeared in the church porch after the service they were given a great ovation. Queen Mary, however, heard the news in her own room, "the only nice thing to have happened this year" as she said. Queen Mary was then in her seventieth year, "happy to be back in her old home". But she was feeling unwell with the personal strain and reaction of the abdication and probably did not realise how closely she would be drawn to her youngest granddaughter.

A minor tradition was nevertheless broken at Sandringham that year, for the new King made no Christmas broadcast to his peoples. Afflicted by a stammer, King George VI felt at first that he could not follow his father's successful custom; and in millions of homes that Christmas Day, people wistfully said that it would be strange not to hear the voice of the old

King. And then, instead, in the one o'clock news bulletin, there came the announcement, agreed by the three doctors, "Her Royal Highness the Duchess of Kent was safely delivered of a daughter at 11.20 this morning. Her Royal Highness and the infant Princess are doing excellently." It was as if the entire nation — and indeed that still sturdy Empire — responded with one voice, "Well, how delightful!" One hundred minutes old, Princess Alexandra thus established her first effective achievement in public relations.

II

Princess Alexandra was born sixth in succession to the Throne. Ahead in line were her cousins, Princess Elizabeth and Princess Margaret, her uncle, the Duke of Gloucester, her father, and of course her elder brother, Prince Edward of Kent. A Princess of the blood royal is received with due honour. At noon on December 26th the customary "Boxing Day" holiday in England, Nurse Louie Roberts, the midwife, felt the windows of her room tremble to the thud of guns, the first salvo of the forty-one gun salute fired by the K Battery of the King's Troop of the Royal Horse Artillery in Hyde Park. Simultaneously, a Territorial gun unit of the Honourable Artillery Company sounded a matching salute from the Tower of London. The Lord Mayor also hastened to his traditional duty of sending congratulations on behalf of the citizens of London and, among other messages, *The Times* singled out the telegram from the Duke of Abercorn on behalf of the people of Northern Ireland. "Grateful thanks," wired back the proud father. "Mother and daughter both doing well."

The Duke of Kent had celebrated his thirty-fourth birthday only five days earlier and to his intimates he announced that the baby girl was the best of birthday gifts. After the Christmas

14

lull of two days without newspapers, the new arrival was also a gift to the Sunday journals, but the tender sentiments of Fleet Street merely echoed the good wishes showered on the newcomer throughout the world. The royal exile, the Duke of Windsor, sent congratulations from Vienna and, illogical as it was, the new Princess seemed to many to be another reassertion of the stability and continuity of the monarchy itself. After breakfast on December 28th the Duke of Kent made his Empire broadcast to commemorate the arrival of the first colonists at Kangaroo Island and the hundred years since the proclamation of the Province of South Australia. His speech was packed with the Imperial sentiments considered suitable in a programme backed by choirs singing "The Song of Australia". But the Duke failed to mention the baby in her cradle upstairs, and thereby decidedly missed a trick with his Australian audience.

In Whitehall, meanwhile, passers-by stopped to read the doctors' second bulletin, posted on the doors of the Home Office. Punctually timed at 11.20 a.m., when the infant was precisely three days old, it announced that "Her Royal Highness the Duchess of Kent and her infant daughter continue to make very good progress". Dated from Whitehall on December 26th but actually issued on December 28th, a *London Gazette Extraordinary* also announced the birth as official news which was hardly a scoop by this time. *The Times* however continued to note the daily progress until a final bulletin on January 4th, when it could be announced that "The Infant Princess is gaining weight steadily". And with this tactless hint of a human vegetable marrow public interest abated.

The Princess had received her first bath in Nurse Roberts' arms in her mother's black and silver bathroom where Joseph Sert's painted shepherds and nymphs stoically watched from their classical landscape. When ablutions were transferred to the nursery bathroom, one of the seven bathrooms that heightened the domestic comfort of 3 Belgrave Square, little Prince Edward looked on in bewilderment. Though only fifteen months old, he showed instant affection for his sister, we are told; and already gushing visitors enjoined him, "You must be good to your little sister while Papa is away." For those who would see the shadow of coming events, the New Year of 1937 was itself only five days old when the young mother found herself temporarily bereft of her husband. As his first duty of King George VI's Coronation Year the Duke of Kent had to attend the wedding at the Hague of Crown Princess Juliana of the Netherlands to Prince Bernhard. The gossips of the day could hardly bear to drop the topic of Princess Marina's baby and cradle-matchers naturally suggested that if Juliana and Bernhard should be blessed in due course with a son an obvious choice for his bride would one day be the new little Princess of Kent.

A more immediate personal ceremony came at six weeks old, with the Princess's christening in the private chapel of Buckingham Palace on February 9th. The day was one of both pomp and informality, for King George VI held the first Levee of his reign at St. James's Palace that same morning and arrived at Belgrave Square with his smiling Queen in time for a family lunch. A night or two earlier, Queen Mary had entertained the young parents to dinner at Marlborough House and had approved the choice of names Alexandra Helen Elizabeth Olga Christabel. Full of memories of thirty-four years earlier when her "Georgie", her fifth and favourite child, had sunned in his pram in the Marlborough House garden, the old Queen similarly did not miss the fact that Queen Victoria's third child, Princess Alice, had been the first to be christened in the newly-consecrated Palace chapel in 1843 and now her own third granddaughter was to be christened in the same private sanctuary.

The conjunction was more apt than she knew, for in 1940 the chapel was wrecked by a bomb in the second Nazi air attack on the Palace, and Princess Alexandra was the last of Queen Victoria's descendants to be named in that unchanged setting. (It was in a new guise, part chapel and part art gallery, the Queen's Gallery, that the reconstructed building served for more recent baptisms after the war.) The centre of the first ceremony in 1843 was the Alice of Hesse whose Mountbatten granddaughter married Prince Andrew of Greece and became the mother of Prince Philip, the Duke of Edinburgh, and Queen Victoria had occasion to note at the christening that the old King of Hanover "arrived just in time to be too late". Now, in the intricate meshwork of royalty, the stork had skipped a generation of cousins and, at Princess Alexandra's christening, Queen Victoria's youngest surviving daughter, Princess Beatrice, was delayed by the aches of her eightieth year from arriving at all and was a godmother by proxy.

Nor was she the only absentee, for a trio of godmothers, besides, waved their wands at long range. The grandmother, Princess Nicholas of Greece, and the baby's Aunt Olga of Yugoslavia, having impeccably supported Princess Marina in the later months, had now not unreasonably returned home. The baby's great-aunt and godmother, Queen Maud of Norway, wrote drily of the compelling need of her presence in Oslo for "the other new arrival" anticipated by her daughter-in-law, Princess Martha, and the boy born twelve days later proved in fact to be Prince Harald, the Heir-Apparent to the Norwegian throne. To some, at the time, this rival birth also seemed full of promise for the Kents, but the days of match-making by cradle were past.

In addition, the baby's Uncle Toto — Marina's Bavarian brother-in-law, Count Toerring — was excused the journey from Munich, and Alexandra's baptism was thus notable for the number of sponsors by proxy. The new King and Queen were, however, godparents in person, and the soldierly figure of the Earl of Athlone — Queen Mary's brother — stood as godfather beside the gold font from Windsor Castle. The lustrous aigrettes, diamond-clasps and boutonnières of the principal guests lacked nothing of royal impress. The witnesses included Queen Mary, the ten-year-old Princess Elizabeth and her awed little sister, Princess Margaret, the Duke and Duchess of Gloucester — newly-weds of little more than a year — Princess Alice of Athlone and the aged Princess Louise of Argyll, Queen Victoria's fourth daughter, who had herself been christened in the Palace chapel in 1848, a remarkable link in time. The Home Secretary was there, also, as indeed were the doctors and nurses and the servants from Coppins and Belgrave Square. The choir boys of the Chapel Royal had filed in, in their red and white cassocks and cottas, and puzzled sounds arose from the youngest guest, Prince Edward of Kent, sixteen months old that very day.

One festive family service in the old private chapel was much like another, amid the cast-iron columns, the sombre crimson and gold flock wallpaper, the gold chairs and red carpeting. Princess Marina fondly remembered it decorated with bridal roses and carnations for her wedding when, after the first ceremony in Westminster Abbey, she and her husband had returned to the Palace to be married under the picturesque Greek Orthodox rites: the hands of bride and groom bound together with a silken scarf, the placing of the nuptial crowns… Now the chapel was decked with spring flowers, for her daughter and, as the baby was proudly borne in by Nurse Smith, a pink little arm flailed at the air.

The infant Princess wore the short-sleeved royal christening robe of white Honiton lace lined with white satin that had been used since the christening of Edward VII — for Alice of Hesse and Louise and Beatrice and babies innumerable — but Nurse Smith was aware that the baby's struggles jeopardised this fragile and pearly heirloom. If the Archbishop of Canterbury, Dr. Lang, had anticipated that the baptism would provide a peaceful domestic interlude between the strife of the Abdication and the spiritual preparation of the Coronation he was faced instead with infant fury. On receiving three scoopfuls of Jordan water, the child resisted so energetically that the assisting Dr. Fisher took a protective step forward. Archbishop Lang had been a friend of the older members of the Royal Family for nearly forty years, and the teasing he genially received on account of Princess Alexandra strengthened the final deep friendships of his life with the young generation. (Eight years later, indeed, he received a Christmas card from the Duchess of Kent on the very last day of his life, and the card was found on his desk after he had collapsed in the street at Kew and been carried unrecognised into the fishmonger's shop where he died.)

But to return to the christening, one guest recalled that the baby "came in with a threatening whimper and went out with a roar". Her brother, Prince Edward, joined her wails in sympathy, and *The Times* next day was solemnly able to record that "the baby cried throughout the ceremony".

This precisely suited the public, who hated to suppose that a baby might be tranquillised for royal formality and were delighted to imagine that Prince George of Kent's two children were lively ones. In every era the popular image of royalty changes and is responsive to the imprint of the changing times. This was the era of the £100 car, the one-child family, of the broadcasting of dance music every night by the bands of the smart West End hotels, and it suited the world to read that the Duke and Duchess of Kent went dancing that very night at the Dorchester, that they "stayed for some time" and that the Duchess looked "quite lovely in black velvet with a silver fox wrap".

The following evening, too, the young parents went to see the play *French Without Tears*, and a few days later, they left for the Continent on a motoring tour, items of news all equally acceptable, for no one wished to think of the pretty, slightly audacious Marina trammelled and tied to the nursery.

Gradually public attention shifted to the first giant panda ever caught alive, and only the local chauffeurs of Belgravia and their wives knew that the baby Princess was taken by car to Buckingham Palace every sunny afternoon for her airing in the Palace gardens. After a six-weeks holiday, the Duke and Duchess of Kent returned unobtrusively to the bustle of preparations for the Coronation, and Princess Alexandra was precisely seven months old when she again burst into public event. This time, too, the effect was dramatic for printed news placards were rushed into the streets with the announcement, ROYAL MOTOR-CAR ACCIDENT.

Travelling to Sandwich in Kent with her children, the Duchess of Kent's chauffeur-driven car had been involved in a collision on Wrotham Hill. It was, in reality, a hair's-breadth miss. All the offside windows were shattered and slivers of glass showered over the Princess as she lay in her travelling cot between her nurse and the Duchess at the back of the car, but no one was harmed, and the baby cooed contentedly while lifted in her basket over a hedge into a meadow. The real distress for her mother came with the discovery that her sapphire engagement ring had slipped from her finger and was missing. She was still searching frantically when the relief car arrived, and she was reluctant to leave. But for this delay the British public might not have discovered that the Kent children were to stay with their nurses overlooking the sands at Bloody House Point. It made another point of contact with the popular-though-foreign-born Marina that she had enjoyed girlhood holidays at Bognor like other English children, and now it was pleasant to discover that even little Alexandra was to be confronted already with the seaside joys of bucket and spade.

The engagement ring was safely retrieved from the hedgerow a day or two later but, for a time, a detective and a burly Kent constable had to protect the children. A freelance press photographer was content to take a view of the empty shelters and tent erected on the beach for the young Kents, and did very well out of it.

III

Undoubtedly, the glitter of Princess Marina's own popularity was seen in the public interest in her baby daughter. Equally, the immediate public affection for Princess Marina reflected the glow of her husband's prestige. Prince George, the Duke of Kent, ranked in national sentiment as Queen Mary's youngest son. (In fact, there had been a still younger boy, Prince John, an epileptic who died in childhood seclusion.) The early nineteen-thirties saw the adoration of the Crown at its apogee, to use Kingsley Martin's phrase, and in the popular conception or illusion of the Royal Family, Prince George, when still a bachelor, was handsome, heart-whole and carefree.

The picture was of a "playboy" with a developed sense of duty, a good sportsman, a good mixer, a good dancer, tall, confident, a Prince Charming; and public opinion would have implied that he was the most engaging of all the King's sons, if one could avow as much without disloyalty to the Prince of Wales.

It may be entertaining, indeed, to trace the beginnings of that public image. Did it originate in the simplicity of the pram glimpsed from the lace-hung windows of Marlborough House? Did a special loyalty devolve upon the infant who awakened to interest amid the splendours of his grandfather's (King Edward VII) post-Coronation year? From the viewpoint of the nineteen-thirties, Prince George ranked as the only adult royalty born within the twentieth century. The day of his birth on December 20th, 1902, placed him twenty-two months beyond the shadow of Queen Victoria. Or was public affection first engaged when, as a nine-year-old in 1911, Queen Mary's alert sense of fitness caused him to appear at his father's Coronation in Highland costume?

The impression had spread that Prince George was the most intelligent of all the royal children. King George V was quoted as saying that his younger son "had the brains of the family" and in his first year at Dartmouth naval college he stood higher in the order of his term than had his two eldest brothers. Unhappily, this early impetus was not maintained, as may be judged from a private letter from the Duke of York (later George VI) in the summer of 1920. "He has kept up the best traditions of my family by passing out of Dartmouth one from bottom, the same as I did!!!!"

The insouciant Midshipman Prince George passed out of public view, first on his training cruise on the battleship *Temeraire* and then with *Iron Duke*, the flagship of the Mediterranean fleet. The Duke of York had been invalided out of the Royal Navy three years earlier, and although Prince George suffered from the same constitutional stomach disorders his gastric troubles were more romantically interpreted as severe bouts of seasickness. His only spell in hospital was for the amputation of his little toes: he suffered from hammer toes and surgeons advised that it would be better to part with the two worst offenders. He recovered in ample time for the first of all the great post-war state pageants, the wedding of his sister, Princess Mary, to Viscount Lascelles in Westminster Abbey, at which he made an appealing figure to the public in his midshipman dress uniform. But when Prince George returned to Malta, he was supposed to be as happy there as his father had been as a young man, although the truth was that he missed the gaiety and bonhomie of London and would much have preferred a shore career at home.

Prince George's distinctive gift in the family was a flair for readily making and keeping a wide circle of friends, a social talent denied at first to his elder brothers, and he probably scored by having been brought up as a junior son, with less sternness and repression. Even the King unbent to him and treated him with an affection and ease never vouchsafed to the other boys. When he was still at Dartmouth, indeed, his father gradually initiated a series of affable letters, explaining and commenting upon the events of the day. "The happiest and greatest event for many years is the signing of the agreement with regard to the settlement of Ireland... It means peace in Ireland. For 700 years the statesmen have all failed to find a solution," King George wrote to him, for example, in a characteristic letter of 1921. "Georgie's" distance from home also encouraged the King into uninhibited confidences on the triumphs or shortcomings of his other sons. "Bertie got through the speech all right, but there were some rather long pauses," runs another typical father-to-son comment after the Duke of York had opened the second season of the British Empire Exhibition at Wembley.

The letters winged or, more often, slowly sailed their way to South Africa, the West Indies, Nova Scotia, Hong Kong and Singapore. "P.G." as he was widely known, served with the battleship *Queen Elizabeth* in the Mediterranean, the cruiser *Hawkins* of the China station, the flagship *Nelson* with the Home Fleet and the destroyer *Mackay* in the North Sea. If in his own letters home he occasionally contrived to hint that he did not feel cut out for the Navy, his overtures evoked no response.

Ultimately, the Prince of Wales came to his rescue by suggesting they should share a visit to Canada in 1927 for the diamond jubilee celebrations of the Dominion. Despite the eight years between them, the two brothers enjoyed the close friendship often found between the oldest and youngest of a family group. "I found in his character qualities that were akin to my own; we laughed at the same thing," the Prince of Wales was to write in his memoirs, when Duke of Windsor. "The two sailors" were greeted in Canada with riotous enthusiasm, and on returning from the lakes, the Rockies and the exhilaration of coyote shooting on horseback near his brother's ranch in Alberta, Prince George shuddered at the thought of his interminable future at sea.

In his misery, he found a sympathiser in Queen Mary's old friend Lady Airlie, who had in fact joined his mother as a lady-in-waiting in the year he was born. "He told me how much he was dreading the next voyage," she wrote not long afterwards. "He wanted to go into the Civil Service or the Foreign Office, but the King would not hear of it... His only reason for refusing is that it has never been done before..."

Lady Airlie shrewdly counselled that argument was a waste of time and would only make the King angry. It would be better, she wisely suggested to the Prince, if he could get the Civil Service examination papers, work on them while at sea and then let his father see the results. The Prince acted on this advice and jubilantly reported to Lady Airlie the following year that both his exams and her strategy had been highly successful.

Prince George retired from the Navy in 1929 with the rank of Commander. After a short spell with the Foreign Office to gain experience, he was then transferred to the Home Office as an Inspector of Factories. Here again it afforded the public a pleasing sense of royal balance to suppose that three of the King's sons were representative of the fighting Services while the fourth served the Civil Service and thus the civilian population. It was encouraging to see that a member of the Royal Family need no longer be content to be politely conducted around a factory, but was armed with real legal power to inspect and amend any shortcomings. Much was said at this time about Prince George inheriting Queen Mary's vigilant eye; but the popularity of his new civilian personality even more mirrored that of the Prince of Wales. This effect was heightened when Prince George moved into rooms at York House, his brother's wing at St. James's Palace, and it was announced that he would join the Heir Apparent's impending "commercial trade mission" to South America. The two brothers assiduously prepared for the eighteen-thousand-mile-tour by studying Spanish together in daily sessions with a London University tutor, yet newspaper readers noted with equal pleasure that the Princes had attended a fancy-dress dance together attired as little boys, an item of gossip in splendid light relief to the undoubted sobriety of the Throne.

The average household, in fact, supported the monarchy on pillars of anecdote, and the world in that pre-war era measured royalty almost solely by the press photograph and gossip column. It was apparent that Prince George was tall and good looking, well-dressed, elegant in the sartorial trend of the day, fun-loving and forward-looking. The daily square inches of newspaper coverage reflected journalistic admiration which in turn built up the beau ideal. Prince George's "press" of the nineteen-thirties tended to report him trying out a car at Brooklands, installing "a wireless set" in his "motorcar" or taking up flying lessons at Northolt in direct rivalry with the Prince of Wales. It was due to Prince George's influence, apparently, that the King and Queen agreed to see "their first talking picture, *The Good Companions*". And the headlines grew wider and deeper when he visited South Africa early in 1934 as "an emissary of Empire" and ebulliently joined in a five-mile run in the hot sun with an athlete who had figured not long before in the South African Olympic team.

At home, Prince George shouldered his own line in royal duty, opening hospitals and town halls, impressionable to any architectural merits, socially facile and extrovert. "George was sharply different in outlook and temperament from the rest of us," the Duke of Windsor has said. "Possessed of unusual charm of manner and a quick sense of humour and talented in many directions, he had an undoubted flair for the arts. He played the piano, knew a good deal about music, and had a knowledgeable eye for antiques. Being somewhat Bohemian by inclination, he had understandably found life in the Navy a bit confining..." With greater social aplomb than his elder brothers Prince George moved in the lighter social-theatrical world of Tilly Losch, June Inverclyde, Adele and Fred Astaire, Noël Coward and Gertrude Lawrence. Even to the Prince of

Wales it was "somewhat Bohemian" of George to disappear into a cinema with a woman friend on a sunny summer afternoon.

The public became obscurely aware of the more romantic side. Queen Mary heard of rumoured flirtations and began to worry about her Georgie's matrimonial future. Her only other married son at that time, the Duke of York, had made a suitable match at twenty-seven, and Prince George at thirty-one had already progressed beyond that family landmark by four years. The Queen's brother, the Earl of Athlone, approached the culprit at dinner one evening with the apparently casual remark, "It's time you thought of getting married…" Prince George said nothing to solace him. He had however already met a girl, royal and beautiful and four years younger than himself, whom he found could not be readily effaced from his mind.

Prince George and Princess Marina of Greece reputedly first met at a dinner party given by the American-born Lady Cunard, that genius among hostesses, although they had in fact briefly seen one another some time earlier when he was a naval sub-lieutenant comically on sick leave after having his tonsils out. Emerald Cunard was adept at making her guests see the best in each other, and George and Marina were minor satellites of her two principal guests of the evening, Marina's eldest sister, Princess Olga, and her husband, Prince Paul of Yugoslavia. The following day, however, Prince George called at Claridge's, and although Princess Olga was out shopping and Princess Marina was at the hairdresser's, he told Prince Paul he was willing to wait. Not long afterwards, according to one chronicler, he confided to a friend, "There's someone with whom I'd be happy to spend the rest of my life. She beats me at most things — and she doesn't give a damn how fast I drive when I take her out in the car."

IV

The British public in 1934 were in need of a fairy tale, given the thesis that an occasional escape from reality may benefit nations as well as individuals. It was the year when Great Britain struggled free from the hunger and distress of the very real and unmanipulated economic depression. It was hailed as a sign of recovery that the muster of two and a half million unemployed shrank by half-a-million, compared with the two million fewer unemployed in Germany or the four million miraculously put into employment in the United States. "Compulsory idleness still remained a grim problem," reported the popular *Daily Mail Year Book*, and then found it "safe to say" that there was "more security for workers" than there had been twenty years earlier. Into this miasma rode St. George in the semblance of Prince George, rescuing a beautiful princess from the dragon of hardship that had dogged her family for years.

When King George V privately noted that Marina was "looking very pretty and charming and will be a great addition to the family", he was precisely echoing not only his consort, Queen Mary, but also the tune of mass sentiment. A waif had been rescued by true love from the turmoil of Europe and brought safe to the bosom of the greatest Royal Family in the world. Or so it seemed to Joe Whelks, of whom Charles Dickens once said that if he could be told a story "by the help of live men and women dressed up, confiding to him their innermost secrets, Joe will unravel a story … and sit there as long as you have anything left to show him."

The announcement of the engagement of Prince George to Princess Marina of Greece and Denmark, the third daughter of Prince and Princess Nicholas, delighted everyone but left millions in doubt. The press faced an initial perplexity in describing the personality and kinship of the foreign princess. "Princess Marina a Great Sport", a *Daily Mail* headline reassured readers and the journalist went on to describe "a tall brunette of infinite charm... She talks English perfectly and is keen on dancing and shooting, of both of which Prince George is very fond. She has visited England on many occasions, and in 1927 attended many dances in London chaperoned by her elder sister, Princess Olga." And in the *Sunday Dispatch* a contributor described as "An Intimate Friend" wrote of the "years of something approaching hardship" and of the Princess's subtle cosmetics, "her complexion only permitted a dusting of a pale, sun-bronze powder".

But the tarnish gathers quickly on hurried journalism, and one recalls that the pressmen were struggling against ineffectual Palace public relations. They had to tunnel against time to discover Princess Marina's early associations with England in her childhood holidays with her English governess at Bognor, and the fact was only gradually excavated that she felt rather better acquainted with England than with the dismantled palaces of St. Petersburg or Athens. Moreover, there were other warm notes for the public organs. Princess Marina's grandfather was that benign King George I of Greece who had been none other than the brother of Queen Alexandra, that beloved bride from over the sea who had also first come to England as a little-known Danish princess. Time had not dissipated the legend, and steadfast hammering on this link by the British press effectively kindled an affectionate welcome for the new royal personality. Prince George's betrothal was announced in the Court Circular of August 28th, 1934, while he was staying in Salzburg with his fiancée and her family. On September 16th Princess Marina landed at Folkestone to the music of the town band, the greeting of the Mayor and the cheers of every man, woman and child who could pack the quays. Along the railway line to London people stood waiting at every vantage point for a glimpse of the Princess and, outside Victoria Station, flowers were thrown in front of her car by the dense, applauding crowds. It was one of the last occasions, historians remind us, when flowers were tossed in front of royal cars in London.

V

The facts about Princess Marina in turn were, of course, dramatic but not quite as the public imagined them. The beautiful newcomer to the Royal Family was more royal by birth, better circumstanced by upbringing and altogether less of a stranger or foreigner than the romantic supposed. It may be convenient to trace beyond the meagre fact that she was the granddaughter of George I of the Hellenes, that Danish prince, bald-pated in early manhood, who was popularly elected King of Greece at the age of seventeen in 1863 and fell to an assassin's bullet fifty years later. In 1868, then, King George married the sixteen-year-old Olga, a Russian Grand Duchess, daughter of the Grand Duke Constantine who, in turn, was brother of the Czar Alexander II, son of Nicholas I and thus grandson of Paul I and great-grandson of Catherine II, the "Catherine the Great" of splendour and romance. As we might expect of such an aristocratic little innocent, the bride Olga was so young and inexperienced that she brought a family of dolls to her new home in Athens and was still attached to them when her first baby was born a year later.

Altogether King George and Queen Olga were blessed with five sons and two daughters between the years 1868 and 1888. The royal flush of sons — the Princes Constantine, George, Nicholas, Andrew and Christopher, in that order — still occasionally bemuse readers of pre-war memoirs. Constantine succeeded to the throne under the impending shadow of the First World War, to be dismissed by the Allies as a political scapegoat only four years later, and he died in exile at the early age of fifty-five. None of the brothers were to enjoy notable longevity.

We may note in passing that Prince Andrew, father of the Duke of Edinburgh, was posthumously a grandparent of the Prince of Wales. Prince George and Prince Christopher long figured in Princess Marina's world as bland and benevolent uncles. George married a granddaughter of the enormously rich François Blanc who founded Monte Carlo Casino, and family tittle-tattle avers that the gambling revenues contributed their mite to Prince Philip's education. Christopher equally married well by espousing the wealthy Mrs. Leeds, the widow of an American tin-plate millionaire, who died only three years later, leaving him the bulk of her considerable fortune. But Marina's father, Prince Nicholas, had already long since set the plush gilt-edged standard by marrying the niece of the Czar Alexander III, the daughter of the Grand Duchess Vladimir.

It was in reality the closest, least-contrived and most natural match in the world, for a sister of Nicholas — another Alexandra — had already married one of the Czar's younger brothers. In addition, Nicholas's Aunt Dagmar was also the wife and Czarina of Alexander III, and we have noted that his mother, Queen Olga of Greece, was a granddaughter of Nicholas I. We need not trouble ourselves with the complex pattern of all these Russian relationships nor attempt to trace every genetic link between Dagmar's sister, Queen Alexandra of England, and the latter's great-granddaughter, the Princess Alexandra of today. It suffices that amid the glitter of a royal wedding in St. Petersburg, Prince Nicholas of Greece renewed his childhood acquaintance with his cousin Helen, who was just a year his junior. Far from proving to be love at first, second or third sight, however, their friendship took thirteen years to mature and it was the 13th June, 1902, before Prince Nicholas and the dark-eyed Grand Duchess Helen — having romantically met again by chance in Paris — at last became engaged.

Two months later, they were married with a ceremony of great splendour in the gold-domed chapel of the palace of Tsarskoe Selo. One of the younger guests, a daughter of the British Ambassador, could still vividly remember fifty years afterwards the radiance of the Grand Duchess Helen, her long train carried by twelve pages, her curls crowned by the pink diamond tiara once worn by Catherine the Great and worn ever after by Romanoff brides. In the enormous ballroom that night, the reigning Czar Nicholas II led the bride in the polonaise to the music of Chopin, and "Cousin Nicky's" gift to the newly-wed couple was a villa to be built to their own specifications wherever they pleased in Athens.

They chose the finest site available, opposite the Royal Palace and slightly aloof from Constitution Square, and as the building gradually rose, balconied, opulent, luxuriantly white, gleaming in a bower of royal gardens, it became one of the wonders of modern Athens. The inquisitive are said to have bribed the builders to show them the bathrooms; and the proud new owners sometimes arrived unexpectedly to find total strangers enjoying a conducted tour, guided by an unabashed foreman. With Princess Nicholas's insistence on perfect craftsmanship, the mansion was not finished for nearly three years and her two elder daughters, Olga and Elizabeth, were accordingly born in the royal country home at Tatoi. Both Nicholas and Helen hoped that Le Petit Palais, as it was called, would be auspiciously ready for a son, but their third child — born while rain lashed the new shutters on the night of November 30th, 1906, by the Greek old-style calendar — proved to be a third daughter, Princess Marina.

By some omission or mistake, cannon thundered and church bells rang as if to welcome a prince, a muddle Prince Nicholas glosses over in his memoirs. It was more ominous that the little Princess Marina first came to England, at the age of three and a half, in time for a State funeral, that of King Edward VII. It so chanced that her five-year-old sister, Elizabeth, had to undergo an operation in Frankfurt, and the parents sent Olga and Marina ahead with their English nursemaid, Miss Fox, who sat on her chair on the beach at Bognor reading of the scenes of mournful pageantry in London while the two little girls built and patted their sandcastles, unaware of this shadow on family life.

When Elizabeth was well enough to travel and Prince and Princess Nicholas brought her to Bognor, they also persuaded their cousin, the sorrowing Princess Victoria, to motor down with them for the rest and change. One can glimpse her, garbed in black darker than the seaweed or the basalt pebbles, gazing mournfully at the sea, though passers-by would not have accorded a second glance at the plain and pallid woman, the spinster daughter of the dead monarch and the best-loved sister of the new King George V. Princess Victoria at this time was just forty-two and cast in an irretrievable aura of spinsterhood. The family knew that twenty years earlier she had fallen in love with a courtier of neither wealth nor title and had been refused permission to marry him. But now she was enchanted by the sweet and affectionate baby Marina, whom she swept into her heart and, in a sense, practically adopted from that moment.

Twenty-five years later, Princess Victoria altered her will in order to leave her country home, Coppins, to Princess Marina and her husband, the then new Duke and Duchess of Kent. It was a cause of family sadness that she did not live long enough to see Princess Alexandra, although in her last illness in 1935 she was comforted by the news of the arrival of Marina's first-born son.

With Princess Victoria in England and a bewildering host of so-called English aunts and cousins, with her Danish-born paternal grandfather in Athens and her German-born maternal grandmother in Russia, it is not surprising if Marina grew up to be markedly cosmopolitan. In the golden age of that pre-war childhood, Meriel Buchanan remembered the annual winter visit of the three sisters to St. Petersburg, the trio of "little princesses driving in an open sledge, their faces rosy with the cold, framed in fur-trimmed velvet bonnets". In Athens itself, the glowing memories were to lodge longest with Prince Philip's mother, Princess Alice Mountbatten, who at that time had three little girls of her own and so was thrown into a deeper communion of understanding with her neighbour and sister-in-law, Princess Helen. The two families visited England together and then there were six children paddling and playing on the seaside beaches under the gaze of their nursemaids. Summer months were spent at a smallish house on the Tatoi estate where the children could clamber in the ravines, and the King's peacocks must have seemed to Marina at dusk to call her mother's name, "Helen! Helen!"

Then there were visits to Prince Andrew's villa on Corfu, Mon Repos, where his only son, Prince Philip, was to be born nearly a decade later and where, at the time of writing, a new group of Greek royal children play in the gardens that run through scented orange and lemon trees down to the water's edge. On one occasion, an exceptional Christmas visit was to Coburg to stay with Marina's great-aunt, the Duchess of Coburg. She indeed was both Duchess of Coburg and Duchess of Edinburgh, her husband having been Queen Victoria's second son. We may see how closely this places Princess Marina, even in childhood, within the hierarchy of the British Royal Family, and we have come far from the concept of an impoverished distant relative reared in a narrow world beyond some feudal Balkan fastness.

Princess Marina and her sisters were staying with their grandmother at Tsarskoe Selo on August 4th, 1914, when the scythe of war cut the great dividing swath in their lives. A legend has sprung up of a nightmare journey endured by the children and their parents through a countryside in the throes of mobilisation. In reality a special train conveyed them, under the direct orders of the Czar, to the Romanian border where another special train was laid on by command of the King of Romania. Family jokes about army fleas were destined to be chronicled in all seriousness but, writing a decade later, Prince Nicholas recalled the only difficulty as the hardships of a local train on the last leg of the journey when "the heat was unbearable, we had no water and the children cried, until at a railway station we were able to purchase a watermelon." We need not believe that the ordeal was too much for the nieces of the King of Greece.

Their uncle King Constantine, had succeeded on the assassination of his father, George I in 1913. When he was forced into abdication by the Allies in 1917, and his brothers followed him into exile, Marina was in her eleventh year. The war had till then been little felt among the dolls' houses in the nursery rooms in the tranquil Petit Palais, and perhaps Marina's most memorable experience was of being shepherded into the cellars of the old palace across the road when the Allied warships were bombarding Athens, just as her daughter was shepherded into the cellars of Sandringham more than thirty years later when German planes were thought to be in the Norfolk sky.

Exile itself at first seemed to the child like a holiday, with her sisters and nursemaids and pets transported by a Greek destroyer to Taranto and thence to a hotel suite in St. Moritz. The one cruel and stupid change came unexpectedly a year later. The family were ensconced in Lausanne and the Princesses' English nurse, Kate Fox, received a summons one day to attend the British Consulate. There she was coldly reminded by an unsympathetic official that the deposed King of Greece was considered a traitor, and she was warned that if she continued in service to any members of his family, she would be deprived of her passport. Poor "Foxy" returned to Princess Helen with tears dripping beneath her pince-nez. She had no alternative but to leave her mistress next day. This was as harsh and senseless an interdict as one can imagine, and on a par with the incident of the stones that were thrown at Princess Marina's car in Brighton some years after the Second World War. She had been visiting a Regency exhibition at the Pavilion when, it would seem, a deranged ex-Serviceman was overcome by the discovery that her maternal grandmother had been born a princess of Mecklenburg-Schwerin.

2: "MARA MAMA"

I

The first exile of the Greek royal brothers lasted, as a wag put it, for "only forty days and months in the wild". Then, much to the chagrin of the moody statesmen of Versailles, a national plebiscite proved to be 98 per cent in favour of King Constantine, and Marina's "Uncle Tino" was recalled to the throne. Packaged with his kingship, however, there was also the intractable problem of the Asia Minor campaign against Turkey, a spluttering time bomb that caused the restoration itself to collapse like a pack of cards within two years.

"We really needn't have bothered to unpack," the sixteen-year-old Marina is supposed to have said. The new phase of exile was, however, to last thirteen years and produced, wisp by wisp, the fable still persistent in the public imagination of the impoverishment of Princess Marina and the Kents. It is true that the family estates around Tatoi were confiscated by the Republic and the income from Greek investments shrank to a trickle. The Russian Revolution had also swept away the unfettered affluence of Princess Helen's family background, although the substance of her marriage settlement still sufficed for a comfortable apartment in one of the more socially exclusive blocks near the Trocadero. But Helen was a good manager, with a financial acumen derived from her mother, that Grand Duchess Vladimir to whom diamonds, if not precisely a girl's best friend, were nevertheless always a wife's consoling perquisite. The portraits of the Grand Duchess, still treasured by her descendants, show a firm-faced square-jawed woman more submerged in jewellery than any present-day royalty at a State Banquet. To a practised eye, the festoons of diamonds and pearls and particularly a pearl drop tiara have a perplexing and elusive air, until one realises that the tiara in altered form is still worn by the present Queen Elizabeth II and that a much simplified necklet of diamonds and pearls is also often worn by Princess Alexandra.

The story of great-grandmama's jewels has indeed become one of the best-loved Kent traditions. The total collection, representing one of the largest hoards ever whisked from under the eyes of the Bolsheviks, was reputed to be second only to that of the Dowager Empress Marie. We know from the remarkable published indiscretions of Sir Frederick Ponsonby, Treasurer to King George V and Keeper of His Majesty's Privy Purse, that the Empress Marie's jewels arrived safe in England in a single box "ropes of the most wonderful pearls ... all graduated, the largest the size of a cherry, cabochon emeralds, large rubies and sapphires...", and were subsequently sold for £350,000. On different ships, both the Dowager Empress and the Grand Duchess Vladimir escaped from Russia early in 1919 via the Caucasus and the Black Sea. Both alike suffered the indignities of house arrest, but the Grand Duchess's home was searched and looted so often that finally the searchers took even her toothbrush in case it concealed diamonds, and she finally had to acknowledge in her letters to her worried relatives in Switzerland that she had nothing left but the dress she had on.

But what she seemed to reveal so carelessly in correspondence was wisely not the whole truth. The Grand Duchess did not mention her jewels which, for all she knew, were still in the very obvious place where she had left them, in the safe in her house in the park of Tsarskoe Selo. She took into her confidence a devoted friend, Bertie Stopford, of the

British Embassy in St. Petersburg, who quietly undertook to recover the jewels if it were still possible. At the risk of discovery and imprisonment, he visited the estate in workman's clothes and found not only that the Duchess's trustworthy old steward was still safely living there but also that he had kept the safe concealed and intact.

They opened this treasure chest together one wintry afternoon, and by discarding the heavy leather boxes and cases and wrapping the glittering pieces in newspaper they managed to cram the entire collection into two old Gladstone bags. Captain Stopford then casually walked through the park to the tramlines, where he presently took a cab to the British Embassy and the jewels were smuggled in cigarette boxes safely to London.

On her mother's death, Princess Helen inherited a fourth share of this collection, a windfall to any average family, but for the Princess a dilemma in the technique of being royal. In the Paris of the 1920s, behind the anecdotes of the Grand Dukes who drove taxis and princesses who scrubbed floors, the plight of many destitute Russian refugees was a pathetic reality. With the proceeds of some of her jewels, Helen founded a school at Saint-Germain-en-Laye where sixty orphaned Russian children could be housed, fed and educated. A fourth share in perhaps £300,000 worth of jewellery sounds enviable but, after philanthropy, Princess Nicholas realised that she would be fortunate to enjoy an income before tax of about £5,000 a year. The jewels could be released on to the glutted market only a few at a time. Queen Mary purchased one of the finest pieces, the tiara in diamond entwined opals and drop pearls, now interchangeable with drop emeralds, which so often nowadays adorns her granddaughter, the Queen, on State occasions. It has also been said that Queen Mary privately bought in a fine diamond clasp arranged as a bow which she subsequently gave to Princess Marina as a wedding gift.

Like any sensible man of middle-age faced with early retirement, Prince Nicholas had meanwhile taken up painting as a hobby and the sale of some of his watercolours — signed "N le P", for Nicholas the Prince — provided what he called "useful pocket-money which at that time was very low". But with the buttress of her investment income, Princess Helen was able to send Marina away for a year to a finishing school at Auteuil and she successfully created a social ambience for the matrimonial prospects of all her young family. Then, as now, different points of view arose between mama and daughters. When the eldest girl, Princess Olga, was still in her teens her engagement was announced to the then Crown Prince Frederick of Denmark, but second thoughts and difficulties arose. The prospect of one day becoming Queen of Denmark did not seem sufficient recompense to Olga for marrying a man she did not love. Prince Christopher was present at one of the family discussions when the rich voice of Marina suddenly enquired, "But why should Olga marry him if she doesn't love him? I wouldn't!"

Thereafter Mama could only set the scene for match-making, as Princess Marina was one day to do for her own Alexandra. During the London season of 1923, for example, Olga met a Cambridge undergraduate who at first gave her his name merely as Karageorgeovitch but who was in fact Prince Paul, the cousin of King Alexander of Yugoslavia. It quickly became crystal-clear that he and Olga had fallen in love and Paul's impetuous wooing led to a remarkably rapid engagement. That October Europe's royalties gathered in Belgrade for a double event. The first ceremony was to be the christening of King Alexander's baby son, Peter, to whom the then Duke of York

(George VI) acted as sponsor. The next day saw the wedding of Princess Olga to Prince Paul of Yugoslavia, with Marina and her elder sister Elizabeth as bridesmaids, and the Duke and Duchess of York — themselves a young married couple of only six months standing — among the guests. These double ceremonies provided the occasion when Elizabeth, the Queen Mother and her husband first met Princess Marina. None could foresee that the Duke and Duchess of York were to be King and Queen of England, or that King Alexander would fall to an assassin's bullet in the streets of Marseilles eleven years later while Marina, in London, was in the very midst of her wedding preparations. Nor did futurity disclose the change of fortunes of the screaming baby at the font when Paul of Yugoslavia, acting as Regent to the young King Peter, would unhappily find little alternative but to compromise with the Nazis and so incur Peter's satiric but bitter denunciation as "the wicked uncle".

The stage of history was indeed being strangely set in that week of christening and wedding in 1923. In the previous year the fifteen-year-old Marina had also visited England for a few months for the benefit of her English, staying in a Kensington hotel with her old nurse, Miss Fox, for a spell and with a friendly private family at Warlingham. Riding into Purley on a red London bus or cinema-going in Croydon, could she have dreamed that she would one day marry in Westminster Abbey? A visit was paid to Queen Alexandra and Princess Victoria at Sandringham and, unaware of coming events, Marina was a guest of her future mother-in-law, Queen Mary, at Windsor Castle. "Marina is charming ... she will be a great help to my son," Queen Mary was to comment to Lady Airlie a dozen years later, with a certainty strengthened by distant first impressions. As we can now clearly see, it was hardly a total stranger who responded with energetic waves to the ecstatic welcome of the London crowds in 1934.

II

Both the intent, nervous embarrassment with which she faced the unaccustomed cameras, and the hint of unprepared gaucherie as she greeted official welcoming parties, equally endeared Princess Marina to the public. The Cinderella element in her public story gave rise to the idea that she achieved her effects with a secret economy, and she became a source of instant fashion. She had first arrived in London wearing a little close-fitting fez-like hat with an upstanding feather quill, and within a week or two copies of the "Marina pillbox", as it was known, were on sale for as low as 2s. 11d. Since haute couture was supposed to depend on exclusive design, she was thought to maintain a constant battle to beat the copyists, and the copyists were "routed", said the newspaper fairy tale, when she appeared in a different hat each day for six weeks running. As if to strengthen the picture, *Daily Mail* readers were regaled with an interview by Margaret Lane with Captain Molyneux, who was designing the wedding gown, "The Princess put a lot of her own ideas into the trousseau and drew them on scraps of paper to show me exactly what she meant…"

A decade had elapsed since the last royal wedding and a new generation realised that they were to share in all the romance and colour of this one. A forest of Venetian masts — oddly topped with spearheads and battle-axes — rose around Whitehall and Parliament Square. But Bond Street was decked unexpectedly with pink, green and primrose canopies hung the length of the street; Piccadilly and Oxford Street flourished banners unequivocally displaying "the colours of England and Greece and the City of London", and the gaiety of these trimmings heightened but did not explain the public sense of participation. Marina contributed a few telling gestures of her own, first with the issue of a studio portrait by Dorothy Wilding showing her without a shred of jewellery and then, as wedding gifts began to pour into St. James's Palace, with an entirely unexpected announcement: "I would like the people of England to share in some way my great happiness on the occasion of my engagement to Prince George. As you know, my years of exile have taught me how much unhappiness there is in the world. Although I should be happy to think that the preparations for my wedding were in some small measure giving employment to those who need it, I should be more than happy for the unemployed, and particularly for their children, to receive any money which has been intended for the purchase of wedding gifts…"

Following this example, a steel scaffolding firm built a grandstand overlooking the Mall free of construction costs and announced that the proceeds from the sale of seats would go to a hospital. On the wedding eve crowds danced in Piccadilly Circus. Shortly before midnight, the jeers at the audacity of a chauffeur who was trying to edge through the throng changed to wild cheering with the astonishing discovery that the couple inside the limousine were the happy pair, who had left Buckingham Palace and come among them, ostensibly to view the decorations.

Above all, the marriage ceremony in Westminster Abbey was the first royal wedding to be broadcast, a facility that allowed every Tom, Dick and Harry — or, rather, every Mary, Doris and Harriet — to attend as a listening guest. Prince George had been created Duke of Kent a few days earlier. The Prince of Wales was best man — the microphone missed a comedy moment when he forgot to hand the ring to the bridegroom —

and the bride's attendants included Princess Elizabeth of York and Princess Juliana of the Netherlands, as well as an assemblage of less familiar but undeniably beautiful foreign princesses. For the public the only flaw was the long wait in the November mists between the return ride down the Mall of the newly-wed Duke and Duchess in their glass coach and the send-off with an escort of Life Guards on their honeymoon drive to Paddington Station. As we have seen the delay was occasioned by the second marriage ceremony, under the rites of the Greek Orthodox Church, in the private chapel of Buckingham Palace, which historically was the first such double wedding for seventy years. "But why do they want to do it twice over?" said a voice in the crowd.

It became impressed on everyone that the new Duchess was a lively personality who did everything thoroughly. Her honeymoon had a superlative non-stop quality, first in the isolation of Himley Hall, Lord Dudley's country seat, and next in the seclusion of Trent Park, loaned by Sir Philip Sassoon, and then in the New Year of 1935 a spell of winter sports around the Bavarian home of Marina's sister Elizabeth and her husband Toto, the Count and Countess Toerring-Yettenbach, who had themselves been married only a year. Finally the honeymoon ran its prolonged course with a cruise in the West Indies. Back in London the young Duchess then began a round of the art galleries, as if indicating the trend she hoped for in her future duties.

In the memory the most trivial incident often gains significance. The new Duchess visited a school in Kent where one of the pupils presented her with a large folded embroidered tablecloth, beautifully beribboned and packed. The Duchess insisted on opening it fully out for the cameras, while she held one end. "You must have a souvenir," she said, "of such a beautiful piece of work."

In the mid nineteen-thirties, there was a Marina era when her beauty, dress sense, talents and charm dominated the newspapers. The Marina pillbox, for instance, held sway for three years. The colour Marina blue dominated its season. There were Marina perfumes, Marina cocktails, Marina dahlias. The ostrich farmers of South Africa presented her with a quilt of ostrich feathers as a wedding gift, and sought her help to restore ostrich feathers to fashion. The "elegant Duchess" wore hats trimmed with ostrich feathers for three days running at Royal Ascot. "She does nothing by halves," people said. In the summer of 1935 she retired into a suitable haze of happy anticipations and Prince Edward — later the Duke of Kent — was born in the early hours of October 9th. Everyone calculated, of course, that little more than ten months had elapsed since the wedding. The clucking approval was equally obvious when Princess Alexandra arrived nearly fourteen months later. "First a boy, then a girl…" — and it was difficult not to be convinced that the pattern was due to the Duchess of Kent's unerring sense of perfection.

III

Number 3 Belgrave Square, the third house facing south along the northern terrace, is at the time of writing the headquarters of ASLIB (the Association of Special Libraries and Information Bureaux) but its royal occupants are still commemorated in a framed photograph, hanging in the hall, of Princess Alexandra's parents leaving for the coronation of King George VI. Elsewhere, layers of recent paint have submerged the past, and a dozen typing desks and filing cabinets fill the room where Alexandra first saw the light of

Christmas Day. Yet the girls who work there pleasantly know of it as her birthplace. In the broad corridor outside there still stand the imposing battery of her mother's huge pine wardrobes, useful today for office stores. On the first floor Princess Marina's drawing-room still knows some splendour as the council chamber though only the chimneypiece of French marble and the chandelier remains unchanged, the latter preserved and mysteriously scheduled in the ground lease as one of the ground landlord's fitments. But when the infant Princess Alexandra took her first view of the world, all seemed secure, fixed and changeless, permanent and reassuring as Nanna Smith's crisp starched apron, though in reality as transitory.

The Duke of Kent's lease, in fact, contained an optional expiry clause and its date ultimately coincided with the outbreak of war in September, 1939. But the Second World War seemed an unthinkable contingency in 1934 when the Duke first took the house furnished from Lady Juliet Duff, two years before the Nazi troops had as much as crossed the Rhine. In those days Prince Arthur of Connaught, Viscount Hambleden, Lord Howard de Walden and Lord Hastings were neighbours, almost the typical tenants whom the architect Basevi has in mind when he designed the classicist stucco-faced mansions for the Grosvenor Estate nearly a century earlier. The Duke of Kent signed the lease with eagerness, for the house was one he had always admired when casually entertained there. It had an atmosphere of Lowther wealth, heightened and transcended by the more fashionable artistic impulses of the early thirties.

Rubenstein had played upon the shawl-hung grand piano in the drawing-room; Somerset Maugham had stammered witticisms about the alabaster swans that swam in green niches in the dining-room. As Lady Juliet showed him around the house, the Duke needed no reminding that she had been just old enough to figure in country-house parties with Edward VII and Alice Keppel and just young enough to inspire romantic verse from Hilaire Belloc. She had been instrumental with her mother, Lady Ripon, in bringing the Diaghilev ballet to London, and it surely intrigued the Duke to think of Diaghilev, Cocteau and Stravinsky spinning the glittering bubble of conversation in these very rooms. Looking back, the eye of memory sees that there were perhaps too many gilded French chairs and consoles matching the flushed and opulent ladies in the Renoirs. In the study at the rear of the house, Lady Juliet would have made her favourite joke, "This writing table belonged to Talleyrand, you know. You will have to write all your important letters here."

It was a nice house to be born in, as Prince Nicholas said, keeping vigil on the night Prince Edward was born. And it was a nice house for the plump little Princess to come home to from her outings, as she grew from the toddling stage, with the footman coming to help her up the four broad steps and the patrolling policeman always near at hand in smiling approval. There would be the quick patter of small feet across the marble-floored hall that stretched the full width of the house and then the rush to the staircase in emulation of her brother, and the commencement at last of the arduous, adventurous climb, unless Nanna insisted on taking the lift. There was also on the ground floor the pale-green room that the Princess seldom entered, guarded by its four alabaster swans. Beyond, deeper in the recesses of the house was the former pantry where the telephone operator Bobby — Robert Beck — kept sentinel over his switchboard...

Inevitably, in that child's world, pictures and objects were friendly as people. On the ground floor was a guest suite where Alexandra, venturing there one day with a maid, was surprised to find her grandmama, Princess Helen, having breakfast in bed. And if one could but succeed in the exploit of climbing the staircase with brother Edward one came into the upper hall, more a handsome apartment than a landing, where a Lowther in seventeenth-century armour gazed from above the fireplace, leather-bound books glimmered on the bookshelves and, to the right, the drawing-room, where it was delicious at times to romp on the deep-cushioned settees, shrieking with laughter. Prince Edward discovered every source of adventure in the house, every tunnel between chair-legs and tables, every climb — and not least attractive the narrow forbidden staircase to the attics above the nursery.

Nanna Ethel Smith had come from Tunbridge Wells, a firm believer in the ethic that children should not trouble "staff" and that staff entered or passed through the nursery domain only on sufferance. Smith was in her forties, a slight little personage, prematurely grey, but indomitable in domestic battle. She had first been in Princess Olga's household in Yugoslavia, bringing up Olga's two sons, Alexander and Nicky, and respectably feuding with Kentish zeal against endless and baffling confederations of Serbs and Croats. When transferred to Princess Marina's staff, it was a source of deep yet reticent pride to Miss Smith that she had "seen it all" from the beginning. She had been on Prince Paul and Princess Olga's staff at Bohinj in the August of 1934 for example, when Princess Marina came to stay at her sister's picturesque chalet and Prince George also arrived on his all-important visit. When the news of their betrothal burst like a carnival firework, Nurse Smith was, by right of her English birth, one of the first of the staff to curtsey and wish them well. The excitement of being in the midst of that romance carried her forward now to the immense satisfaction of having charge of the children.

Amid these duties, "Foxy" played an ambiguous and affectionate role. Supposedly in retirement, with a little flat of her own in Hampstead where the Duchess went to tea with her now and again, Miss Fox had become a devoted friend, part nursery aide, part companion, the characteristic niche so often filled by the old family nurse. On Nurse Smith's day off, she needed no bidding to lay aside her film magazines and arrive at Belgrave Square to take charge, and she assumed a nominal but unquestioned authority whenever the Duke and Duchess were abroad. Even Princess Helen respected her idiosyncrasies rather than allow them to mar the pleasures of being a grandmama. Occasionally the other grandmama, Queen Mary, also called at No. 3 when the Kents were away, and there was more to this visit than her token promise to look after the children. Having "lost a son" in the Duke of Windsor's abdication, the old Queen had in the self-same month gained a granddaughter in Alexandra and the compensation factor nurtured an interest in the child that flowered in affection.

But, more often, Kate Fox's belief in plenty of fresh air and sunshine saw the nursery transferred to Coppins, the Kents' country estate, one remove from the family supervision in town. The normal flow of royal duties seldom detained the Duke and Duchess away from home for more than a night or two but as confidence in Foxy deepened their pleasure trips abroad grew more frequent and prolonged. The Duke adored continental travel and seized any excuse to whisk Marina from Paris to Munich, Belgrade and Athens, and so alleviate her sense of separation from her family. In retrospect, one knows that the popular Kents of the 1930s were to be spared fewer years of happiness together than John and Jacqueline Kennedy in their own context in the 1950s, and it was sometimes as if the Duke heard the sounding trumpets. The prospect of another jaunt would set him conning timetables or road maps with schoolboyish zest, but four or five weeks of travel invariably edged his nerves with ennui; and then he returned with new satisfaction to the children, the fun and friendship, the music and inward tranquillity of Coppins.

IV

Coppins and the Kents have come to seem inseparable, although in reality the modern dukedom was no more than a year old and the Duke and Duchess were already looking for a country house when they heard that Princess Victoria had left the Duke her home at Iver, Buckinghamshire, just as it stood. The young couple had lunched with "Aunt Toria" at Coppins shortly after their honeymoon; and they wanted always to preserve the same air of welcome, and a little of the same aura, too, with the grave marble bust of Edward VII in the entrance hall, among sweet-scented pyramids of humea, the incense plant. Though so much else was changed, these remained. Marina and her husband took over an ivy-clung, tile-hung, Victorian villa of rain-stained red brick in a dense shrubbery of laurels and yew, hollies and box. The interior was shaggy with red Turkey carpeting, shadowy with dark paint and lachrymose wallpapering, thick with photographs and stuffy with Edwardian furnishing. But the miracle of Coppins was, and still is, its situation in a tiny rural enclave midway between the industrial wens of Uxbridge and Slough. On a calm night, on the southerly side of the house, one can hear the distant surf of traffic on the M4 motorway; and of recent years a grouping of council houses has encroached, midway between the royal estate and the Georgian cottages and half-timbered inns of Iver village. Yet the ancient title Copynsfield was inscribed in manorial rolls in the year 1374, and the essential country scene has altered with merely sluggish rhythm through six hundred years.

The surrounding meadows, flat and arable, are much as they were when a Bond Street bookseller named John Mitchell built the present house in the eighteen-fifties. ("Our lawns are just a glorified field," Princess Alexandra once said.) Mr. Mitchell was attracted by the "elegant estates" of the neighbourhood — Delaford Park, Langley Park, Black Park — but he fortunately kept a variant of the old name, Copyns, and the style of his long, low, multi-gabled country home was pleasantly influenced by the mid-Victorian craze for Swiss cottages. A man of considerable taste and energy, John Mitchell founded his fortune when he began selling theatre tickets as a sideline to bookselling — hence one still refers to ticket agencies as "libraries" — and when Queen Victoria became an early patron his star was in the ascendant. He organised the productions of Italian opera at the Lyceum that delighted the Queen in her teens; he introduced Rossini's *Stabat Mater* to London and was licensee for twelve years of the old St. James's Theatre. Whenever Victoria and Albert went to a playhouse, other than the Theatre Royal, Drury Lane or Covent Garden, Mitchell always attended in person to ensure that arrangements went smoothly; and through his junior, George Ashton, he ultimately founded the firm of Ashton and Mitchell which has held the royal warrant as theatre and concert ticket agents through four reigns.

Court officials were entertained at Coppins in the way of business, and no doubt their host constantly anticipated a summons to Windsor for a knighthood. The call never came.

John Mitchell died in 1874, unsatisfied, and then, with a touch of theatrical irony, the house was bought by Lady Jane Churchill, a lady-in-waiting to Queen Victoria, and the Queen herself was entertained, too late, under his very roof. Lady Churchill was the Queen's closest and last intimate friend, and when she died at Osborne on Christmas Eve, 1900, a chaplain expressed the pious hope that she had but gone ahead to prepare a place. Sure enough, the old Queen herself died precisely four weeks later, and perhaps John Mitchell welcomed them at the gates of paradise to ensure that things went smoothly.

Insistent that a lady-in-waiting must herself be waited on by a large staff, Lady Churchill had doubled the size of Coppins by adding a guest wing and servants' quarters; and Queen Alexandra thought it eminently suitable as a country house for her spinster daughter, Princess Victoria. As it turned out, "Tora" remained her mother's patient companion at Sandringham for nearly a quarter of a century and did not fully take up residence at Coppins until 1926, when her brother, George V, was nearing the sixteenth year of his reign. It was from her Buckinghamshire home that the Princess used to telephone her brother daily at Buckingham Palace, invariably commencing her conversation with the sally, "Hello, is that you, you old fool?" Which once led to the notable response from the telephone operator, "One moment, please, His Majesty is not yet on the line."

Such, then, was Coppins, very truly Victorian, cluttered and overcrowded, when it first passed to the Duke and Duchess of Kent. They unified the fussy exterior, the bay windows and porches, the tiles and bricks, with coats of pale colour wash. They transformed the large unused library into a music room, and the two sitting-rooms shimmered with new light and space. But a great boon was a day nursery wing for Prince Edward and Princess Alexandra, opening direct into the garden through new French doors, so that the Princess with her first steps could totter from the house on to the lawns, and her early summers seemed divided between the sunshine outdoors and the cool of the house. Nor was it far down the passage to the housekeeper's room, where ever since Lady Churchill's regime a portrait-print of Queen Victoria in a black and gold frame had presided over the daily tribute of newly-baked cakes.

One unexpected consequence of the children's freedom was that passers-by could crane to see them over the old garden brick wall, the height of which accordingly had to be increased with strategic fencing. Fortunately, the private entrance to Coppins lay in a cul-de-sac which saw little local traffic, and Queen Mary frequently came unobserved to see her grandchildren, sharing her son's enthusiasm and enjoyment in choosing colour schemes and selecting each new piece of furniture for the house. When Mama and Papa were away, Eddie — Prince Edward — organised his ball games with the butler or chauffeur or followed one of the gardeners along the herbaceous borders with his own little wheelbarrow. His sister was at this time attached to a little black-footed toy lamb and a squeaky toy duck. Among Princess Alexandra's earliest memories is the sweet bustle of her parents' homecoming, and as always when they were at Coppins the house seemed to fill with music and people.

Far from being hemmed in her nursery, Alexandra could climb into the lap of any familiar or welcoming giant. She made mountains of the Mountbattens, Dickie and Edwina, of Queen Ena of Spain, Malcolm Sargent and her obliging schoolboy cousin Prince Philip. She scaled her father's close friend and equerry, Lord Herbert, his knee and shoulder favourite footholds in the list of human ladders, hillocks and well-connected scaffolding. Perhaps she grew confused at the affectionate terms "Mara" or "Ma'am" so often used by the grown-ups, for an early story is that she linked the two for herself and improvised the charming endearment of "Mara Mama".

In terms of doll population, too, Alexandra's nursery was more crowded with much-hugged little creatures than had ever been seen in the better endowed but more regulated nursery of her elder cousins, Elizabeth and Margaret. Old memories dwell on groups of dolls in national costume, Polish, Greek, Yugoslav and Austrian but the adults alone may have had special cause to endow these with significance.

The Polish dolls might recall that when their little mistress was only eight months old and most of the Royal Family had retreated to Balmoral after the arduous Coronation season, the Kents continued to hold public interest by a summer visit to Poland. An old friend, Agnes de Stoeckl's daughter, had first casually mentioned the invitation over the lunch table, suggesting that the Duke and Duchess might visit her country home near Katowice, but the fervour of the Coronation had spread its ripples throughout Europe and the Kents' journey assumed unmistakably momentous undertones. No member of the British Royal Family had ever before visited Poland, and the nation had recently lost its foremost leader in the death of Marshal Pilsudski. The Kents motored through Germany in holiday mood only to find crowds waiting to welcome them at the Polish frontier, where the first dolls and flowers were presented as to a conquering hero.

The private country-house visit developed into a gala week at the fabulous palace of Lancut, home of Count Alfred Potocki, the head of the oldest and noblest of all the great Polish families. On arrival at a private railway station, the visitors were met by a procession of open carriages with liveried postilions and, as the Baroness de Stoeckl wrote, "Louis XIV's time at Versailles was revived and perhaps even surpassed." All eleven dining-rooms of the palace were used in rotation, there were performances in the private theatre, and fancy-dress dinners and balls were held every night. And besides there were dolls in profusion, dressed *a là polonaise*, dolls dedicated to hope, for all aristocratic Poland shared in a dream in those remarkable weeks that the Duke of Kent might become their future Kling. The prospect remained one of the minor might-have-beens that constantly colour the paths of royal history. But the Kents were at Sandringham for Princess Alexandra's first birthday party and King George VI could not resist including the Garbo film *Marie Walewska* in his programme of entertainment, so strong was its topical connotation.

The Greek dolls were to evoke the events and equally unavailing daydreams of the following year. The birth of Prince Edward of Kent in 1935 had coincided with the events of the restoration of the monarchy in Greece, but the new King George II was without a direct heir and the wedding in January, 1938, of his brother, Prince Paul of the Hellenes to Princess Frederika of Brunswick was thus of dynastic consequence. The Kents had cause to ponder the dynastic implications for their own two babies, whom they left in the Sandringham nursery while they left to attend the wedding in Athens. When Frederika's first child, Princess Sophie, was born in November, 1938, not very long after Prince Edward's third birthday, the matrimonial possibilities of the remote future seemed to require no clairvoyant powers. The matchmakers could not help but be disappointed for little

Alexandra's sake that the new Greek Princess had not been born a boy.

No one could know that the fates were already inserting different bridal threads in the tapestry. In September, 1938, the Kents were staying on the Balmoral estate when a grandson of their friend, Lady Airlie, celebrated his tenth birthday at Cortachy Castle. Although the twelve-year-old Princess Elizabeth and eight-year-old Princess Margaret travelled from Deeside for this event, their little Kent cousins were evidently too small for an invitation. The Duke and Duchess of Kent were probably content to observe the occasion by sending ten-year-old Angus Ogilvy a birthday card.

Perhaps one should mention here an incident no less trivial that also holds its inconsequential place in our narrative. After the royal wedding festivities in Athens, the Duke and Duchess broke their homeward journey for a week or two of winter sports in St. Anton and on their very first morning in the Alpine sunshine the Duke found a gold cigarette case lying in the snow. "This must be my lucky year," he remarked and, on handing his find in at the police station, he was delighted to learn that the owner, a French businessman, had offered a hundred francs reward. The Duke collected the cash and donated it to a local fund for the poor. Still chuckling, he returned to the hotel — and to the news that his father-in-law, Prince Nicholas, had died in Athens. Still wearing their travelling clothes, the two holidaymakers had hurriedly to return to Greece for the funeral. The pattern had occurred so often, this strange mingling of happiness and grief, in Marina's family. Attempting to lessen the sadness, the Duke could not resist telling friends of his winter-sports luck. The anecdote was still serviceable when he returned to London; and the propitious omen remained in mind, golden and shining in the snow, when he took his baby daughter in his arms.

3: A WARTIME CHILDHOOD

I

In the early autumn of 1938 an Air-Raid Precautions officer called at Coppins to fit the children with gas-masks. From a cardboard box he produced a selection of glassy-eyed snouts that made Eddie and Alexandra shrink with timidity until they were tempted into the fun of trying them on. Then Alexandra discovered that piglike snorts resulted when she breathed out through the fins, and she ran about wildly, attempting to make the noises and shrieking with laughter. The A.R.P. officer descended to the small stone cellar and approved it as an air-raid shelter; he advised that in the event of danger all fires in the house should be extinguished as a precaution in case of a gas attack, and then he took his departure, leaving a part of his heart behind with a tiny princess, aged less than two, still glowing with fun, who had given him her chubby hand in farewell.

The Duke of Kent was present in the House of Commons to hear the Prime Minister make his dismaying speech on the vanishing hopes of peace and he watched Mr. Chamberlain open the dramatic last-minute telegram announcing that Hitler had agreed to a conference in Munich. "I firmly believe war is averted," the Duke telephoned Coppins. "The world is saved." Stunned men and women everywhere believed with Neville Chamberlain that it meant "peace in our time". To the Kents, however, the sweet prospect of peace itself entailed an intensive change in their lives, for the Duke had been appointed the designate Governor-General of the

Commonwealth of Australia and was due to take up office in November, 1939.

It would be wonderful for the children, the Duke and Duchess agreed, and the nursery arrangements at Yarralumla, the Government House at Canberra, were among their first enquiries. Edwin Henderson, the architect, airmailed every plan and detail of the proposed alterations to the Duke and Duchess, and put nothing in hand without their approval. The Duke revelled in choosing furniture in contemporary style, selecting designs for pieces to be made in Australia and choosing new fabrics within the government budget. Two spacious guest-rooms were set aside as the day and night nurseries, and lists were drawn up of the toys the children should take. Certainly they should have their shared Shetland pony, Farino. Should the Duke's thirteen-year-old Alsatian, Alexandra's beloved friend and guardian, Doushka, be included? A list of the Princess's favourite playthings drawn up by her nurse included some of the dolls, a dog on wheels, a worn box of building bricks which she had appropriated from Prince Edward and an array of floating bath toys sufficient, as her father said, to sink a swimming pool.

The preparations steadily progressed amid a welter of State engagements. In 1938 and 1939 the Duke and Duchess of Kent were principal aides to the new King and Queen, particularly when the Duke and Duchess of Gloucester were absent overseas, and Lord and Lady Herbert found that as the aides and closest friends of the Kents they in turn led exceptionally busy lives. One looks through the old engagement books now with some astonishment. King Carol and Crown Prince Michael of Romania had no sooner concluded a State Visit, with all the accompanying banquets and receptions, than Prince and Princess Paul of Yugoslavia arrived on a public visit to Buckingham Palace and a more private week at Coppins. By a melancholy coincidence, they reached England within twenty-four hours of the shock to the Royal Family of the sudden death of the Duke's aunt, Queen Maud of Norway, in a London nursing home, and throughout the visit the family wore the full black of Court mourning.

It made the Kents ponder the prospects of other well-loved figures whom they might never see again after three years' absence, among them the Duke's aged great-aunt, Princess Louise, to whom they were devoted. The Duke also "got in his hand" for Australia by undertaking a royal tour in the Midlands. The multiplicity of private business in connection with Australia, indeed, seemed endless; and among other details a photographer named Baron Nahum arrived at Coppins to prepare some photographs for official use.

Although he had first snapped the Kents earlier that year, Baron had never before made portrait studies of British royalty. His family were in cotton; his great-grandfather had shipped bales of merchandise by camel across the Sahara, and when his mother gave him a Leica he eagerly secured some scoop shots of old King Gustaf of Sweden playing tennis, only to find that in his excitement he had superimposed his pictures on top of each other. As a professional he specialised mainly in portraits of theatrical celebrities until he gained the attention of Edwina Mountbatten, who recommended him to the Kents. The garden photographs were of the simplest kind, but when Baron went to Coppins for the Australian pictures, more than camera history was being made. He did not dream that in ten years he would take the bridal and wedding group portraits of the then scarcely acquainted Princess Elizabeth and Prince Philip. Princess Marina might have thought it inconceivable that a young man, no matter how well connected, would one day become Baron's assistant and would ultimately marry her niece, Princess Margaret. Perhaps a great deal depended on the quality of the photographs but in retrospect it hinged principally on Princess Alexandra's naughtiness.

Accustomed to cameras as she had become, Princess Marina apparently imagined herself in the realms of State portraiture when it came to arranging the colour session for the children. Edward was dressed in a silk suit suitable for a small page at a fashionable wedding. Alexandra, too young for bridal grandeur, wore one of her usual little embroidered frocks ... but she was at the height of ebullient self-expression and she "acted up". She raced about and refused to pose; she rolled on her back on a couch, flouncing fat knees; she scorned any set piece and her misbehaviour almost reduced her elder brother to tears. But Baron clicked his camera, rejoicing, and the sequel was a set of colour photographs of such royal freshness and spontaneity that they were widely reproduced. But for the war, this episode would have launched Baron's highly profitable royal career. But in effect the war only created delay in recognition, and it may be that the public impression of the amusing and unpredictable streak in Alexandra's character was never erased from that moment.

II

In that last summer of peace of her early childhood, Princess Alexandra and her brother went to stay with their grandmama, Queen Mary, at Sandringham. As generations of royal children had done, they adored visiting the dogs in the old kennels, watching the wildfowl on the lake, playing hide-and-seek in the shrubbery and gazing down on their own view of the world from the high nursery windows. Like so many others amid the uncertainties, the Duke and Duchess of Kent also enjoyed another travelling holiday together, cruising in the Aegean and visiting Belgrade, but suddenly the war clouds seemed ominous and the Duke was summoned home. He returned alone, leaving his wife an extra day to make her dreadful *adieu* to her sisters, none knowing, if war came, whether they would ever meet again. It had been agreed that in the event of mobilisation Queen Mary should go to her niece, the Duchess of Beaufort, in the West Country at Badminton. The Duchess had been Lady Mary Cambridge, eldest daughter of the Queen's brother, Adolphus ("Dolly"), Marquess of Cambridge. She was a bridesmaid to both Princess Mary and Elizabeth Bowes-Lyon shortly before her own marriage in 1923, and an affectionate cousin was always much in the inner family circle. Her husband's invitation to Queen Mary naturally extended to her Kent grandchildren, and on August 28th, four days before the fatal German invasion of Poland, the Duke and Duchess of Kent both hastily travelled down to Sandringham to decide what might be for the best.

Tiptoeing into the night nursery to peep at her two sleeping cherubs, Marina nearly broke under the emotional revolt against separation. There were many such moments at this time when close friends saw her "cling to her husband", as one said, "her eyes bright with suppressed tears". In the anxiety, Coppins itself seemed hardly safer than Belgrave Square, where everything was packed up, the Duke having decided to relinquish the lease. It was thought that, if war came, an immediate total onslaught from the air would be encountered from the enemy, an horrific bombardment of high explosives and poison gas. Under this terrifying illusion, on Sunday morning September 3rd, Britain heard the solemn radio voice of Neville Chamberlain telling the nation that, as Hitler had not answered the ultimatum to withdraw his troops from

Poland, Britain and Germany were at war, and he had hardly finished speaking than the air-raid sirens wailed their chilling, wavering signal of alert over the metropolis and countryside alike.

At Coppins, where the Belgrave Square staff had joined the country household, some forty people crowded into the tiny cellar, including an Italian maid carrying a case full of bandages and surgical tools. At Sandringham, Queen Mary and most of her Marlborough House servants were in church, but the nannies hurried with Prince Edward and Princess Alexandra into the enormous cellars beneath the house. The two children were open-eyed at a hidden world of coal bunkers, logs and wine bottles that they had never seen, and reluctant to leave it when the "all clear" sounded. The alarm proved merely to have been a test alert, and everyone laughed at the muddle. That night, however, when an unidentified plane caused the sirens to wail at 2.45 a.m. the entire household hurried down to the basement, Queen Mary being the last comer for she had stopped to dress, while her detective waited outside the bedroom door. "The children behaved beautifully," the Queen recorded. "At 3.30 we heard 'All clear'."

Immediately after breakfast that Monday morning, Queen Mary and her staff left for Badminton as arranged, with the little Alexandra and Eddie and their nurses, and the Queen could not resist a chuckle at sight of the cars massed in the Sandringham forecourt. "Quite a fleet", she noted. With the Kent nursery conclave and her staff, numbering sixty-three together with their dependants, more than twenty cars and luggage wagons set out across country to Gloucestershire via Peterborough and Northampton, Oxford, Swindon and Chippenham, on that memorable drive. The Grand Duchess Vladimir would have no doubt approved, for none of the cavalcades of Princess Alexandra's Romanoff forebears could have matched this royal progress. A stop was made for luncheon at the stately pile of Althorp, Northamptonshire, where Lady Spencer had foreseen the nursery contingencies even to rice pudding. (She had been a Hamilton before marriage, incidentally, and some fifteen years later one of her nieces was to become one of Alexandra's foremost friends and lady-in-waiting.) Towards evening the procession of cars reached Badminton House and, as James Pope-Hennessy has told us, the Duchess of Beaufort "watched the arrival of her aunt's massive convoy with a certain apprehension."

Two days later, Marina herself hurried to see the children on the first of the weekly visits she paid her son and daughter throughout that autumn and winter.

III

The Badminton estate spreads over some fifty thousand acres and at its heart stands the imperious mansion of creamy Cotswold stone, which was already the home of the Beauforts before Charles II created the dukedom for one of his richest subjects. In recent years the park has become celebrated for its annual horse trials, so often attended by the Queen and all the Royal Family, and the house itself ranks as a major showpiece among England's stately homes. The usual bus-loads of sightseers troop through the state apartments: the entrance hall, the oak room, the first Duke's dining-room, the red room, the yellow drawing-room, the library, the great drawing-room. The guides immediately gain attention by mentioning that the dimensions of the original badminton courts were the same as the entrance hall, for the family first evolved the game there as a wet-weather pastime. Elsewhere there are saloons by Wyatt, a notable drawing-room seventy feet long, Chinese-style bedrooms and so on, the whole embellished by Grinling Gibbons woodcarvings, Van Dycks and Reynolds and *objets de vertu* without number. Most of the state rooms were however closed through the war, their gilt and marquetry furnishings turned to the wall for safety.

Within the nine-miles circumference of its park, the Badminton of the war years was almost a private world. A corner of the grounds contained the army hutments of Queen Mary's guard and other military units and the Birmingham evacuees in the village were timidly unwilling to intrude. The nursery rooms of Badminton House itself were high on the second floor, commanding a view of woods and lakes. The Duchess of Beaufort lacked children of her own, but the suite was always in readiness for her younger visitors, furnished with the solid cupboards, shining fireguards, scuffed rugs and scrapbook screens of an earlier generation.

Princess Alexandra, though only three that Christmas Day of 1939, was never to be omitted from any activity in which her brother figured, and Eddie was seldom left out of any expedition savouring of fun for the children. Under their grandmother's tutelage, they went chestnut hunting, carefully picking up the prickly husks, and Alexandra is remembered excitedly rushing for attention one day, crying "Look, I can curtsey!" To their nannies' horror, the Kents were not kept away from Queen Mary's "ivy clearing" when walls and trees surrendered their burden of ivy in gleeful showers of ancient leaves and dirt. To save petrol, Queen Mary travelled to the more distant working sites in a farm cart, drawn by two horses, often with the children also crowded aboard, pretending to hold the reins. "Aunt May, you look as if you were in a tumbril," remarked her hostess, one day. "Well, it may come to that yet, one never knows," Queen Mary happily replied, as the cart jolted off.

The matching dungaree playsuits which "Mara Mama" brought the two children tended to become their Badminton uniform. The onslaught on menacing weeds and ivy had still not palled when Queen Mary launched her Salvage, as she called it, combing woodland walks and shrubberies for rusting tin cans, old bottles, scrap metal and, as the Queen testified, even old bones. The Birmingham evacuee children helped in these efforts, and it may be that little Alexandra's first eager acquaintance was blocked by her inability to cope with their singing accents, though her own popular social centre quickly developed around the rubbish-filled wheelbarrow, the paper dump and the rubbish heap. When hardly old enough to sit still, she was taken to singsongs in the troops' canteen. At Christmas Queen Mary distributed small presents from an Army bran tub and, mysteriously concealed in the sawdust, the Princess also found gifts from the soldiers to herself.

At an early age, in this way, Alexandra unconsciously absorbed royal standards from her grandmother, that most considerate and regal of ladies, and the tiny child came in for her own share of the local devotion that Queen Mary inspired. The Queen's old friend and equerry, Sir Richard Molyneux, was to remember the tableau at "picture book time", with the children with their spun-gold hair leaning intently at the knee of the old Queen; and the veteran of Khartoum felt himself moved by the link of youth and age and family resemblance. These were the moments that Queen Mary evidently missed when the children returned for a time to Coppins, for it then became Lady Cynthia Colville's duty to read aloud instead, while the Queen did her needlework.

After the fall of France, it was felt that they would all be better protected closer to Windsor Castle. Queen Mary actually packed her things but then decided that she would prefer to remain at Badminton, come what may. The Kents' personal furnishings from Belgrave Square had been put into store at the outbreak of war when the lease was surrendered and, at Coppins, their silver, pictures and other treasures were first packed, then unpacked. The Duchess of Kent also precisely shared the dilemma of her sister-in-law in deciding whether her own two children should be sent to greater safety in Canada. The then Queen decided not to be separated and, as everyone knows, she philosophically summed up the problem, "They could not go without me, and I could not possibly leave the King." At that time, however, circumstances might be envisaged in which the central group of the Royal Family could be taken prisoner or dethroned. The next in succession were the Duke of Gloucester — at that time without children of his own — followed by the Duke of Kent, Prince Edward of Kent and then Princess Alexandra. Until the birth of Prince William of Gloucester just a week before her own birthday in December, 1941, Alexandra thus still remained sixth from the Throne, a factor which strengthened the argument for transfer to Canada, but the Duke and Duchess demurred. The emergency plan for the safety of the Royal Family included the evacuation of the children from a western airfield, but this precaution was reserved for a final extremity, and even when the threat of invasion deepened Eddie and Alexandra travelled no farther west than Badminton.

Both were now of an age to be boon companions, revelling in the ever-changing joys of country life, searching for truant hens' eggs, gathering windfall apples, helping to pick berries and becoming more juice-stained than seemed possible, and romping amid the straw in the great barns. The harvests of wartime merge in all its yesterdays, but Lady Colville gives us a picture of the Princess standing in a haycart, in a blue frock with a large straw hat, "the reins in her hand, feeling entirely responsible for the dignified progress of the bulging crop … she made a delightful figure as a rural driver." Though still so small, Alexandra was no more afraid of horses than her cousin, Elizabeth, and indeed, Lady Colville affirms, she was "as brave as a lion".

It seemed natural enough in England in wartime that the whistle and crash of an exploding bomb should be scarcely more disturbing than a crash of thunder in peacetime. It was always accounted a blessing that one of Badminton's most critical air raids resulted in nothing worse than a batch of unexploded bombs in a potato patch. These were dealt with by a bomb disposal squad and the children were warned that there would be a big bang when they exploded: the young Kents never made less noise than when waiting to see just how big such an announced bang would be.

When a large ground-floor room at Badminton House was reinforced as a shelter, the children were usually carried down fast asleep during night alerts, and remained sleeping soundly in their blankets while Queen Mary, fully dressed, sat in a chair doing crossword puzzles. Becoming accustomed to the drone of enemy aircraft, the adults presently preferred to remain in their beds though the children were always taken to comparative safety. Meanwhile, Princess Marina regularly travelled down from London in the overcrowded trains, snatching a day or two to spend with the children during her spells off duty from nursing work at the University College Hospital. Not even the deputy Registrar at U.C.H. knew at first that Nurse Kay in No. 16 ward, dealing mainly with women raid casualties, was the Duchess of Kent. The public learned of her nursing work only after the Duke of Kent as President had officially visited the hospital and accepted a practised curtsey from Nurse Kay without a flicker of recognition. One of the pressmen, however, heard of the rumours rife among the patients, and published the story of Nurse Kay's identity as soon as it could be stamped "passed by censor". The story has contributed to the popularity of the Kents even at this distance of time.

The Paddington stationmaster began to recognise the Duchess's off-duty schedules by the train she caught to Badminton and he used to escort her down a subway, bypassing the crowds, to the one reserved royal compartment, although the exalted travellers invariably squashed up sooner or later for standing passengers and strangers. One such journey in the blackout was shared with Lady Airlie when she was going down, full of news, for her rota as lady-in-waiting to Queen Mary. Conversation had to be discreet. Lady Airlie's young grandson, Angus, was a safe subject and the old lady was proud that, following in his grandfather's footsteps, he was now in Butterwick's house at Eton. As the packed train jolted through the dark, anonymous countryside of the blackout, where even the stations slid past without place names, the Duchess could not have known that they were discussing her future son-in-law.

The Duke of Kent similarly had no inkling of that, although he may have briefly met the boy if it is true that Angus, while at an Ascot prep school, came to Coppins one Sunday. Like the other children of wartime, Alexandra did not see her father for months on end. The Duke made a long tour of Canadian air training bases and of aircraft factories in the United States, flying the Atlantic in a Liberator bomber, but that his family were always much in mind was evinced one evening when a department store was specially opened after hours for him so that he could buy toys to take home. One of his great successes was a speech he once made extempore to a vast crowd of the 13,000 American workmen at the Glenn Martin aircraft plant. "Every hour you work saves the lives of women and children," he said. "The more materials you give us the quicker we shall win."

They cheered him to the echo. After visiting President and Mrs. Roosevelt, he returned with their parting gift, a box of oranges and bananas sufficient for every child in Badminton village, fruit that his own children probably could not remember tasting in their lives. Sharing the characteristic conjuring trick of all Service fathers, he appeared as if from nowhere, dropping into the family circle. Characteristically, he loved to spend part of his leave making expeditions to antique shops in Bath and elsewhere, and when, as Air Commodore, he made a tour of R.A.F. welfare units in the West Country, this furnished one of the last opportunities of his married life to pop the children into the back of the car.

In the summer of 1941, the onset of German "Baedeker raids" on Bath and similar centres made it seem prudent to withdraw the children temporarily from Badminton; and a family reunion ensued at Coppins. Baroness de Stoeckl, who then lived at Coppins Cottage, was always to remember the tall white-shirted figure of the Duke at ease in his own home: "His delight was chopping trees and weeding, the two children running around and the Duchess helping him." In the last golden days of autumn, Marina was able to ask Alexandra whether one day she would not like a baby sister or perhaps a little brother.

Prince Michael of Kent was born at Coppins on July 4th, 1942, an afternoon arrival, when Prince Edward and Princess Alexandra were again at Badminton. "The Duke seems to love this tiny infant," Agnes de Stoeckl noted in her diary a few days later. "Every evening, instead of sitting late as usual, he leaves the table shortly after ten o'clock and carries his youngest son to the nursery and lays him in his cot and stands watching and watching. Nannie told me that each night she discreetly leaves the room, but she can hear the Duke talking softly to him." His other children were brought home to greet their little brother as soon as possible and they attended the christening in the private chapel of Windsor Castle on August 4th. With another war raging, it seemed inconsequent to note that this was the anniversary of the outbreak of the First World War.

Watching the Duke and Duchess leading Alexandra and Edward by the hand up the aisle, one of the guests felt a gust of emotion, "they all four looked so handsome". King George of Greece and King Haakon of Norway attended as godfathers and the proud father stood as proxy to President Roosevelt. The King and Queen, Princess Elizabeth, Princess Margaret, and Queen Mary were present, but the occasion was a completely domestic one. The baby slept placidly as he was given the names Michael George Charles Franklin. The third given name might seem to be Princess Elizabeth's innovation but was in reality the private family patronymic of King Haakon.

Queen Mary considered it "a successful day" and recorded the party afterwards in the green drawing-room that there had been "lots of old friends, servants, etc." King George of Greece, however, priding himself on his social acquaintance, surveyed the well-dressed champagne-drinking throng in puzzlement. "It is so strange," he murmured, "I do not seem to know anybody here today."

"No wonder," he was told. "They are the staff from Coppins."

Princess Alexandra did not know that her handsome, charming and indulgent father had hoisted her shoulder-high for the last time, that there would be no more toys to unwrap when he returned from his journeys, no more of those never-forgotten moments when he sat both children on his knees to tell them stories. Three weeks after the christening, on August 25th, when Edward and Alexandra were perhaps sharing a summer holiday with the Herbert children at Wilton, the Duke of Kent was to make a tour of inspection to Iceland. The day of his departure, as Agnes de Stoeckl noted, was one of perfect sunshine, "the ducks quacked, the turkeys laughed, the cocks crowed … the whole of Coppins seems a mass of flowers". At the front door, after kissing his wife, the Duke paused to stroke his favourite Chow and said smilingly to the butler, "What will you do with him when I'm gone?" A strange question to echo unanswered, as he set out on his journey.

The following evening, the Duchess had retired early when she heard the ring of the telephone downstairs. She heard Miss Fox answer it, and presently noticed her heavy footsteps toiling on the stairs. Before a word was spoken, the young widow knew what had happened. Her husband's plane never reached Reykjavik. Its wreckage was found on a mountainside at Morven in north-west Scotland where the aircraft had crashed and the Duke and his secretary, John Lowther, the pilot and all except one of the crew were instantaneously killed. The Duke of Kent had been in his fortieth year. "He was killed on Active Service," wrote his brother, the King, in the first footnote of grief, and presently, in the House of Commons, Winston

Churchill spoke words that were simple, exceptional and true: "The loss of this gallant and handsome Prince, in the prime of his life, has been a shock and a sorrow to the people of the British Empire, standing out lamentably even in these hard days of war."

At Badminton, too, bracing herself from the incredulity of the first overwhelming shock, Queen Mary's immediate thought was for her daughter-in-law. "I must go to Marina tomorrow," she told Lady Colville, who later wrote of the poignancy of "the thought of the children who could not yet realise the meaning of the loss they had sustained..." The new baby prince, seven-week-old Michael, would never know his father. Not yet six, Princess Alexandra was only old enough to know that her father would never again be coming home and that to help her mother to look after Michael was to be a new attainment. The first tangible consequence in her own small world was that her Aunt Olga suddenly appeared, an aunt whom perhaps she barely remembered. The King had arranged for Princess Olga (Princess Paul of Yugoslavia) to be flown home from South Africa to help give comfort in the dark valley of despair.

This began a close affection between Alexandra and her aunt that never ceased. Presently it was thought best that the two elder children should return to Badminton. They knew nothing of the ordeal of ceaseless public commiseration which the Duchess had to face month by month when she resumed her duties. "I must pull myself together," she told a friend, "I am just one among thousands of war widows."

V

There are clocks in childhood, but no calendars. In retrospect, Princess Alexandra's war years merge into the flowing seasons at Badminton and Coppins; the juvenile crises of hay fever and measles, a spell in hospital for the removal of her tonsils, and always the changing games and timeless rivalry with Eddie. When half a head taller, he liberally encouraged her to take his toy motor cars to pieces in order to enjoy his own expert satisfaction in always being able to put them together again. In an earlier phase they had shared a yellow plush cat with glass eyes which lit up when the tail was pulled. When this favourite was rediscovered, in retirement in a cupboard, Eddie to his sister's horror took it apart to see how it worked, but then was compelled by his elders to put it together again, even to sewing the velvet.

When Alexandra was four she rode astride a toy llama, and at five she and Eddie rapturously raced on the Coppins lawn hopping on bouncy rubber beach animals stored since some bygone summer holiday. The six-year-old who joyously received a Red Cross uniform for her birthday grew into the six-and-a-half who had her dolls "vaccinated" in emulation of her baby brother Michael. But under Eddie's influence, Alexandra also outgrew her dolls at an early age, excepting the rubber-skinned Christabel who accompanied her even on car rides with Queen Mary.

It has come to seem remarkable that Servicemen seldom recognised the Queen when her car paused to give them lifts on the country roads of Gloucestershire. The extra passengers nevertheless saw merely an old lady, her chauffeur and her grandchildren. Everyone was enjoined to move up closer, and probably Alexandra as a small child sat on more laps than any princess in history. "We were packed like sardines," Lady Airlie remembered.

Towards the end of the war, the Queen had little medallions made to give as a souvenir on taking leave of her extra passengers, but this moment of truth itself left unsolved the puzzling identity of the blue-eyed little girl. Lady Colville once found Princess Alexandra and Prince Michael together at Badminton "and both in their different ways most attractive. The young Princess struck me as being very pretty and extraordinarily lively, attractively mischievous, with the brightest eyes I have ever seen," she noted. "She got on admirably with her grandmother, Queen Mary, who was at moments taken aback by her energy, but fascinated too, and who bore with her granddaughter's exuberance with amused fortitude."

At Iver the elderly local shopkeepers regarded the Coppins children with an amused, proud benevolence, and the appearance of their brightly polished little bicycles outside the village shop where Mrs. James sold both small toys and rationed sweets was an accepted sign that all was well with the Duchess of Kent. The children expended their sweet coupons only after deep discussion in balancing both their pocket money and the candy ration. On one occasion, Eddie returned from shopping looking so unusually solemn that Queen Mary enquired what was worrying him. The young Prince sighed deeply and replied, "Rising prices!"

A popular children's comic was also on weekly order from old Mr. Johnson, the newsagent. Eddie followed a serial about a boy Commando with dire results when, in an access of realism, he camouflaged both his own and Alexandra's face with greens and yellows from his mother's paintbox. Princess Marina had often drawn picture strips for her children as a preliminary to bedtime and now found herself expected to keep pace with a host of new heroic characters. Her whole life hinged upon her identity with her family. "Mother always makes fun out of everything, both for herself and for us," Princess Alexandra once said soberly.

The old Coppins pony and trap was put into service to eke out the petrol ration, and in an anonymous countryside shorn of all signposts that might assist the enemy, the children discovered the barges of the nearby Grand Junction Canal. "Wotcher!" Alexandra would shout across the water, picking up bargee bonhomie as readily as she had picked up mumps, measles and colds. The local butcher allowed the two Kents into his back room to see sausages made. "It's a good sausage," Alexandra once unexpectedly announced at lunch at Windsor Castle, "It's a Woolton!" At the home farm, brother and sister supposedly took over the chore of feeding the chickens — when they remembered it. Then each were given a calf of their very own, a responsibility demanding such energetic grooming of the animals that a grown-up suggested a competition for the glossiest coat. This contest Alexandra won, perhaps unfairly, by using a whole bottle of brilliantine.

Happily, the stringently compressed wartime newspapers had no space for anecdotes of the Kents. As a rule, only the conductor recognised them when the children boarded the local bus to Slough or Windsor. For a treat they once visited Pinewood Studios two or three miles away in the old Heatherden Hall estate, where they met Nelson and Lady Hamilton, alias Laurence Olivier and Vivien Leigh, and were thrilled by the battleship sets of *In Which We Serve*. But this too was unpublicised and the youngsters took an unheralded part in local horse shows. Princess Alexandra was eight years old when she won a prize at an Aldershot gymkhana, driving her white pony "Tony" in the small ponies' private turn-out class.

After an interlude at Badminton during the flying-bomb era, Iver also conveniently solved the growing problem of the children's early education. Alexandra and Edward were enrolled in the private classes held in various homes by a Mrs. Parnell, sharing lessons with the local doctor's twin sons and the children of other local gentry. Offering the advantage of a large spare downstairs room, the classes were for a long time held in a small stuccoed red-roofed house, on the corner of the local hospital turning, called York Cottage. Thus, by a strange coincidence, in a world torn apart by change, the young Kents took lessons in a house of the same name as the royal York Cottage at Sandringham where their father had studied under his redoubtable tutor, Mr. Hansell, thirty-five years earlier.

There were, in addition, private French lessons, music lessons and dancing classes, all in a favourable, companionable local atmosphere never enjoyed by royal children until that time. This trimmed away shyness. Rushing in breathlessly from the garden to meet her cousin, the new Queen of Yugoslavia, Alexandra disposed her curtsey with formality and grace but presently launched into a series of disarming questions, "Do you like being named Alexandra? Were you once Princess Alexandra? Shall I become a Queen?" King Peter's young wife was merely echoing family assumptions when she told her that she might well be, one day. The royal ambience was as natural as the wind in the elms; and adult contriving would one day suitably help destiny to provide a royal husband for the daughter of the house, just as surely and reliably as the already evident fact that there was to be a royal bridegroom for Princess Elizabeth at Windsor.

As the war drew to its close, Coppins became a hub of expectant royalty, each with their different hopes. King George of Greece was almost a permanent resident, so much of the domestic scene indeed that before returning to Athens he sought the advice of Bysouth, the Kent steward, on his choice of a Palace butler. Prince Philip came, giving no quarter on the tennis court but ingloriously defeated, to all appearances, one day when he simultaneously took on both Eddie and Alexandra. Later on, when Princess Elizabeth visited Coppins, in the days when curiosity about her romance began to blaze, it was again an advantage that one entrance of the house stood in a leafy cul-de-sac where intruding cameramen were conspicuous if they defied the signpost, "No through road".

TOCCATA

"A touchpiece … a composition intended to exhibit the
touch and execution of the performer."
— *Grove's Dictionary of Music*

4: GROWING PAINS

The coming of peace in Europe brought Princess Alexandra her first experience of State events when she was still barely nine-and-a-half years old. The kinsfolk of the Royal Family gathered at Buckingham Palace for the rejoicings of VE Day, and from a window alongside the balcony the Duchess of Kent and her two elder children looked down at the flower-like swirling and altogether astonishing spectacle of the jubilant crowds. The following week, at the King's wish, Alexandra and her elder brother rode in the State procession to the City for the National Service of Thanksgiving at St. Paul's, the Princess acknowledging the cheers of Fleet Street with such unbounded energy that at one point her mother was seen to lean forward in gentle admonishment.

After this unparalleled excitement in her young life, it must have been dismaying to return to the Palace to a nursery luncheon in which parsnips were probably again served as a staple vegetable. "I don't like them! I was forced to eat too many as a child," the Princess once remarked with a shudder. The disappearance of this repugnant item could not be expected in the endless rationing. The peace in the Pacific was still to be won; clothes rationing and the policies of "make do and mend" persisted, and the frocks that Alexandra wore on holiday that year were recognisably hand-downs from Princess Elizabeth and Princess Margaret.

The peace also brought the Princess a sharper deprivation in the departure of her brother Eddie to a prep school at Wokingham, where he was to be a boarder. Though not far away from home he returned only for holidays and at half-term and an afternoon every fourth Sunday. These were red-letter days in his sister's life. She vowed to write to him daily, a resolve she maintained unremittingly until adults puzzled her by hinting that a sister's ceaseless correspondence was not the best equipment for a schoolboy. She nevertheless continued to send him her horse-show programmes and pieces about her mother clipped from the newspapers, the two cherished items that most involved an unselfish sacrifice in parting with them.

In return, Eddie enquired about the white pony, Tony, and perhaps told of his own exploits, and it may be that he could boast of being spanked for drilling an experimental hole in a lavatory cistern. Alexandra deeply envied such adventures. Her old dreams of becoming a circus bareback rider came as near to realisation as they would ever do, that summer, when she won three or four gymkhana competitions. Though often up to mischief, she never excelled her early recorded naughtiness in the notorious upsetting of a loaded tea trolley when she was in one of her rushing-about moods. Queen Mary once described her granddaughter to Lady Spens as "highly strung and somewhat emotional", with a straight face.

Visits with her mother to the ballet, which she adored, meanwhile prompted Alexandra's girlhood ambitions of becoming the first royal ballerina. She was heard stridently advancing the argument that ballet training would help her to become less clumsy, and books on ballet at about this time solved every gift problem. The Princess's small share in some of the events of the victory year also set her aglow with admiration at the unsuspected and godlike powers of the King, her Uncle Bertie, though they also provided a distasteful revelation in the pains as well as the pleasures of being his niece. Arriving at Ballater for the summer stay at Alt-na-

Guisach on the Balmoral estate, she scrambled eagerly from the train to pump the arms of the stationmaster and welcoming estate staff, for these were her acknowledged friends. But one observer subsequently noted her "horror of being noticed". When crowds lined the approaches to Crathie church, peering into every royal car, Eddie ducked his head out of sight in embarrassment while Alexandra huddled miserably against her companion. "It's no good saying they're not looking at me. I know they *are*, and it's too awful."

At home, in the well-loved vicinity of Coppins, however, there were few strangers faces. In the friendly atmosphere of Iver church, Princess Alexandra's early arrival was always notable, glowing as she was with enthusiasm, turning a beaming smile on everyone she knew, with a smile of special intensity for Mr. Thorp, the organist, as he emerged from the vestry. At Platts, the corner grocery store in the village, she greeted assistants and customers alike with a clarion voice audible in the rear stockroom. The only time she was still and hushed, one neighbour recalls, was when she stood near the bacon-slicing machine, tightly clutching little Prince Michael's hand, unwilling to disturb his fascinated absorption as the rashers slipped from the knife. At bedtime, at Coppins, it was said similarly that her prayers rang down the stairway, with her supplications to bless "Auntie Ag and Uncle Bertie and Aunt Elizabeth and Lilibet…" and a long list of relatives named to the Almighty by their nicknames until at long last she ended, "And, God, please bless me and make me more tidy."

Too young to stay up late for grown-up peacetime junketings, young enough to revel in the pantomime "Beauty and the Beast" at the Theatre Royal, Windsor, Alexandra was at an awkward and impressionable age in the summer of 1946 when a romantic couple arrived unexpectedly at Coppins. This was Marina's younger cousin, Princess Katherine of Greece, and the tall and handsome British Army officer, Major Richard Brandram, who had first met on board ship en route to England three weeks earlier and become secretly engaged after a breathtaking courtship.

The entire household was flung into a whirl of romantic speculation and joyous delight at this enchanting example of love at first sight so close in their midst. Infected by the excitement, Alexandra must have discovered that a Princess did not necessarily have to marry a Prince and that the couple were "old enough to know their own minds". Perhaps she dreamily suggested that she might be a bridesmaid and was no doubt childishly vexed to learn that the wedding was still too far in the future for anything to be promised.

At this juncture, an unexpected ally appeared in "Uncle Dickie" Mountbatten, as efficient in coping with juvenile problems as with the strategic riddles of Southeast Asia. His eldest daughter, Patricia, was to marry Lord Braborne at Romsey Abbey in October, and Lord Mountbatten could hardly resist the prospect of a trio of princesses of the House of Windsor tending his daughter's bridal train. Young Alexandra, on receiving her bridesmaid's invitation, was breathless with delight and wonder. "But will my dress really be the same as Lilibet's and Margaret's?" she asked, incredulously.

It was indeed identical, even to the floral tiara and the double string of pearls which were Lord and Lady Mountbatten's private gift to the three attendants. Alexandra had been one of the junior guests at the wedding of Mrs. Vicary Gibbs and Andrew Elphinstone at St. Margaret's, Westminster, earlier that same year, and she was at the reception at the Savoy at which Prince Philip and Princess Elizabeth chanced to be photographed together for the first time. But now she had a role to play before a thousand guests as well as a long, chilly and unforeseen wait with her cousins for their car, prominent and visible in that unliked public eye. Afterwards, at the reception in the long dining-room at Broadlands, she revelled in the festivities evidently unaware of Uncle Bertie's somewhat critical glance. The King already had his plans for her future education, and the Duchess of Kent realised that it was now time for Alexandra to have a full-time governess. At this juncture, Marina's sister-in-law, the Duchess of Gloucester, came to her aid by knowing the very girl.

The Duchess recommended a young Scotswoman, Miss Katherine Peebles, then in her mid-twenties, whom she had first known through her lady-in-waiting in Australia, Lady Clive. Glasgow-born, Miss Peebles had been governess to Lady Clive's daughter, Davina, as well as to Susanna Cross, daughter of Sir Ronald Cross, then Governor of Tasmania. Moreover, at the first interview, Miss Peebles proved to have qualities outweighing her one disadvantage, her lack of a university degree, and her manner indicated a quiet smiling insistence that seemed to explain her success with children. Alexandra took to her at once, nicknaming her "Bambi", after the endearing Walt Disney cartoon fawn, "because she has such nice brown eyes". Katherine Peebles was to become an important element of the Coppins household for the next seven years, first supervising the studies of Princess Alexandra and then continuing with Prince Michael. In the present reign she stepped into a more exalted circle, for the Queen appointed her governess to Prince Charles in Coronation year and she became successively governess to Princess Anne, Prince Andrew and Prince Edward.

Miss Peebles believed in trying to understand a child before attempting to mould the character and one of her maxims was "firmness and fairness". As rewards, it was her custom to produce unexpected treats, such as a cruise on a river-steamer from Hampton Court or a journey all the way to London to visit Madame Tussaud's. The Princess considered the royal waxworks gruesome but found excitement in a pin-table, winning a penny from a small boy which she promptly returned to him.

No doubt the King noted an improvement when he suggested that Alexandra might spend a little time that year with the Windsor Castle house-party for royal Ascot. To Alexandra's already decided tastes, however, the anticipated treat turned out to be boring. "Eton boys stand around and we stand around," she said, "and you never see anyone for more than five minutes. First they're changing, then you curtsey, then they're off to the races. About the only thing to do is to eat up the strawberries and cream."

But the inactivity of royal Ascot was the prelude to a whirl of excitement. At Patricia Mountbatten's wedding Princess Elizabeth had no doubt been asked to keep an eye on Alexandra and now she ardently wished her young cousin to be one of her own bridesmaids at her own coming wedding to Prince Philip in Westminster Abbey. Prince Michael, too, was to be a page. Meanwhile, Princess Katherine had married her Major Brandram at the royal palace in Athens and in doing so, like Princess Marina, she assumed British nationality. Over the breakfast table at Coppins it could be explained that Uncle Bertie had sorted out problems of precedence by granting Katherine the style and precedence of the daughter of a Duke, so that she would henceforth be called Lady Katherine Brandram. At the same time, in order to marry Elizabeth,

Philip had settled down to plain Lieutenant Philip Mountbatten but no doubt presently would again be a prince.

It must have savoured somewhat of "Alice in Wonderland" to Alexandra, and even "Bambi" was powerless to give full explanations. And before everything could be puzzled out, even the exciting plans for Princess Elizabeth's wedding were diminished by a new consideration. When Eddie returned home for the summer holidays, Alexandra was able to greet him with the surprising, thrilling news that she, too, would soon be going away to school.

II

Princess Alexandra was the first British princess ever to go to boarding school, and it was at King George VI's direct wish that she established the great precedent of the break from the swaddling-bands of nannies, governesses and tutors. The King apparently left no memoranda on his motives but we have Princess Marina's own statement that he "strongly felt that Alexandra should have every chance of being an ordinary child while she could". Perhaps his own daughters would not have been pent up for so long with their governess, "Crawfie", at Windsor Castle if the war had not resolved the question. The King may have been presciently looking ahead to the welfare of his own future grandchildren, and Marina respected his decision, which she felt at heart was the right one. Nevertheless, she confessed that she dreaded the thought of being without Alexandra at Coppins, although she privately admitted, "It's the best thing really."

The difficulty was the choice between the older academic schools such as Cheltenham and Wycombe Abbey or the secluded advantages of Benenden or Cranborne Chase. Heathfield offered immense pros and cons. That other

Alexandra, the now exiled Queen of Yugoslavia, had been desperately unhappy there before the war and went on an alarming hunger strike until her mother took her away. On the other hand, Princess Alexandra's closest friend, Diana Herbert, had been a pupil there for several months and was ecstatic in her reports. The then newly-wed Tina Onassis, a bride of eighteen, had only recently left the school and was full of laughing, glowing reminiscences of the rivalry between Heathites and Fieldonians, one school building versus the rest. Although Heathfield was reputed an expensive, exclusive haven of daughters of the rich and privileged, the Herberts chuckled at its inner history. Founded in the eighties by a schoolmaster's daughter, as an extension of her good works in the East End, an exercise in the moral guidance of the poor, the school had changed direction in the naughty nineties when a friend had argued persuasively, "You're slumming at the wrong end, my dear. The poor, after all, have the Salvation Army. The upper classes need your guidance most."

One advantage for the Princess was that Heathfield did not then require a Common Entrance examination. Despite the skill of Miss Peebles, the Duchess was doubtful of her daughter's scholastic standing and a private tutor, Mr. Wilfred Edwards, came in for a time to give special coaching on mathematics. Alexandra was strongest in English literature, history, music and languages. Calling at the school for the first time, Marina found that its white-columned portico and pleasant classical lines reminded her of her mother's home in Athens. This was auspicious, but the Duchess felt nonplussed on first meeting the headmistress, Miss Kathleen Dodds, who seemed scarcely older than "Bambi" herself.

At thirty-one, Miss Dodds was in fact the youngest public schools headmistress in the country. Faced with this outwardly cool, soignée and smiling brunette, there was nothing to remind Marina that Miss Dodds had been at Heathfield less than a year and, indeed, the Duchess perhaps never realised that only one of the teaching staff had worked there longer than three terms. Equipped with a Holloway College honours degree, a teaching diploma from Bristol University, the strength of her own personality and a varied experience of elementary, secondary and grammar schools, it chanced that Miss Dodds had taken the £600-a-year-headship of Heathfield at a dire turning point in the school's history.

Heathfield has been called the "super potting shed of the English rose", but in 1945 Kathleen Dodds had not been warned that the roses were completely out of hand. On the first night of her first term, on her own account, the entire school of seventy-five pupils staged a fantastic skilfully planned revolt. At bedtime none of them could be found in their right rooms or dormitories, and they scampered up and down the passages giving false names when questioned, knowing no one could be recognised.

At ten o'clock at night, when some girls were skylarking in the moonlight on the flat roof, Miss Dodds ordered the whole school to assemble in the gym, dressed or undressed, and there icily threatened to expel anyone who disobeyed. The whole school, she reminded them, could be expelled and replaced from the waiting list if necessary. Her very sincerity quelled the rebels. She had won her first battle in a campaign that restored discipline and staff morale and she magnificently reorganised the school into renewed success.

But the Duchess of Kent's anxieties were not those of average Heathfield parents. "I should like to make sure that Alexandra is given exactly the same treatment as all the others," she said. "It is really important that we avoid extra privileges and fuss." Miss Dodds reassured her, not without reason to suppress a grim smile at thought of some of the privileged children of Heathfield. There were new girls so accustomed to having everything done by their nannies that they sat in their bathtubs waiting to be washed. There were girls who did not know how to brush their own hair or tie a shoelace.

The Duchess enquired whether many of the parents were very rich. "We are not," she told Miss Dodds firmly. "And we can't afford expensive outfits for Alexandra." This hurdle was cleared, for only three items of wear were permitted in addition to the uniform wardrobe. Alexandra arrived with only the standard off-the-peg outfit, from her gym suit to navy blue uniform and red winter cloak. "I'm expected to wear my cousin Margaret's clothes," she candidly told the Australian matron, displaying a well-pressed flannel suit. "How does anyone expect me to get into them? She's so small and I'm so *huge...*"

"A hefty child" was indeed Miss Dodds' first impression when "Alexandra of Kent" was listed among the new entries at Heathfield that autumn term. "She was very warm-hearted and demonstrative and expressed absolutely everything she felt ... she could never hide her feelings ... a sunny outgoing nature." And to her first impressions the schoolmistress was to add later that Alexandra "couldn't bear to hurt anyone's feelings and she adored helping others...", while the child's other disarming qualities included "an irresistible sense of humour" and her "utter truthfulness. She never lies about anything." But Miss Dodds was then assessing the sum total of the schoolgirl rather than the "naturally unrestrained" innocent who arrived at Heathfield breathlessly eager to get to know the other girls, ebulliently enjoying everything, rushing about and using her "clear, carrying voice at maximum power, always and everywhere".

Despite the presence of young Diana Herbert as a mentor, the newcomer had, as Miss Dodds said, "scarcely any idea of how to behave in a school". A remonstrance from the matron about a forgotten clothes hanger would cause the Princess to fling her arms around the startled matron and cry, "Oh, darling matron, I'm very sorry." A teacher who provided an extra notebook would be fervently embraced with, "Oh, it is so kind of you."

All the staff, I think, found Alexandra intensely shy of being singled out as a princess. Fortunately the other girls immediately took her for granted and accepted her as a new girl rather than a royal. It caused only a companionable excitement when the school discovered that she was to be one of Princess Elizabeth's eight bridesmaids, and nothing came of a giggling conspiracy for a mock ceremonial during which she was to be presented with a poem based on the school motto, "The distinction of one is the honour of all".

The new pupil indeed, discreetly kept the news to herself until the announcement was made from Buckingham Palace. The chief fitting for her bridesmaid's dress was arranged at Norman Hartnell's at mid-term, and the royal schoolgirl was enchanted by the most beautiful dress she had ever seen, a creation of ivory silk tulle with a fichu of tulle around shoulders and corsage and with a full flowing skirt glistening with a milky way of small star-shaped blossoms, embroidered in pearls and crystal. A final fitting was given in some secrecy at Heathfield itself, allowing Miss Dodds and one or two other teachers not only a privileged glimpse of the dress but also a revelation of the potential attractiveness of their budding pupil.

But the Princess, the youngest of the bridesmaids, seems to have thought herself the ugly duckling of the group. Perhaps it was as well that her bashfulness found diversion, during the ceremony in the Abbey, in sisterly concern for Prince Michael, who though only five was on his best behaviour as a page. At the Palace Princess Alexandra missed her cue for the balcony appearance, being more anxious to give attention to dear old Princess Helena Victoria, who was unable to leave her chair and had indeed approached the closing months of her life. It was one of those instances of consideration that continually endeared her Kent granddaughter to Queen Mary, who would often say, "She is a sweet child, a very sweet child." Yet back at school Princess Alexandra had really very little to say about the wedding party, beyond her impressions of "the absolutely gorgeous food". In that first division of personality with the wider world, her expansive and unrestrained nature was already watchful of the royal need of reserve and discretion.

Besides, Alexandra was constantly and emotionally concerned lest her unavoidable status as a Princess should seem to be showing off. When a film of the wedding was shown the following week in Ascot, the teaching staff agreed that the whole school should go and see it, but the horror of being seen in the movie reduced the Princess to floods of tears. Her housemistress felt unable to do anything with her and ordered her to go to the headmistress's study. "But I can't, I can't, go to the picture," she tried to explain between sobs. "I'm in the film. They'll all see me."

Miss Dodds murmured reassuringly that it would be fun. "Oh, no," cried the weeping child. "It will be so dreadful. Please don't make me go. I can't bear it."

It was difficult to reason that bridesmaids always appeared with the bride and difficult to sympathise against the public watchfulness which would be a lasting part of the Princess's life. Miss Dodds could only conjure up a penalty by saying, rather sternly, "Well, Alexandra, if you do not feel able to come to the film, you must go to your room and lie down until we get back." To her surprise, the Princess immediately smiled through her tears and said fervently, "Oh, thank you. Oh, how perfectly wonderful!"

III

Heathfield girls who became bridesmaids generally availed themselves of the privilege of a night away from school, but Alexandra was back in her dormitory as usual on the night of Princess Elizabeth's wedding. Her mother thought her still "much too young to go to the evening party".

There were then four dormitories for juniors at Heathfield and some fifty single rooms for the older girls, and Alexandra opted to remain with her own dormitory group of six girls as long as she could. More than the average proportion of her fifty-shillings-a-term pocket money was spent on midnight feasts and the matrons had to be vigilant that she did not help other girls unduly with their allotted tasks of cleaning, tidying and other disciplines. For a time the Princess had the job of sweeping her form room and went rushing round the corridors with a vast grin, brandishing her broom and proclaiming, "I'm Mrs. Mopp and can I do yer now?"

Ringleaders of mischief were usually made head of the dormitory in the hope that responsibility would temper high spirits and Princess Alexandra was an early "dorm head" or "dorm demon". One night the matron brought an unusually violent pillow fight to an end with the news that the combatants had nearly brought the chandelier down in Miss Dodds' sitting-room, immediately beneath them. "And the head of the dormitory is to see Miss Dodds in the morning and apologise," the matron ended, severely. "Oh, gosh!" said Alexandra, with visions of an enormous candelabra, such as those at Windsor, swaying perilously.

Next day, in "Doddy's Room", the culprit's first glance was at the bronze chandelier. "Oh, it's only a little chandelier," she said with relief. "I imagined it was like the huge ones at Windsor..."

"All the same," Miss Dodds replied, "I like it, and I'm not having it crashing down by your dormitory's behaviour." The Princess was immediately contrite. "I'm so sorry, Miss Dodds, I didn't intend to be rude." But Miss Dodds felt that the apology was more for hurting her feelings in unwittingly slighting her small chandelier.

Heathfield had already smoothed the Princess slightly to pattern. She soon no longer said her bedtime prayers aloud although, wearing her muslin cap in chapel, she knelt at her private devotions noticeably a few seconds longer than other girls. "She obviously had more to say," one teacher suggested. Disliking to be different, the Princess basked in reflected glory, however, when burglars broke into Coppins, for the other girls' parents also had burglaries. The Princess could even enjoy schoolgirl one-upmanship in that her mother was away from home and the thieves took nothing except the police whistle that the Duchess always kept at the side of her bed, an extreme oddity. In February, 1948, too, Alexandra could enjoy schoolgirl homage in having appendicitis, when she was rushed home to Coppins for an operation and wallowed in a welcome furore of "Get well" cards while she comfortably recovered.

Yet conformity was all. It was satisfactory, presently, to have an elder brother going to Eton, to be average in rounders and tennis and in due course to be in the second XII "Lax"

(Lacrosse) team. Hearing that visitors would be watching a game, she enquired anxiously, "They won't recognise me, will they?" When petrol rationing eased, there were form outings by coach to London, the Houses of Parliament, the Tate Gallery, to theatre matinees and to Hampton Court where Alexandra, camouflaged in her group, did not shrink when an American tourist called "Oh, Elmer, some genuine British schoolgirls! Can we take a photo?"

It was all to merge in the memory, in the words of another Old Girl, "the curtains of apple green silk, the sunny common room with the Bechstein grand, the Chapel lit up for Compline, the rose garden where we construed Ovid to the sound of the mowing-machine, the crusty head gardener who watched over his plants like the dragon guarding the golden apples..." And there were events like the St. Nicholas tea when all the girls held a sale of work, the Saturday afternoon film shows in the gymnasium, the invitations to the annual Wellington College ball, the occasions like the traditional Halloween party that would find Alexandra pelting along the corridors, panting to any teacher she met, "Oooh! Isn't it gorgeous!"

Meanwhile, the separate lives of Coppins and Heathfield, of home and school, of royalty and privacy, went on side by side. Alexandra undertook one of her first public duties even before Heathfield, when she was still only eleven and Queen Mary decided that it would be a suitable experience for the Princess to join her in a tour of a section of the British Industries Fair at Olympia. The royal group also included the Duke and Duchess of Gloucester and the Duchess of Kent. Circumspectly, the schoolgirl held tight to her mother's hand until on reaching the toy section she clearly realised what was required of her and zealously inspected and tried out the playthings like a model

Princess in the best of toy worlds. Offered a choice of toys as a souvenir at one stand, her mother suggested a little mascot toy cat but young Alexandra pointed to a cat nearly of her own size which had been made for display purposes and formed the central feature. A roar of laughter went up, and the Princess ruefully accepted a small painted dog instead. Queen Mary must have been a little disconcerted to find that the incident swallowed up most of the space accorded the royal visit in the meagre rationed newspapers the following day.

The story made the Princess appear a little younger than she was. Prince Michael was still devoted to the thrills of a travelling circus at Ballater, but the Herberts matched Alexandra's taste perfectly when, to celebrate Princess Elizabeth's twenty-first birthday, they took her to see *Annie Get Your Gun*. The illusion of the theatre was to become a life-long enjoyment; and love of the changing scenes of travel developed in a gradual progress from the English seaside to the Channel Isles. After the Cartier atmosphere of the first post-war Sandringham Christmas, the Duchess of Kent swept her children off to an out-of-season holiday at Bexhill, where the Princess enjoyed signing the hotel register "Alexandra Kent, The Coppins, Iver, Bucks, British" and the Duchess walked the promenade while her family scrambled in and out of the poles and girders of the rusting invasion defences of 1940.

It was not until 1949 that Princess Marina could publicly visit her sister Elizabeth in Montreux. As with Prince Philip and his sisters, an obtuse, unthinking public suspicion hung around all the so-called German connections of royalty in those immediate post-war years. While Eddie was at Balmoral, that summer of 1949, Alexandra and Michael circumspectly took their holidays in Jersey, which turned out to be an unfortunate choice, for polio was reported and the young Kents hurriedly flew home. The Duchess was disappointed for, despite Bexhill and other visits, she still longed for her family to experience the carefree friendly children's seaside holiday that she herself had known. In seeking alternative accommodation, a hotel at Clymping, Sussex, was telephoned. "Are there other children in the hotel ... because the Duchess particularly wishes her children to have companions." The young Kents arrived with a chauffeur and seven-year-old Michael's nanny, and Princess Alexandra, with Heathfield composure, asked to see her young brother's room "to make sure it is comfortable" but also no doubt to satisfy her love of exploration. The hotel staff kept an interested eye on their young but self-reliant royal, and were rewarded to note an envelope addressed to "His Majesty the King, Balmoral".

The interrupted holiday in Jersey was resumed the following year, its highlight perhaps the sunny Monday morning, when they scampered back to the hotel every hour for messages until, shortly before lunch, they learned that their cousin Lilibet's second baby was a girl (Princess Anne). As soon as they returned home, a visit was paid to the new baby at Clarence House. The Duchess now made her own visits to relatives in term-time, when the children would not miss her: travelling to see her mother, Princess Helen, in Athens or meeting her sisters via Montreux. In October, 1950, all the enjoyments that Heathfield could offer Princess Alexandra were probably outweighed by envy when she learned that her mother and Michael and "Peebie" — as the governess had become — were all flying off to meet her grandmama Helen in Rome. Marina could hint that they would all have a holiday abroad together the next summer. But from that moment a number of small things began to go wrong.

IV

Alexandra planned to invite Eddie to the Christmas dance at Heathfield. Instead, early in December, he had to have a small operation on his foot, just as his father had done, though he manfully swore to be ready to dance in time for the end of term: and he could have kept his vow ... except that he went down with measles. It was such an absurdly childish ailment for a fifteen-year-old brother, and to his sister's mingled chagrin and sorrow he had to be isolated over Christmas, during her own fourteenth birthday. Possibly Alexandra argued that they could make up for it at Easter but the perceptive Heathfield matron had noticed the Princess's unromantic habit of snoring heavily at night, a clue to recurrent throat troubles, and at end of term she had an operation for the removal of her adenoids. "Everything happens to me," sighed the sufferer, rather unreasonably, and her only comfort was that she wouldn't want to snort and snuffle before Grandmama and perhaps Uncle Bertie at her Confirmation for which she was to be prepared, with other girls, in the ensuing summer term.

Princess Alexandra looked forward to this event with sincere piety until, as the day approached the intended simplicity was threatened by the requirements of royal guests. Red carpet was laid down all the way from the main hall to the Chapel and the dining-room, and chocolate cake was baked to Queen Mary's special recipe by the school chef.

Miss Dodds naturally anticipated that presumably Queen Mary and the Duchess of Kent would be entertained to tea with the other parents, but this was not quite the case. A Marlborough House secretary telephoned to explain that Queen Mary and her lady-in-waiting would take tea with the Duchess of Kent and her lady-in-waiting and with Princess Alexandra and her headmistress alone — and the secretary added persuasively that Queen Mary would be delighted if the visitors, children and all the school servants would like to assemble to wave goodbye to her as she left. Then, at the eleventh hour, Alexandra had the dismaying news that after all her grandmama would not be coming, because she had influenza — a disappointment instantly forgotten when another telephone call added that the Queen — Elizabeth, the Queen Mother — would be coming instead. "And would Her Majesty care to stay to tea — with the other parents?" Miss Dodds enquired tactfully.

"Yes, certainly," said the voice at the Palace.

The next morning, however, disaster struck dramatically. The matron found Alexandra in frantic tears, and covered from head to toe with the unmistakable rash of German measles.

Her Confirmation, of course, was postponed. The Queen's visit was cancelled, and it was no consolation to the victim to hear her illness announced on the radio news bulletin. Four weeks passed before the Princess was convalescent and could reply to a letter from the King. Uncle Bertie suggested that it was a pity to wait another year and he proposed that Alexandra should be confirmed at a private service in any chapel she preferred. The Princess chose the little Victorian chapel in the grounds of Uncle Bertie's home at Royal Lodge, Windsor, and for four of her school friends, as for other guests, it was an occasion of friendly family charm. The King had undergone the pressures of a busy season, together with a bout of influenza and symptoms of lung infection, and he was showing signs of strain. Just before the choirboys filed in and the service began, his voice was heard raised in lively argument with his Consort. "Oh, dear! They're off again," said Alexandra, with one of her inimitable grimaces. "Why can't they wait till I've been done?"

But the then Queen could always soothe her husband and the King was a genial uncle at the tea party afterwards around the oval table in the dining-room. This proved to be one of those rare occasions when he expressed his wishes on the growing girl who was, after all, his only niece. "I wanted Alexandra to have the broadest possible education to learn how to rub shoulders with the world and keep up with it," he told Miss Dodds.

Nevertheless, there were other aspects in education, and Alexandra went through an adolescent phase of acute self-consciousness at her own clumsiness, and a shame-faced certainty that she could never live up to the heroine she most admired, her own poised and graceful mother. When she learned that the promised holiday in France in 1951 was to include a dinner party with the Comte de Paris, which she and Eddie were both to attend, she struggled in vain against tears. "I'm not — I'm not looking forward to it," she told Miss Dodds between sobs, "I'll knock something over. I dread meeting new people. My hands go so clammy and I can't think what to say. They'll put me next to some elderly prince who can't be interested in me and he'll think I'm stupid. If mother wasn't going to be there it wouldn't be so bad…"

The Duchess of Kent would have been distressed had she known, at the time, the effect that her beauty and elegance produced on her daughter. The headmistress talked quietly to the troubled girl and sensibly gave her the good advice that people like to talk about themselves, that one had but to ask questions to start the ball rolling. "But won't questions be rude?" Alexandra objected. "Not at all," said Miss Dodds, and suggested that the Princess should just try the remedy. And after the holiday an excited Alexandra told her delightedly that her advice had worked. "They talked and talked. It was gorgeous!" It had been from first to last in fact a wonderful holiday with her mother and Michael and Eddie, not only in Paris but also in Provence, where they had stayed at an old villa, a converted mill, near Grasse. Going up the Eiffel Tower, sitting at a cafe, exploring the southern countryside, they had done all the things that are so exciting to do for the first time.

Eddie, too, was in a mood of uninhibited gaiety for it had been agreed that his Eton career should close. At Eton he had seldom ceased snuffing with hay fever, and it seemed best that he should spend a year at Le Rosey in Switzerland. Then, if all went well, plans were maturing for a "fabulous" tour with his mother in the Far East. From France, after the young people's delighted discovery of the atmosphere of the Continent, the Kents went to Balmoral and they were still at Deeside when their "Uncle Bertie" flew south to learn of the necessity of the operation on his lung.

V

On the day that King George VI died, Prince Michael of Kent and Miss Peebles had only just returned to Coppins from Sandringham. The young Duke of Kent was at Le Rosey and his mother was in Munich with her sister, Elizabeth Toerring. It was perhaps for the best that Princess Alexandra, then fifteen years old, was at Heathfield, able to sob her young grief in Miss Dodds' arms, but presently, resilient, seeking her opinion of the pencilled draft of the letter she wished to send her grandmother. The task came of writing to the bereaved Queen Mother was more difficult. "I can't think what I should say," she said. "I'm so anxious it should be right." Presently, later in the day, another thought crossed her mind with youthful directness, apropos of the new Queen's advisers. "Do you think they'll make me wear mourning in school? They might insist on a black school tie. They think of these things!"

She still had her schoolgirl horror of appearing different. Her mother and Eddie were able to reassure her when they flew home from Europe, and Alexandra was dressed only in sombre colours on the day when she tiptoed with them into Westminster Hall and saw, unforgettably, the catafalque in the candlelight, with the people quietly streaming past. For Eddie the ordeal lay ahead of walking, as the head of his family, behind the gun carriage in the funeral procession that made its slow progress through London. Princess Alexandra had never before been more consciously proud of her elder brother than when she watched him that day.

It was strange, at Clarence House, to curtsey to her cousin Elizabeth for the first time as Queen, her cousin only ten years older than herself. Although a decade was a yawning gulf between the girl of fifteen and the young woman who would soon be twenty-six, the Princess read with horror of Elizabeth's mounting duties and responsibilities. One of the questions she asked was whether, if her father had been alive, he would have had any extra duties to do. She could see for herself that, as with her Uncle Harry of Gloucester, there would have been an extra super-imposed task of supporting and serving the young Queen. "Can't *I* do anything?" she asked. Eddie went back to Le Rosey not only mourning his uncle but also heavy-hearted and a trifle alarmed lest the wonderful promise of the Far East tour with his mother should be cancelled, now that everything was different.

Everyone concerned felt a great relief when, after the Queen had consulted with the Prime Minister, Winston Churchill, when it was decided that the fabulous tour — from Singapore to Kuala Lumpur, Sarawak, Brunei and Hong Kong — should go forward as arranged. For the first time, Alexandra was also experiencing the conflict between her dislike of appearing royal at school and her sense that royal responsibilities should not be shirked. Eddie would, after all, be acting as his mother's chief aide, and Princess Alexandra was not altogether satisfied with reassurances, from both her mother and Philip Hay, that she would one day be "old enough" herself. No doubt Mr. Hay did his best to explain that the mantle of the Queen's former duties among youth organisations fell mainly upon Princess Margaret. The would-be volunteer persisted and, in the course of an Easter visit to her grandmother at Marlborough House, fruitful results emerged in a talk with sympathetic old Lady Airlie. The dowager Countess, though relinquishing the ties that had bound her through half a century of public service, was still a member of the executive council of the Red Cross. And in August, 1952 — during school holidays lest she might be thought to be showing off — it was announced that Her Royal Highness Princess Alexandra had become Patron of the Junior Red Cross.

It seemed enough to begin with, and her emergent sense of dedication was strengthened two weeks later when, from Balmoral, the Duchess of Kent fulfilled a compact she had long since made with herself and took her young family to visit the scene of their father's death. Flying north to Wick in a Viking of the Queen's Flight, they motored to Berriedale and Braemore and then walked two miles through the heather-clad hills to the granite memorial cross. They were left to themselves and lingered there through the long summer afternoon, alone with the curlews and the sighing wind, but someone who was close to them that day noticed for the first time that Princess Alexandra was a fraction taller than her mother and seemed to assume a tender adult responsibility.

5: THE TEENAGE PRINCESS

I

One might say that the full-vestured ceremonies of Coronation Year compelled Princess Alexandra to dive into the tasks of royalty at the deep end. She left Heathfield at the end of the winter term of 1952, just before her sixteenth birthday with, as her headmistress, Miss Dodds, finally summed up, "all the lovable qualities of quick sympathy, affection and generosity, laughter and total honesty still there in abundance…" Returning from the great success of the Far East tour, her mother was honoured with a civic luncheon at the Mansion House and the Duchess of Kent shortly afterwards gave a reception at Coppins … and for the first time Alexandra was in the receiving line.

She had formerly moved quietly among such gatherings, handing round nuts and biscuits at a Wren reception or a neighbourhood cocktail party, but now her self-control in concealing nerves and embarrassment were taxed to the uttermost, especially when she realised that Miss Dodds was there and was indeed about to curtsey to her. Yet one observer noticed how smoothly Heathfield had turned her out, without stamping a pattern, and Miss Dodds, on meeting her at local official functions, noted how the "knowing look of recognition fined down to an imperceptible glance and a skilful indication that if I could get over to a corner she would join me there for a talk". Alexandra was never within sight of being a deb of the year. She gave an astonished glance at one of Norman Hartnell's early sketches for her Coronation gown and murmured, "I wish I *could* look like that. It doesn't really look like *me!*"

Mr. Hartnell designed, as he said, "a diaphanous garment of white lace and tulle lightly threaded with gold", and with his usual poetic touch the embroidery of the train repeated the starry motif of the dress she had worn as bridesmaid to Princess Elizabeth more than five years before. As the fittings progressed, the modest, self-deprecating Alexandra showed an astonishment that deepened to delight and real pleasure. "Drifting", "glinting" were the adjectives Norman Hartnell chose to sum up his impressions when the Princess made her entrance in Westminster Abbey. Looking down from the Queen's Box, the couturier realised with pride that the Duchess of Kent and her daughter were the first royal ladies to appear wearing his creations.

The Kents left Buckingham Palace at 9.40 a.m. in the "procession of members of the Royal Family" that seemed to the crowds to be the most graceful and charming of all the secondary processions, consisting as it did of two of the smaller glass coaches and an elegant state landau, with an officers' escort of the Household Cavalry. The first coach was occupied by the Princess Royal and members of the Gloucester family, the second by the Duchess of Kent and her family of three. Then, in the Abbey, over the carpets of blue and gold, they enacted their romantic role in the measured pageantry of the family procession: the Duchess of Kent, her train borne by Lady Rachel Davidson, her coronet carried by Philip Hay; and then the youthful and dignified groupings of the Princess Alexandra, her train borne by the Hon. Katherine Smith, the Prince Michael of Kent and the Duke of Kent, his coronet carried by his page, Henry Herbert. It may have been noticed by those versed in the symbolism of heraldry that, as a princess not of age, Alexandra did not yet rank a coronet.

Posterity must wait upon Princess Marina's thoughts as, from the Royal Gallery, she watched the crowning of her niece. Sadness was there, that Queen Mary was no longer alive to enjoy the transcending young beauty of all her three granddaughters. A mother's pride was there, as her seventeen-year-old son was third to kneel in homage to the crowned Queen upon her throne, his one small error the omission to remove his gloves. And was there also perhaps in a mother's reverie the expectation, the dream, that her own daughter might one day take part in a similar ceremony ... if another land should ever institute the coronation ceremonial of a Queen consort?

For Princess Alexandra, as for the Queen, the immense beauty and solemnity of the day reinvigorated her deep-felt sense of dedication. But for the child that still lurked in her, with feet very much in both worlds, there were the celebrations afterwards and the fun. Late that night, when the crowds waited outside Buckingham Palace undaunted in the drizzling rain, Princess Alexandra stood squashed among them, chanting with equal fervour, "We want the Queen! We want the Queen!" The sudden increase of the floodlights on the unpeopled balcony had been the signal for her little group unobtrusively to cross the Palace forecourt and squeeze against the railings, Alexandra wearing a headscarf and dark coat over her party frock with her wartime protectors, the Duke and Duchess of Beaufort, and with Viscount and Viscountess Cobham and others, some looking very much a part of the crowd in their raincoats. "Palace servants, I suppose," said a man making way for them near me, for I too that night had thought the crowds the best fun. "Servants of the Queen, at all events" I told him. And then we were all lost in the fervour of cheers as the great glass doors opened beyond the balcony…

Princess Alexandra had begun at the top with her share in the State Banquets, receptions and family celebrations of Coronation week, culminating in that stately progress beneath the sophisticated eyes of the five thousand in Westminster Abbey. But she had served no apprenticeship, and had still to begin as she should, at the beginning. Naturally unrestrained, always saying the first thing that came into her head, Alexandra was dismayed at the thought of transforming herself into a gracious royal lady who above all must conform. "You don't have to change," she was told by one of her mentors. "You will be as great a success as your mother in your own way. It will all come gradually."

And so, the month after the coronation, the sixteen-year-old royal lady rode in her mother's best limousine just down the road from Coppins; to the little county secondary school in Iver, in fact, on the occasion of an "open day" when she was to present the prizes. She remembered to congratulate, question and praise the children and subsequently royally toured the classrooms, pausing to examine the drawings on the walls, bending down to talk to young prefects. Alas the Princess was about to have tea in the domestic science room when her teacup dropped at her feet, smashing to fragments. Amid the dismay of the education officials, the Princess picked up the pieces. As a beginning, it was highly characteristic.

That sunny August, too, the Duchess of Kent fulfilled a longstanding ambition, a much-discussed plan, by taking Alexandra and eleven-year-old Michael to visit their grandmother, Princess Helen, at her home in the Athens suburb of Psychiko. It was, of course, an ordinary private visit but British Embassy officials and King Paul's equerries were represented in a welcoming party at Athens airport. There were some people who considered that Princess Alexandra's first arrival on Greek soil held special significance, not least in her first meeting in his own land with the young Crown Prince Constantine. Yet for Alexandra herself the plane flight over the Alps and the Adriatic was the overture of an exciting whirlwind round of people and places, cousins and classics. "Uncle Palo", the King of Greece, was in reality Marina's cousin, and his children, the Crown Prince Constantine, Princess Sophia and Princess Irene, were therefore Alexandra's second cousins. Sophia was two years younger than Princess Alexandra. Irene had been born only two months before Michael. Constantine — "Tino" as the family called him — was three and a half years Alexandra's junior, a plump dark schoolboy of thirteen to her tall sixteen years. The difference dismayed and vexed those who wished to make farsighted dynastic plans, members of an elder group who could shrug their shoulders and murmur, "After all, what is three years — when one is in one's twenties?"

But Alexandra was unaware of these spinning webs of anticipation as she first saw the bitter orange trees of Constitution Square, the kiosks and cafes in the roar of traffic, the slopes and villas of Lycabettus, the Parthenon and the waiting museums. And above all, perhaps, royal Athens: the giant Evzone guards of the new Royal Palace; and her mother's birthplace, the Petit Palais, so unexpectedly akin to Clarence House in its stucco and its site overlooking the royal gardens. They drove out to Tatoi — "Just a bit like Coppins", it could be agreed — and Auntie Freddie, the Queen, invited confidences. Princess Marina was radiant with remembrances of her childhood; and Princess Helena, among her dogs and cats, and portraits happy that her English grandchildren could at last enjoy her own world. A wonderful week was spent in Corfu with a family reunion at Mon Repos, the enchanted cliff-hanging house where Prince Philip had been born, and where Michael and Constantine rushed up and down the steep paths so wildly that Alexandra had every reason to fear they might hurtle into the sea. All this and much more must have packed that first Grecian holiday to glowing completeness.

Princess Alexandra so much more at ease with her royal status, indeed more sure of herself on returning home, that in October she set out without qualms to share a tour of duty with her mother. Observing the maxim that the royal tyro should progress in a series of level steps, this new graduation was a two-day tour in East Lancashire at the behest of the Cotton Board, visiting the Board's official colour, design and style centre; a textile training college at Kirkby; and then spinning mills at Chorley and Bolton. In Accrington the crowds awaited them in driving rain and, rightly or wrongly, the story was spread that Alexandra admonished a chauffeur, "Let's drive slowly; they've waited so long." At a calico-printing works, the two royal ladies donned aprons to print their own souvenir handkerchiefs with the Accrington coat of arms.

The tour was concluded with a mayoral tea party at Manchester Town Hall, a function which would formerly have surely — and fatally — appealed to Alexandra's sense of humour, but all went well. The joke to strike her with full comicality came next day with an account of the tour in *The Times*, ending with the announcement "Photograph on Page 11". But the promised picture was absent. "They've spiked us!" said the Princess. "We must have looked awful!"

Yet possibly this was true — and it may not have been a joking matter. Marina was aware of attributes in her daughter that needed polishing, and in Athens she had discussed with King Paul and Queen Frederika a proposal for Alexandra's "finishing" in Paris. The Duchess and her daughter flew to France immediately after the Lancashire tour, and the cameras caught an admittedly gauche and awkward young princess, still with some signs of the hobbledehoy English schoolgirl, tweedy and flat-heeled. They were met at Le Bourget airport by Princess Olga, who now had a house in the quiet and demure Rue Scheffer, on the aloof and pleasant verge of Passy. Here, for a week, Alexandra settled in with her cousin, Princess Elisabeth of Yugoslavia, discovering once again the sights and sounds of Paris, window-shopping along the Victor Hugo, and visiting Elisabeth's own friends. As it happened, King Paul and Queen Frederika were also in Paris, stopping over just before their much-publicised visit to America. But now Alexandra was to have her own minor measure of publicity and both the British and Greek newspapers made a "splash" of the announcement that the Princess "was to make a stay in France, taking lessons in French and music" and that she would be staying with the Comte and Comtesse de Paris and their family.

II

If eyebrows were raised at the acceptance of the French Pretender as Alexandra's host, in the touchy climate of post-war opinion, it must be remarked that the Duchess of Kent in reality was no more than drawing upon her inexhaustible family connections. The Comte's sister, Françoise, was Marina's aunt-in-law, being the second wife of Prince Christopher of Greece. Moreover, it had to be admitted that Princess Marina was lodging her daughter with the most aristocratic family in France and with the most unconventional, left-wing and forward-looking of royalists at that.

Henri d'Orléans, Comte de Paris, could trace his descent direct from the brother of Louis XIV, the Sun King, and was the great-great-grandson of the Louis Philippe who restored the Bourbon dynasty to the throne of France in 1830–1848. Princess Alexandra knew sufficient of French history to appreciate the ingrained pride, as well as the royal paradox of humility, in these antecedents. His wife moreover was of the house of Orleans-Braganza, of Portuguese, French and Bohemian blood, and a granddaughter of the ill-fated Dom Pedro II, the last Emperor of Brazil. The Comte's worst enemies could not suppose him an effete claimant, clinging with lustreless aspirations to a throne that could never exist. On the contrary, even staunch republicans could concede him an aura of gallantry. First and youngest of royal air pilots, he had found himself prohibited in 1939 from joining the French Air Force or Army, and had enlisted incognito in the Foreign Legion. Since the war, the Comte de Paris had continuously enlarged his sphere of political influence with optimism and energy ... with the result that in 1950 the French government revoked the law of 1886 barring the Bourbons from France, and the Comte was able for the first time to return from his family's sixty-five years of exile.

Only a year or two before Princess Alexandra's visit, the Count and Countess had found and fixed up a tumbledown mansion at Louveciennes, near Versailles, and restored the old name, the Manoir du Coeur Volant, the Manor of the Flying Heart. Its fifteen rooms afforded space for the more important family portraits; and the conversion of an extra cottage in the grounds, the Blanche Neige, afforded space for all the family. The situation of the Manor was akin to that of Coppins, near a motorway though secluded within its own acres on the rural western fringes of the city. For a day or so Alexandra evidently found the names of all the Comte's eleven children inextricably confusing, and she explained with nervous comicality that she had never realised anyone could have so many. The unorthodox ménage of fun, variety and originality, nevertheless appealed to her immensely and she must have felt at first that she was re-living her initiation at Heathfield *a là française*.

The eldest girl, Princess Isabelle, was twenty-one and was working for her final State nursing exams. Her brother, a year younger, the Dauphin, Henri, was bent upon taking his science degree. The nineteen-year-old Princess Helene quickly inveigled Alexandra into piano duets, and was full of advance information on "Mademoiselle Anita's", the school in Paris which they were to attend together. Next came tall and handsome François, who was tragically to meet his death in the Algerian war, and fifteen-year-old Anne, the "potters' thumb prodigy" of the family. The eldest five had all been born in Belgium, while the others asserted that they formed a United Nations by right of birthplace. The Brazilian one was the ballerina, thirteen-year-old Diane. The twelve-year-old twins, Jacques and Michel, were away at boarding school, but it was an oft-told family story that they had been born in Morocco when the Comte was unexpectedly away from home and the Comtesse had frantically driven herself to hospital in an ancient and rattling Renault. Neither of the youngest children — Claude, the Spanish-born Chantal or the Portuguese-born seven-year-old Thibault — spoke English, which seemed the best of reasons for giving Alexandra a room in the Blanche Neige, Snow-White, the pink-washed little house which they shared with their governess, Mdlle de Montlaon.

The English visitor at times thus had no alternative to French conversation. The parents prohibited television and the family made their own fun, from Isabelle's painting in oils to

Thibault's preoccupation with model cars. There was even for a time a family newspaper *Nous Onze* printed on an ancient printing press which the Comte had bought as a bargain in America, the self-same press, incidentally on which the young Rudyard Kipling had once printed his own short stories. I owe this information to a biographer of the family, Miss Bromberger, who has also told how the youngsters in fiesta mood would raid the collection of Brazilian records, dress up in old skirts and scarves cherished since the war and dance frenzied sambas. When Alexandra settled in, however, the Frere Jacques' *Barbara* was more in vogue and a song about onions had been wildly adopted by the smaller fry. The English princess, merry, adaptable and yet with her underlying seriousness, was quickly at home. Her alarm clock was set for 7.15 a.m. and life was soon as real and earnest as for any student.

Methodical and business-like, it was the Comte's custom to leave for his office in the Rue Constantine early every morning by car, and the Princesses, Isabelle, Anne and Alexandra became his regular passengers. Isabelle occasionally completed the journey to her hospital near the Porte d'Italie by Metro, while Anne and Alexandra, three days a week, were usually dropped near the top of the Rue de l'Amiral d'Estaing where they strolled down to the mansion that was "Mademoiselle Anita's".

There is still no brass plate on the door of No. 10 to indicate that it is not a grim block of flats like the rest, and nothing proclaims that it is probably the foremost young ladies' finishing school in Paris. Adjacent doorbells announce the Baronne A and the Vicomte X; and in nearby streets the elegant salons of the couturiers Jacque Fath and Guy Laroche display circumspect striped awnings to impress potential clientele. Alexandra was to come to know the Amiral d'Estaing in every aspect: the convent garden across the way waving bleak wintry branches above its wall, the same trees starred with blossom, the young children skipping to their own school around the corner in the Rue Lubeck, and, dominating everything as the princesses walked down the hill, the superb near view of the Eiffel Tower, framed in the grey façades. All the English girls were careful to walk to Anita's, one observer was quick to note, while the Americans arrived chauffeur-driven in their Buicks and Cadillacs. Outwardly cordial but guarded and stiff as her starched high collar, the ageless Anita parried all questions about Alexandra. "Which princess? I have five in my school." Anita's curriculum ranged from the arts and current affairs to languages, typewriting and gymnastics, and was defined with an epigram. "I give lessons in all the arts, but chiefly the art of living."

Alexandra studied French literature under the Rev. Mother Borel on Thursdays, Russian literature in French on Fridays, French grammar and dictation on Saturday mornings, and this linguistic stress was carried into the classes on cookery and dressmaking and pervaded the afternoon excursions to the Louvre and the art galleries, the days at Versailles and the "brainwashing" — as the girls called it — in French décor at Malmaison and Fontainebleau. It was an education of which Princess Alexandra's father would have approved. No other English royalty had ever similarly received the opportunity of being versed in the fine arts with such skill and polish.

Nor was this all. At Anita's, one remained the schoolgirl, still intangibly fettered to the Heathfield contingent, but on Tuesdays Alexandra became the music student, climbing with her music case up the hillock of the Rue Paul Valery. Here was the studio of Mlle Labroquere, who was herself a graduate of the celebrated music school of Marguerita Long and Jacques Thibaud, and had the privileged entrée for her students of the little white Long-Thibaud salon in the Rue Molitor, where the lines of wooden chairs were packed with music-lovers for the sessions "de virtuosite and d'interpretation". These became a favourite with Alexandra and her friend, Anne, and the youthful Alexandra specially looked forward to a Beethoven concert in which her own teacher was to be the chief soloist. It provided one of her few occasions for ruefulness in Paris when she fell ill with mumps and was unable to go.

The cameramen who tracked her first arrival with impatient excitement — even to thrusting a ladder over the wall of the Coeur Volant — soon forgot about her. There were sessions at her Aunt Olga's house; hours of window-shopping and confidences with her cousin, Princess Elisabeth of Yugoslavia, and an occasional evening out with Olga's two sons. Flying freight planes in and out of Le Bourget as a pilot with B.E.A., Elisabeth's eldest brother, Prince Alexander, displayed only the casual friendship of a man of thirty for a cousin of seventeen, but his dark-eyed younger brother, Prince Nicholas, was only seven years older than Alexandra herself, and Nicky had an air of knowing everything and everyone.

Eddie also came over after completing his pre-cadet Army training course at Sandhurst, and they were all having tea with Isabelle at Angelina's on the Rue de Rivoli one afternoon when a man with a Leica snapped the young Duke but missed his scoop by failing to recognise the girls. To Alexandra's happy satisfaction, the subsequent newspaper photograph showed only her sleeve, almost hidden behind a waitress. But apart from the patisserie at Angelina's or Rumpelmeyer's, Alexandra's Paris was the city of the *carte d'identite scolaire* — the student's half-price ticket — as well as the purse-tempting

Paris of the shops of the Faubourg St. Honore. It was a milieu of well-circumstanced social acquaintance, with the Duke and Duchess of Windsor and a covey of American students as the opposite poles of magnetic attraction. One writer rather inadequately summed it up as "the Metro, museums and music".

Yet a tougher reality was evidently glimpsed through Princess Isabelle in her hospital training at the Croix Rouge Peupliers. Part of her apprenticeship had been served as a compound of home help and district nurse in the workers' flats of Ivry, juggling with the household chores of pregnant chars, and coolly equipped to don an apron and provide a temporarily motherless family with a well-balanced cooked meal for six. Now she was qualifying in "Casualty", at times so unreticent in the horrors of traffic accidents, factory mishaps and would-be suicides from the Seine that the family dubbed her "Frankenstein". The Alexandra who had played in nursing uniform as a child listened avidly to these candid professional reports. Sometimes she would go to meet Isabella when she came off duty, catching unprepared unroyal glimpses of out-patients in the white-tiled corridors and halls of the hospital, amid the smell of iodoform and blood and poverty.

But Isabelle believed equally in the counterbalance of Balmain and Dior; her sister, Helene, was in the midst of proclaiming a cult of originality, while the younger Anne excused everything by asserting that above all one must be oneself. The two eldest girls bought their own clothes with a monthly allowance, and Alexandra was at the most receptive age to benefit from their French and essentially feminine wisdom. Above all else, she longed to return home at last looking a credit to her mother, whose poise, beauty and dress sense she so admired. Princess Alexandra spent six months in

Paris, apart from the Christmas interlude at home. She had gone there schoolgirlish, tweedy and flat-heeled. She returned glamorous, elegant and composed "sleek ... faultless ... with the latest..." as one fashion writer gasped. The features editor of the world's largest circulation newspaper the *News of the World* telephoned my literary manager. "We'd be interested in a series on Princess Alexandra," he said. "By Helen Cathcart? Not just yet — but soon!"[1]

III

The Kents gathered at Coppins for that Christmas of 1953 with a sense of significance that, on sadly looking back, they were to realise was not unfounded. Princess Alexandra and her mother were to remember it ever afterwards as the time they were all together. They had all been separated — Alexandra in Paris, Edward at Sandhurst, Michael at prep school, and Olga's sons, Nicky in London, Alexander away flying — and now they revelled in being united, all the young Kents and their Yugoslav cousins and all "Auntie Ag" Stoeckl's family, friends of a lifetime, the Koziells from Coppins Cottage. Alexandra's birthday on Christmas Day also carried the special importance of entering her eighteenth year, that mystical shore of young womanhood. Her brother Edward was jubilant in having passed his exams, and even eleven-year-old Michael seemed invested with a charming new manly independence. For the Duchess of Kent, there was the happiness of having under her roof her sister and brother-in-law, Prince and Princess Paul and their family. Olga and Paul arrived together with Elisabeth and, despite some initial uncertainty of air schedules, Alexander

---

[1] In the event, the *News of the World* preferred to serialise the author's book *The Queen and the Turf*, and her series on Princess Alexandra appeared in 1955 in the now defunct *Sunday Chronicle*.

came rushing in on Christmas Eve, bubbling over with mysterious hints of an Italian girl friend in Lisbon. Nicky, too, was jaunty with the probability that his firm, the City branch of Niarchos, might allow him an extended oil-tanker trip to the Far East, a journey anticipated as so prolonged and leisurely that he hinted some doubts whether he would be home for next Christmas.

Coppins echoed with merriment, music, talk, laughter and companionship. Everyone agreed it had been a wonderful Christmas when, late on the 27th, the two brothers, Alexander and Nicky, had to return to London, roaring away down the drive in Nicky's silver-grey sports car. Next morning, Marina and Olga and the others left to join the Queen Mother's house-party at Sandringham. (It was, of course, the winter when the Queen and Prince Philip were away on their first long Commonwealth tour.) When the Kents returned to town after New Year, another family party culminated in an evening at Covent Garden when they all occupied the royal box for a performance of *Le Coq d'Or*. Only Prince Alexander was absent, his air duties happily coinciding, no doubt, with the wishes of the mysterious lady in Lisbon.

Princess Alexandra flew back to Paris with her Aunt Olga for her second term at Anita's, though not before indulging in a serious business conversation with Philip Hay, who was charged with the negotiation of future royal engagements. Lady Moyra Hamilton, daughter of the Duke and Duchess of Abercorn, who had been a maid of honour to the Queen at the Coronation, now, at twenty-four, agreed to become Princess Alexandra's lady-in-waiting. Ahead of the family announcement, the young men of the family no doubt attached some levity to the news that Alexandra was to become vice-patron of the Y.W.C.A. and her impending patronage of the

National Association of Girls' Training Corps and her presidency of Guide Dogs for the Blind were equally greeted with hilarious puns that the namers of these worthy organisations had not intended.

These good-humoured remarks failed to disturb the Princess's resolution to make a success of this "first" royal year. Her engagements were to commence after Easter and she gave some thought to the wardrobe that, well within the budget, she hoped would please her mother. Only the day before she returned, however, the death occurred of Crown Princess Martha of Norway, and so when Alexandra stepped from the plane on April 6, and was greeted by her mother, both of the royal ladies were dressed in the black of Court mourning. It was a curious omen of the tragedy that, to the fatalists, may have evinced its first faint tremors even at Christmas.

The weekend before Easter the two sisters, Marina and Olga, were again at Coppins. Nicky was staying with friends at Winkfield but on the Sunday, April 11th, he motored over to accompany his Aunt Marina and his mother to Iver Church. After lunch he returned to Winkfield for an afternoon's tennis and stayed on until nearly midnight when he set out to return to London, alone in his car. Shortly afterwards, residents on the outskirts of Datchet heard screeching brakes and a crash. The car overturned into a flooded ditch, the engine running, the radio playing, the driver trapped, and before help could come Prince Nicholas was dead.

As on that other terrible night, twelve years before, the Duchess of Kent was in bed when the news was brought to her, and she had immediately to brace herself to break the shock to Olga. In an instant, the house was a vacuum of grief. Instead of the Easter house-party, there was Nicky's funeral service at the Serbian Orthodox Church in Bayswater. It seemed inconceivable.

The memories of Princess Alexandra's father belonged in distant childhood, and she had never before wept for the loss of anyone so close in age and kinship. A Red Cross official sympathetically suggested that the Princess might wish to defer her royal commitments. Philip Hay responded with the Princess's thanks and appreciation but said that she would prefer the arrangements to stand. On May 5th, only two weeks after the funeral, her name for the first time headed a Court Circular announcement issued from Coppins to the effect that Her Royal Highness had visited the headquarters of the British Red Cross Society and that Lady Moyra Hamilton was in attendance. A week later the Princess accompanied her mother to the British Industries Fair at Olympia.

The world was of course unaware of private sadness and, during the Princess's first royal engagements that summer, the accompanying journalists found it profitable to ascertain her smiling asides. At the Chelsea Flower Show an official enquired what she would like to do next, and she eyed a lily pool wistfully. "Jump in there and have a swim!" Visiting a Guide Dogs demonstration, she suggested she should be blindfold to help her inspect them in the right way. Officials demurred, and she produced a black mask ready prepared from her handbag.

Though the press loved these touches of unorthodox showmanship, Alexandra was perturbed that the papers invariably emphasised the "unconventional" side of her personality. The magazines, both monthly and weekly, palpitated with a rash of articles: "A Princess Prepares", "The Princess Nobody Knows", "Princess Alexandra Grows Up" ... one can trace the elements of rising prestige in the titles. Royal initiation always occurs in the more sheltered reaches of events, and towards the end of May the Duchess of Kent undertook a four-day programme in Northern Ireland, and Princess Alexandra accompanied her mother. They flew to Belfast in one of the lush aircraft of the Queen's Flight and found a guard of honour of the Royal Ulster Rifles drawn up on the tarmac for inspection: it was a royal visit with all the trimmings.

One objective was the Ulster Show, where Princess Alexandra gazed with dexterous interest at the prize livestock parade and presented rosettes to the winning horses. This was familiar ground, and Alexandra was equally at home with her hosts, Moyra Hamilton's parents, the Duke and Duchess of Abercorn, with whom the royal ladies stayed at Baronscourt, Newtownstewart. Indeed, the friendship can be traced to the days when the Duke's married sister, Lady Katherine Seymour, had been Queen Mary's youngest lady-in-waiting. Moyra also had two brothers, Jimmy, the twenty-year-old Marquess of Hamilton and the eighteen-year-old Lord Anthony who doubtless, as elder folk hoped, unobtrusively drew Alexandra's mind away from the poignancy of Nicky. But she had learned, too, the royal essential of masking her thoughts and she blazed with smiles on the last day of the visit in Belfast when she accompanied her mother on a visit to open a Methodist College extension, unveiled plaques and planted trees at an old folks' home and was lunched in the magnificence of City Hall by the Mayor and Corporation.

IV

In the afternoon sunshine of June 10th, 1954, a trim figure in the navy-blue belted officer's uniform and beret of the Red Cross stepped from a royal limousine at St. James's Palace, accompanied by her similarly-attired lady-in-waiting. The date is not unimportant for — preceded though it was by the May 5th inspection — officials rated this Princess Alexandra's first important public engagement on her own. The occasion was a rally of the Junior Red Cross and a public demonstration of the good work achieved by this young element in helping the sick and needy. The organisers considered that the Princess acquitted herself superbly: spending just the right amount of lingering time on each display stand, busily asking questions, smiling broadly, even to showing extra interest, as a local Princess should, in a stand manned by juniors of her own county. She made a short speech with just the right touch of embarrassment and modesty and presently, meeting a group of deaf and blind demonstratively shook and held the hands of every individual, so that their tenseness turned to pleasure. Oblivious of the difficulties of her apprenticeship and eager for a characteristic slant on the story, the press reported that she "mislaid her handbag, twice dropped her gloves, spluttered pink-cheeked through her speech and then escaped with obvious relief to the sandwiches and eclairs". Such distortion were often to dog the Princess, "inaccurate rather than untrue", as Philip Hay tactfully explained. But this was the occasion that a boy greeted the Princess with "Wotcher!" and received an instant "Wotcher!" in response. Young and old alike could agree that the Princess had left a glow behind her. "I wish her grandmother could have seen her," one official said.

Her great-grandmother, Queen Alexandra, would also have approved could she have seen her namesake touring the Alexandra Rose Day depots. The tempo was increasing. At the Dockland Clubs Ball old Princess Marie Louise sponsored her debut into evening engagements, though Alexandra was a trifle disturbed that — at Marie Louise's punctilious insistence — her precedence as seventh in the succession caused her to enter the ballroom ahead of the old lady. She was becoming accustomed to presentation lines, her tempo timed by one observer that evening as shaking 145 hands and returning 145 smiles in fifteen minutes. The requests for patronage flowed in faster, now, and the Royal Soldiers' Daughters' School and the Royal Alexandra Hospital for Sick Children were among the early acceptances. "I expect I shan't really rank until I've launched a ship," she had once said jokingly. This duty, too, was hers when she was still only seventeen.

"Her Royal Highness will be received at the shipyard of Messrs. John Brown and Company by the Lord-Lieutenant of Dunbartonshire..." Normally the Princess would have read the long minute-by-minute schedule with a flutter of nerves followed by days of increasing stage fright. On this occasion, the mounting tension was eclipsed by the family panic of a motoring accident which befell the Duke of Kent, fraught as it seemed, only two months after Nicky's death, with such disastrous possibilities, Edward had passed his driving test the previous year and was alone at the wheel of a shooting-brake driving from Sandhurst one morning when he collided with an estate car travelling towards him. Both drivers were knocked insensible but the Duke was thrown head first towards the road and the police, on telephoning Coppins, reported him still unconscious.

His mother foresaw the frightening possibility of a brain injury, and an ambulance rushed her son to the National Hospital for Nervous Diseases in London. As it turned out, the young Duke had suffered only concussion and, just before she flew to Glasgow, Princess Alexandra had the immense relief of learning that he would be home safe and sound the following day. It was a jaunty Princess indeed at John Brown's yard who scored "a direct hit with the bottle" against the tanker *British Soldier* and then went down into the crowds to talk to the men who had built her.

Princess Alexandra had always got on exceptionally well with her elder brother, and his accident revived an ambition, already fanned by Princess Isabelle in Paris, that she should have some nursing experience. The Duchess of Kent suggested that even if her daughter's mounting engagements allowed the time she was still too young and should wait a little. Ahead loomed another adventure, for Alexandra was to accompany her mother to Canada. Besides, whenever Elisabeth of Yugoslavia was in London, every minute was pledged to help her cousin not to mourn Nicky. Their elders, I suspect, themselves drew comfort from their youthful resilience. The two girls would go off together on long explorations of art galleries and museums, and Alexandra lingered over showcases with all Queen Mary's old engrossment. When they privately visited Luton Hoo, Lady Zia Wernher had cause to notice her young guest's improved knowledge and discernment of her Fabergé and other treasures.

Elisabeth's companionship was rewarding also in the enjoyable though exacting task of selecting the "expense-account wardrobe" for the Canadian visit. Princess Alexandra wished to go to one of the younger couturiers and, chiefly on the retired Captain Molyneux's recommendation, her choice fell on John Cavanagh. With a touch of his native Irish blarney, Mr. Cavanagh has asserted that he began his career by picking up pins in Molyneux's salon. The truth was that he had worked eight years with Molyneux and four years with Pierre Balmain before opening his own showroom in London. Princess Alexandra was, he found, an engaging client who lacked neither the imagination nor the words to describe what she wanted: moreover, her youthful knowledge of fabrics was quite extraordinary. Although she asked for everything "as simple as possible, please", Mr. Cavanagh was unaware that she still felt the influence of Mdlle Anita's interdict against buttons and bows, and one design caused concern because it featured three buttons. The Princess enquired if the dress could be made without them and was only reluctantly persuaded that they were functional, not ornamental, and part indeed of the very construction and tone of the frock.

John Cavanagh little dreamed that in less than nine years he would have the honour of designing Princess Alexandra's wedding gown, and his royal client did not divine the significance of events that were already shaping her future. It was under Sir Harold and Lady Zia Wernher's hospitable roof, at a house-party at Luton Hoo during the summer, that the Princess and Mr. Angus Ogilvy first definitively met one another. They had also met more casually at an Eton Beagles ball and had probably seen each other during previous summer visits to Birkhall. He had been asked once before to escort her to a party, "But why me?" he had asked. "I'm no debs' delight."

From this point, however, their impressions of acquaintance needed no further reminders. "A charming child," was the way Angus spoke of the Princess, from his lofty stature of twenty-five years. They are remembered at Luton Hoo playing tennis and dancing in a group of young people, although it must be added that Angus played a rather capricious game owing to a sprained knee muscle, and the Duke of Kent, apparently, drily described his sister's style as "smashing". The Princess, nevertheless, began taking lessons from Dan Maskell, the coach for the All-England Club, on the Wimbledon courts, and perhaps convinced herself that her easy Coppins style was inadequate and unsatisfying, not only for Angus but also for the Hamilton brothers at Baronscourt. Her mentors, at all events, had achieved a successful exercise in diversion. In the early summer, when the sunny days were still shadowed with memories of the foursomes with Edward and Tilly Laycock and Nicky, the Princess had said she could never play tennis again.

V

As late as the summer of 1954, many of the itineraries and announcements of the Canadian tour were issued through the Duchess of Kent's office in Marlborough House. Queen Mary's old home was being dismantled, but the Kent secretariat nominally stayed on, like a bridgehead between its royal past and its Commonwealth future. During the fleeting visit to Balmoral that year the Kents had also spent a day with old Lady Airlie, who now lived in only two or three rooms at Airlie Castle but opened up all the unused rooms for a few weeks to entertain her grandchildren and their friends. There the Kents again met Angus Ogilvy's elder brother, Lord Ogilvy, who was paying his grandmama a visit with his blonde American wife, Virginia, and her parents from New York, Mr. and Mrs. John Ryan. The Americans were entranced with the little castle, turreted and towered although only one room wide, and they revelled in its draughts, erratic electric lighting and hazardous plank flooring. Even more they were enchanted to meet Princess Alexandra and warmly insistent that the Duchess should adapt her plans while in New York and stay with them for a week, rather than the day or two planned with the Pierson Dixons, the British U.N.O. representative and his wife, out at Riverdale. In reality, their friendship solved a difficulty, for the Pierson Dixons were unavoidably preoccupied in refurbishing for an impending visit from Queen Elizabeth the Queen Mother.

The Royal Canadian Air Force laid on one of their V.I.P. planes for the Kents' transatlantic flight, and a festive holiday atmosphere developed in the lush pearl-grey cabin. So far as I know, only Lady Rachel Davidson, Marina's lady-in-waiting — a sister of the Duke of Norfolk — had crossed the Atlantic before: the Duchess of Kent and Princess Alexandra, Lady Moyra Hamilton and the maid from Coppins were all first-timers. The North American press had shown signs of being nonplussed by the royal visit: whether to treat it as top-level royal, to highlight the Duchess as the world's best-dressed woman or to focus on Alexandra as a young "rival to Margaret". In the plane, the air hostess handed out the latest copy of *Maclean's,* and Alexandra discovered that Canada's top magazine had made her the main feature. The article began by claiming that beautiful princesses were once almost as plentiful as Wampus baby stars. "Now what's a Wampus baby star?" the Princess asked Lady Moyra.

She was learning fast. The time-trick of five hours back enhanced the magic of leaving London in morning sunlight and enjoying tea in Quebec. Vincent Massey — then the Governor General — received them at the airport and whisked them up to the Citadel. That evening, in the dusk, it was delectably adventurous to steal out by a side door with one of the sons of the house and take one of the horse-drawn cabs, so unexpected in the New World, to explore the narrow clambering streets, realising that by Greenwich time it was two a.m. Next day Hart Massey grinned when he found himself described as a handsome young attaché, with whom Alexandra had been romantically alone (though at one point, it seemed, she had asked the driver to move over while she took the reins). The exaggerations had already begun. During the Atlantic crossing she had spent a few inquisitive minutes in the control cabin, but the press view was that she "took the controls". Her mother, it was said, remained confident that the automatic pilot was in operation. This could have sharpened the real story, for the automatic pilot had failed when two hours out of London.

Trivialities can, however, cast a floodlight on character. Towards the end of the tour the Duchess of Kent was to unveil the new Montreal University war memorial and lay a wreath, and at the crucial moment she discovered that no wreath was to hand. It was one of those hazardous slips in detail that so frequently threaten to embarrass royalty and so seldom do. Before the officials could show their consternation, Alexandra with perfect aplomb took her mother's ceremonial bouquet from Moyra Hamilton and walked forward with it to the Duchess. Only an accustomed English reporter noticed the incident, so small and yet significant to the Kent entourage in proving that Alexandra's mind had been on the job. Far from her old wool-gathering, the Princess had truly grown up and was royally of age.

The principal event of the Canadian visit was the inauguration by the Duchess of Kent of a new generating station at Niagara Falls, which would make the power plant the second largest in the world. Thousands of onlookers obligingly lined the route and cameramen dashed like greyhounds around the sleek royal car. Out of the public eye, in one of the turbine rooms, however, Alexandra's sense of the ludicrous impelled her to borrow an Army cameraman's flash camera and turn it on the jostling photographers themselves. Unaware that photography was one of the Princess's prime hobbies, they expected a spoiled plate and it turned out otherwise. "Princess packs bigger punch than Niagara," said a Detroit news caption the following day. It happened that a Toronto newspaper, noted for its private feuds with the Ontario Hydro Commission, had decided to compress its coverage of the switch-on as much as possible. But the irresistible appeal of Alexandra snapping and being snapped turned the affair into a special edition.

In Toronto, Alexandra had an engagement of her own at a reception of the Junior Red Cross, in contrast to the major event of the day when her mother had opened the National Exhibition with all the full pageantry of red-coated Mounties, Scottish pipers and while-silked drum-majorettes, that the vast stadium could produce. When Princess Marina snatched Saturday morning to drive out to Cooksville to see her mother's first cousin, the old Grand Duchess Olga of Russia, Alexandra dropped out of sight to visit Moyra Hamilton's own friends. If she had thought it impossible to merge private fun and public functions, the tour now proved otherwise. As princesses are expected to do, she clambered on to the footplate of a C.P.R. loco and supposedly drove the train. At Detroit the Mayor met the Kents in the middle of the International Bridge while the fire-floats put on a water display that made their backdrop of skyscrapers appear to rise from a sea of fountains.

Next, the tour took in a flight to Halifax, when Alexandra once again allegedly took the aircraft controls, and they visited St. John's and Fredericton before returning to base in Montreal at the Windsor Hotel. The elderly room-service waiter particularly wanted to tell Alexandra that he had known her father. "He wanted to shop for you, being Christmas and then was nearly mobbed in the department store. So they opened up the store specially for him after hours and he came back with all the toys and tried them out right here on the floor." But the waiter wondered whether she remembered her father, and Alexandra told him quietly that she remembered very well. All over Canada there were people who remembered him, a reminder of the sober importance and durability of one's work beyond and above the speeches and presentations, the photographers and the crowds.

In mid-September the Princess and Lady Moyra paused for a pleasant weekend in the Laurentians with other young folk before joining the Duchess of Kent in New York. The Ryans' penthouse, with its fabulous view over the East River, displayed the sophisticated comfort equated with quiet good taste that one comes to expect of wealthy Americans. (John Ryan was the grandson of the aptly-named multi-millionaire John Fortune Ryan and his wife was a daughter of financier Otto Kahn.) And like her mother, Alexandra was immediately made to feel at home in the friendliest possible way, for the three Ogilvy brothers, David (Lord Ogilvy) Angus and James beamed from family photographs, and in the wedding group of Virginia Ryan and David Ogilvy she knew nearly everyone, Beits and Baileys and Brocklehursts and Airlies, and not least her own dear mentor, now in her mid-eighties, the dowager Mabell, Countess of Airlie.

Princess Alexandra was given Virginia's old room, and the future inscrutably treasured its happy secret that she was the second Ogilvy bride to sleep there. The Ryans set out to show their guests New York as only local folk can, whirling them from the Battery at the tip of Manhattan to the top of the Empire State Building. The weekend was spent at Moorland Farm, the Ryans' country home on Rhode Island, where Mr. Ryan amused his guests by projecting his colour slides. It turned out that he had spent a lot of time photographing the Ogilvy brothers against the granite archways and battlements of Cortachy and Airlie, and now the Kents shared the oddity of watching them, in another hemisphere, in the curious frozen solidity of the colour transparencies. Perhaps for the first time Alexandra felt a nostalgic inkling that she had been away for long enough and, for the first time, she may have wondered what it would be like to be away from her native land for always. The wonderful holiday had come to an end, and a gala performance at the Metropolitan gave a brilliant gloss to the final evening before mother and daughter sailed for home on the *Queen Mary*.

6: A PRINCESS IN KENSINGTON

I

Princess Alexandra and her mother returned from Canada to the fresh interest of creating a London home of their own in the south-west wing of Kensington Palace. This was the outcome of an old promise. King George VI had first offered the so-called Suite One to the Duchess of Kent as a grace and favour residence twelve years earlier, shortly after her widowhood. He had in fact even discussed the prospect during her husband's lifetime, as one of several attractive possibilities that might be realised for them both after the war. Queen Elizabeth II renewed the offer to her aunt. No one more merited the advantages of a grace and favour residence: rent-free, with no expenses to meet save rates and customary tenant's outgoings, and put into pristine order for the new occupant. Yet for a long time Marina expressed reluctance. "What should I do with all those rooms?" she said.

Suite One was indeed reputed the largest and most old-fashioned and inconvenient of all the apartments in the Palace. Queen Victoria's daughter, Princess Louise, had occupied it for a quarter of a century and, on surviving her ninetieth year, she was said to be chatelaine of a room for every year of her age. No doubt this quaint estimate included the dungeon-like kitchens and other "astonishingly poor and humble rooms", as one surveyor found, where the draughts were "vicious and persistent" and "coal and water had to be carried laboriously along endless corridors". But it was a wild exaggeration.

Princess Louise died in 1939 and, on the night of October 14th, 1940, at the height of the blitz, incendiary bombs showered on the palace roofs. Only the heroism of firewatchers and civil defence workers, clambering among slipping tiles and burning rafters, saved the building. In the State Apartments, heavy toll was taken of seventeenth-century panelling, elaborate William-and-Mary ceilings and woodcarvings by Grinling Gibbons. But the attics of the private suites were hastily patched with roofing felt, shattered windows were boarded up and the insidious depredations of damp and dry rot began in the untenanted rooms.

The Duchess of Kent's first visit of inspection with Princess Olga was gloomy and daunting. The walls were damp and mildewed, the papers stained and peeling, the hearths filled with rusting iron; and all the rooms, universally dark, seemed either too large or too small. Accustomed before the war to leaving even minor decorative detail to her husband, the Duchess must have felt at a loss. Princess Alexandra, however, with a share of her father's flair, raced through the apartments in a ferment of enthusiasm, seeing everything as it could be. There were far too many rooms, she admitted, but it would be nice to have some of them.

The architects found a happy solution in subdivision, and Suite One became both 1 and 1A and more besides. (Number 1A Kensington Palace was, of course, destined to become the home of Princess Margaret and Lord Snowdon.) The need to dry out the Palace and warm both the newly-restored State Apartments and the London Museum beneath them in the east wing, also provided a bonus in a newly-installed communal boiler plant, piping heat to every room. The structural alterations involved a year of building chaos, and then suddenly the transformation was all but complete, and the Kents were entranced with a graceful three-storeyed house, where the new plaster in each of the twenty rooms was ready for paintwork and even the little neglected walled garden invited the task of planting bulbs for the spring.

One might say that the rehabilitation of Kensington Palace rounded off two and a half centuries of royal history although, if we could turn back that span of years, we should merely find Queen Anne admiring her new Orangery and discover that Wren had completed his southern red-brick Palace façade ten years earlier. It was in fact in 1689 that William III bought Nottingham House, on the outskirts of the village of Kensington, and began beautifying it as an escape hatch from the crowds and smoke of Whitehall. "A very sweet villa, having to it the park," Evelyn noted, and the pleasure of enlarging and furnishing their Kensington home was to last William and Mary for life. Sir Christopher Wren was commissioned to add four pavilions at each corner of the main building, and then a portico and a gatehouse running into a western courtyard. At one time, indeed, his clients hurried him with so many demands at such a pace that the work was scamped and part of one new building collapsed just after the Queen had left it.

George I and George II in turn both lived at Kensington Palace, the first adding decorations by William Kent and the second gleefully constructing the Round Pond, after encouraging his Queen Caroline to filch hundreds of acres from Hyde Park to fence and include within his own gardens. Closer to our own day, King George V admired the situation so intensely that he dreamed of pulling down Buckingham Palace and making Kensington his own headquarters. Did he foresee that his Kent grandchildren would live there? If Princess Alexandra "felt at home from the start", it was because Kensington Palace was in her bones. Her great-great-grandmother, Queen Victoria had been born in a bedroom in the south-east wing which was somewhat the match of

Alexandra's little suite to the south-west wing. Closer still in kinship, Queen Mary was also born in Kensington Palace in 1867, in the same bedroom as Victoria, and Princess Alexandra heard from her grandmother's lips stories of that other Kensington childhood in the magical gas-lit London of the seventies.

Queen Mary had been responsible for the meticulous pre-war restoration of Queen Victoria's nursery suite, even to printing lengths of the old wallpaper from the original blocks, and now her granddaughter dedicated much of her time to perfecting the decor of the new Suite One with an equal though modern enthusiasm. Through the winter months of 1954–55, she and her mother hunted happily in the shops for the precise fabrics and additional pieces of furniture they required. The Duchess indulged her daughter and the Princess ebulliently enjoyed finding the accessories that would freshly set off her mother's wedding gifts from Coppins.

A continuous search centred, for instance, on Georgian chimneypieces in pine and marble. The Ministry of Works had provided the dining-room with an exceptionally fine carved Adam chimneypiece bought for £525 at a country house auction, but this installation evoked such a fury of distasteful questions and comment in Parliament that the Duchess decided to purchase her own chimneypieces and ultimately invested in seven. (In reality, nevertheless, such "renewals of the fabric" were a Government responsibility.) Princess Alexandra does not share her mother's drawing ability, but mother and daughter first envisaged the dream rooms in discussion and the Duchess then sketched possible alternatives. The result of this care and forethought was to be justified.

As at 3 Belgrave Square a fine staircase sweeps from the blue-carpeted entrance hall to a spacious first-floor foyer where, when the Duchess first moved in, one's eye was caught by a romantic and splendid portrait in oils of the three Kent children. From this hospitable focus open three handsome apartments, the largest, the drawing-room, a delight of white and gold, glittering with chandeliers and mirrors. The second was intended as a State dining-room but the large dining-table was long since invaded by business papers and tended to become a reception room and adjunct of the office. The third room, a family sitting-room, similarly began with formal aspirations only to become dedicated to the music and magazines, books, drawings, records, flowers and photographs of crowded family life.

Of the six bedrooms, two were guest-rooms. The others were formed within over-large rooms as self-contained suites, each with a dressing-room and a bath. Pile carpets, chintz curtains and coverlets and a feminine scattering of finely-worked petit point rugs set the atmosphere. Princess Alexandra chose a background of white wallpaper decked with pink and red carnations tied with green ribbons, colours which she echoed in her curtains and dressing-table. A problem piece was a gilt settee which seemed to fit nowhere else in the house. The Princess tried it at the foot of her bed, where it nestled perfectly.

Alexandra was to live in Kensington Palace for eight happy years, awaking each morning to the chirp of the Cockney sparrows. It is a pleasant amenity that Palace residents are secure from sightseers as they step from their front doors opposite the grassy expanse of Palace Green. There is only the salute and smile of the sentinel policeman, and one might be in the eighteenth-century close of a distant cathedral town rather than in the heart of London.

II

Princess Marina could not help but feel a maternal satisfaction at the social embroidery of friendships developing around her daughter. Months before Kensington Palace was ready for house-warming, Angus Ogilvy invited Princess Alexandra to a cocktail party at his tiny flat in Chelsea which seemed to be a representative welcome to London. Formality was quickly abandoned and most of the guests ended up sitting on the floor, listening to records. Two parties later, Alexandra and another girl were the first to arrive, to help with the sandwiches. Virginia Ogilvy invited Alexandra to dinner-parties at the little house in St. Leonard's Terrace which her parents had given her as a wedding gift. There were girl friends of Alexandra's own age group, Henrietta Crawley and Mary-Anne Hare, school friends, mostly, such as Carina Boyle, Charlotte Bowater, Janet Hamilton and Elizabeth Rhys, Camilla Straight and Teresa Crossley. There were young men like Jocelyn Stevens (nephew of Edward Hulton, the publisher), James Macdonald-Buchanan, David Bailey (who was another Airlie cousin) and a contingent of Sandhurst friends of the Duke of Kent. They all moved in the same social swirl of Chelsea mews houses and Belgravia mansions, and of weekends involving air hops to Ulster and house-parties in the Shires.

Alexandra, it became evident, was subject to sudden swift enthusiasms, like her incursion into hunting country when she rode with the Strabane and Pytchley Hunts. With the latter, she had the misfortune to be thrown and, muddied and blooded, she was probably nauseated to read in the newspapers that she had "appeared unharmed at a country house dance" and, another time, that she had "won her spurs by jumping an eight-foot dyke, downfall of many crack riders". It was exasperating to discover that three unconcealed visits to

Baronscourt amounted in press arithmetic to "rumours of a romance" with the Marquess of Hamilton. "We have been seen together!" the Princess would announce dramatically, to sundry young men, but at times the joke thinly concealed her dismay.

The New Year of 1955 was celebrated at Coppins with a family party, culminating near midnight with the old Slav custom when molten lead poured by the guests into cold water was supposed by its twisted shape to foretell the future. Laughter sprang from the fun of invention, grotesque or otherwise, when it was safe to prophesy that Elisabeth of Yugoslavia would be at a splendid wedding, that Alexandra would be subject to engagement rumours, that Edward would be in a car mishap. At midnight the Duchess opened all the windows to let the warmth of the Old Year out, and the chill of the New Year swept her shoulders.

Ten days later came the news that her sister Elizabeth, the Countess Toerring, had died in Munich, aged only fifty. It was a cruel blow, for the family had been together at her birthday party and were all bent on reunion at the coming wedding of her nephew, Prince and Princess Paul's son, Prince Alexander. At first it seemed that the wedding would be postponed but the plans were far advanced, two thousand guests had been invited and as so often in large families, the knife-edge of personal grief yielded to wider rejoicing.

Prince Alex's pretended secret attachment to an Italian girl in Lisbon was now in fact splashed across the pages of *Paris-Match* and every other photo-scoop magazine in Europe, for the young lady was the Princess Maria Pia of Savoy, eldest daughter of ex-King Umberto of Italy. When at least £4,000,000 of his family fortune was happily secured to the retired monarch by a favourable judgment in the Italian courts, he had made his home at Cascais on the Estoril in one of those "modest villas" that require a staff of twenty-five servants. In brief, Maria Pia's nuptials were one of those solid-gold-Cadillac weddings that served as excuse for a glittering reunion of ruling and exiled royalty alike. The British contingent was headed by the Duchess of Kent, the Duke of Kent and Princess Alexandra.

Buzzing with gossip, one hundred Majesties and Highnesses sat down to the wedding breakfast. Paul Weiller, the French aircraft tycoon, was lending the young couple his house at Versailles for as long as they wished. The Onassis and Patino families had competed in giving them gold boxes studded with diamonds. The eighteen-year-old Alexandra looked round the decorated, befeathered and diamond-decked throng and may have reflected that this, too, was a part of her life. "You will be next!" she was told by sundry elderly ladies, but the proposition must have seemed premature. Her cousin, Crown Prince Constantine of Greece, was as yet only a naval cadet of fourteen. On opening the airborne copy of the *Sunday Express*, however, Alexandra found that an editorial had the same theme in mind. In another age, amid the royal dynasties, the leader-writer noted, "Princess Alexandra would have had high hopes of one day becoming a queen." Then the editorial stressed the brighter side of the shortage of thrones. "The Princess need feel no despondency," it ended (as if she did!). "She has the right to marry a man of her own choosing."

In point of fact, personal romance was far from her thoughts in her quicksilver personality. She hurried home to deputise for the Queen Mother at an inter-hospital rugger match at Richmond, and the press made much of the photographs of the Princess "inspecting the two husky teams". No one noticed that she also quietly went to a rugby match a few days earlier, to be instructed in the finer points of the game by Mr. Angus Ogilvy.

III

Studying her press clippings, Princess Alexandra read of her public self — "The New Princess with her Grace of Youth… The Princess whose Lead Young Girls Follow" — with the unreality of a newspaper-created character who did not seem to be herself at all. My own Kemsley (Thomson Newspapers) series, "The New Princess Charming" can scarcely have been an exception, although I understood that she admired the accompanying photographic artwork.

It caught her droll sense of fun to note how frequently the columnists described some unfortunate young socialite as "the debutante of the year, other than Princess Alexandra". The Queen had not then abandoned the Presentation Parties in the white and gold Throne Room at Buckingham Palace and it was true enough that, as seventh lady of the land, Alexandra sat on the dais "close at the Queen's side, unabashedly studied by two hundred debutantes". It would have been equally correct that she also unabashedly flashed a special smile to each of the Heathfield contingent. The attributes of "unaffected spontaneity and naturalness, humour and lack of starchiness, approachability and ease", that public image which a Mass Observation survey reported to be hers in the mid-sixties, were already clearly fixed in people's minds in the mid-fifties. Within this role was also her shining popularity as a royal willing horse, ready to stand in for Princess Margaret or even Prince Philip, a deputy taking over at an instant's notice, yet always to be depended upon to face the most hackneyed royal duties with an assumption of verve and originality. As we have noted, Princess Alexandra's insistence at Leamington one day on inspecting guide dogs by being blindfold was typical. When she visited a paratroop training centre, experienced reporters almost swallowed the rumour that she would change into full gear and undertake a practice leap from the beginners' tower, and later she did in fact ascend in a tethered balloon to share at least a fraction of the visual experience.

She agreed to become patron of the Royal Empire Society's junior section, of the Twentieth Century Group of the Royal Overseas League, of the National Heart Hospital and the London Junior and Senior Orchestras and the word got around that Princess Alexandra might give quicker royal sponsorship, and certainly royal attention, to lesser organisations that might otherwise wait years for notice. She was willing to open new Y.W.C.A. flats at Highgate or unlock the door of a new London youth hostel. She was prepared to say a few words — in a warm mezzo-soprano voice that had now completely gained bright confidence — on behalf of a local blind society or to present prizes to nurses at the Liverpool Infirmary. She was as ready to open a new department of Eastern art at the Ashmolean as to judge millinery at a fund-raising Easter Bonnet parade at the Dorchester and she had the knack of accepting a scarifying crafts-embroidered handbag with flattering appreciation of all the time it had taken to make. She always arrived, attended by Lady Moyra Hamilton, looking as glamorously Hartnell-gowned or Cavanagh-clad as anyone could have wished. She planted commemorative oaks, tapped mallets on foundation stones and invariably looked pleased and surprised if the curtains parted without hitch at an unveiling.

The story got around that she skilfully bought many of her duty clothes off the peg, which seemed to give the impression of a Princess sauntering between the racks looking for bargains. She indeed bought her jeans and other casuals at

Harrods but I cannot believe the tale that the highly practised sales staff at the store failed to recognise her or were startled when she asked, "Can you please send them to Coppins, Iver, Bucks?" The fact remains that Alexandra was the first Princess to wear mass-produced ready-mades as a deliberate accent of an overseas tour: a child of our age, too, in preferring the wider, quicker choice, more readily discarded budget-wise, of ready to wear.

Her mother early initiated her into the mysteries of direct purchase from manufacturers and three or four firms such as Susan Small were regularly patronised over the years. The Princess made an appointment to go along to the showroom at a time of day when things were quiet and the models paraded past her, as they would for any wholesale buyer. The one difference was that the manufacturers were ready to ring as many changes for their royal client, who bought only one of each, as they would for a store buyer ordering in dozens. "Could you provide this dress with a separate jacket?" she might ask. "For summer weather, do you think this tweed would look equally well if done in linen?" From a bulging handbag the Princess produced fabrics she would like matched in colour. "She has a genuine clothes sense," said one manufacturer. "Her ideas often inspire something that catches on." He cited a knitted coat which the Princess saw in palest yellow rather than the more practical tones and once she was seen wearing it, the sales notched four figures.

The manufacturers would gladly submit dresses to Kensington Palace, but the Princess, one suspects, enjoyed the special atmosphere of a showroom, much as we all enjoy a peep behind the scenes. At a favourite milliners' she was one of the few clients to ask if she might visit the workroom, and the work girls gained an impression not only of a sweetness of which she was unaware but also of above-average expertise in the mysteries of spartra and wiring. I once mentioned in my rough draft of a magazine article that the Princess had sometimes made her own hats, and an indignant hand pencilled on the manuscript "Never!!" One must accept the correction. But Alexandra as a young girl had the know-how of making her own dresses, and a similar Heathfield skill was applied one wet holiday to retrimming some of her mother's old hats with wisps of net and tulle.

Amusingly, when Princess Marina took her to Madame Vernier's for her first "couture" hat, she was only ten years old. Madame forbore to mention that she did not usually make hats for children and devised the pretty little hat, with spring flowers beneath the brim, which the Princess wore at the Victory Parade. Since then more than twenty-one years of trendsetting hats have passed through Princess Alexandra's wardrobe, and one is tempted to think of the attractive exhibition that could be staged for charity — preferably at St. James's Palace, so seldom seen by the public — of her panorama of millinery innovations!

When fashion writers were critical during one phase that Alexandra's hats were too small for her coiffure, they noticed that the fault was speedily remedied. Unlike one royal lady who has her hairdresser expensively flown to wherever she may be, Princess Alexandra has always set her own hair, another highly practical accomplishment learnt from her mother. Princess Marina when younger took tuition in pinning and combing from a hairdresser, and indeed at one time regularly set the hair of that most glamorous royalty, Queen Marie of Romania. Princess Alexandra has been a patron of Riche and René of Mayfair and Alexandre of the Faubourg Honoré, but her own useful knack was to avert many a crisis on overseas tours, and I believe she was similarly the first of the younger royals to wear a wig.

As the wife of a highly mobile air-minded businessman, Princess Alexandra's ability to pack and fly off at a moment's notice is a notable asset, but this is to look ahead. At the gate of her twenties, one recalls that an unexpected holiday similarly blew up from across an empty horizon. In February, 1956, the Queen and Prince Philip had just returned from their tour of Nigeria, and after only six days in London, Prince Philip sailed in the *Britannia* to join the combined Fleet exercises in the Mediterranean. It was one of the rare occasions when the Queen was able to act on impulse. At barely ten days' notice she decided to fly south to join her husband and invited Princess Alexandra to accompany her. Perhaps, also, Alexandra merited the interlude after her astonishing high-pressure year of royal endeavour. Joined by a few friends, they flew south in a Viking from London Airport on March 1st to rendezvous with the royal yacht at Ajaccio.

From then on, the ship's course was secret, but it must be said that the cruise proved disappointing. If one excepts Edward VIII's odyssey with Mrs. Simpson in the Adriatic, it was the first time that the Sovereign had made a Mediterranean cruise since George V went south for health reasons back in 1925, and the royal holidaymakers had hoped for brilliant spring weather. Instead the Med presented itself in its most sullen mood. Mist or cloud veiled the cliffs and capes of Corsica, and cold winds and rain lashed the travellers whenever they ventured on deck. Squalls swept the royal yacht through the Straits of Bonifacio, and Alexandra borrowed a seaman's oilskins and had to peer through the rain to glimpse the precipitous shoreline. Two days out, the sea grew so rough that the *Britannia* was driven to shelter in the La Maddalena estuary.

During this respite, an enlivening view of a fishing village in fiesta mood, and a brief sight of the mountain peaks of Sardinia glistening with snow, rewarded the small party — including the Princess — who ventured ashore, and they returned to the ship with a handsome presentation of traditional dolls. But then the rainstorms swept down again and the voyagers necessarily settled down to make their own fun.

Alexandra had never been more in demand at the piano. Every evening after dinner, also, the panels in the dining-room were pushed aside and the guests settled down to watch, among other films, the movies that the Queen and her husband had made in Nigeria. Princess Alexandra was thrilled by the amazing spectacle in colour of the durbar at Kaduna, culminating in the charge of the Jahi horsemen to the very foot of the royal dais, and the entrancing kaleidoscope of the ten thousand painted and masked dancers of Lagos.

The Queen evidently suggested that Alexandra would perhaps see it for herself one day, and within four years the Princess was indeed Her Majesty's representative at the new independence ceremonies of Nigeria, witnessing in vivid reality all the splendours that the Queen had filmed. For the moment, however, African travel occupied but a minor corner of her young aspirations. Above all else, she never ceased to press her elders with her ardent wish to become a hospital nurse, and effective arguments were now to hand to demonstrate that "the young Kents" were growing up. For one, her nineteen-year-old cousin, Countess Helen Toerring, was old enough to get married. Her bridegroom would be the Archduke Ferdinand of Austria, first cousin of the Archduke Otto, and the wedding at Castle Seefeld the following month would see a great gathering of Hapsburgs, Greek royals and, of course, all the Kents. (The Queen also had a more personal interest in this romance, for Ferdinand was Prince Philip's exact contemporary and had been his room-mate at Salem, in the pre-Gordonstoun days.) For another argument of mature responsibility, also, it was undeniable that in another six months the Duke of Kent would celebrate his coming-of-age.

IV

It invariably pained Princess Alexandra in the 1950s that her elder brother received, on the whole, a sharp-toned press. Their boy-and-girl rivalry had soured in the popularity polls. Edward of Kent really worked in his Army career but press-wise could do little right. Alexandra now sailed effortlessly through her royal duties in contrast with the nerves of her debut, and Fleet Street never faulted her. Edward adored his sister's popularity and shared her annoyance at ill-founded rumour and her sense of comedy that made her tolerant of the oceans of inaccuracy awash around the rafts of fact. His own headlines nevertheless tended to steam with the "playboy Duke". Only one editor of my acquaintance ever sought an article on the Duke's future career, based on his posting to the Royal Scots Greys, but I sidestepped not a few requests to write on the "eligible bachelor" and his "girl friends".

Shortly before Alexandra's Mediterranean cruise, a particularly spate of gush had bubbled around the Duke's kiss for Jane Sheffield when she met him at Klosters, that peck on the cheek which the cameras recorded in frozen immobility. It is possibly news when a prince publicly kisses a girl, though Edward had known Jane as a friend of Alexandra's for years. It is news when a peer has a car crash, and the "speed-loving Duke" was involved in three within thirteen months. Edward's tastes ran from a Sunbeam Talbot to a Sunbeam Rapier … to a trade-in for a second-hand Aston Martin and later a vivid red "Jag". The columnists droned that he was the "envy of his speed-loving friends". But in reality the Duke devoted the precious time of his weekend passes to teaching his sister to drive in the Coppins grounds, although she did not apply for a driving test for some years. He enjoyed the satisfying excitement that his tuned-up cars accorded his young brother Michael and indeed similarly gave him driving lessons at Coppins when he was still only thirteen. Yet there was a time when a malicious gremlin dogged the news columns. The young Duke was reported to be having a wonderful time in Dublin when in reality he was tank-training in Dorset, and it was alleged that the Queen had banned him from driving, a criticism so hurtful and false that he was driven to grant a newspaper interview to ensure that an informal denial went into print.

Yet half-truths and untruths were not always corrected so readily. In May, 1956, newspaper readers were titillated with an account of a Chelsea river party when guests were thrown — or pushed — overboard fully dressed and — I quote — "laughing on deck was the Duke, among the first to toss a lifebelt".

All the Kent family fumed, the Palace was consulted and the unprecedented step was taken of issuing an announcement from Kensington Palace with the totally different reality: "The private secretary to the Duchess of Kent is authorised to say that although His Royal Highness was present for about an hour ... he was in no way involved in, nor indeed, a witness of the actions attributed to him." This caused the collapse of that stout party, Madame Rumour, and it was a prelude, as it happened, to a summer of shrinking publicity that provided a lull before the storm. But the Duke of Kent's celebration of his twenty-first birthday party at Coppins was to be infused with exceptional annoyance.

Every hostess knows the mischance fated to occur on a big occasion. Only two days before the party, the Duchess of Kent was joining in a family foursome on the Coppins hard tennis court when she slipped and sprained her ankle. Fortunately, her local doctor, Dr. Stafford Saint, made a work of art of the bandaging; and her old housekeeper, Mrs. Keeble, came out of retirement to help her to cope. On the great day Alexandra and Elisabeth of Yugoslavia turned a series of exuberant cartwheels on the lawn and Prince Michael was brought home from Eton in time for the birthday tea.

At nine o'clock thirty or more family guests sat down to the birthday dinner party, among them the Queen and the Duke of Edinburgh, the Queen Mother, the Gloucesters, the Harewoods and Lascelles, Princess Olga and her family, and the Poklewska-Koziells, the Hamiltons and other friends. Indeed, the only notable absentee was Princess Margaret, who was in East Africa. Nearly two hundred other guests also gathered for what the invitation cards termed "a small party" afterwards, including a lady whom the footman did not recognise and whom he had to direct to the ladies' cloakroom at the top of the stairs. The intruder was, in fact, a newspaper reporter who had come past the police patrols in the boot of a car.

The footman reported her presence and a lady-in-waiting went to interview her. "I'm so sorry I've forgotten my invitation card," the uninvited guest explained, "but I am a personal friend of the Duke." Edward was thereupon consulted at dinner; the name mystified him and, as an official statement later described the scene, "a member of the Household went upstairs to escort her to the front door. As he approached the stairs she was descending immediately following two lady guests, but on seeing him approach she turned and ran down a corridor until she discovered it led nowhere. She was then taken to the front door and the police escorted her off the premises."

Nor was this all. As the guests gathered, two strange men, who were seen in conversation separated mysteriously as if to avoid detection. This couple, in turn, turned out to be journalists: one had even parked a parcel with a camera and flashlight equipment, which he asked if he could collect before he left. It was indeed a gross intrusion, and more than a hint of the Queen's anger lingered in the letter of complaint which her Press Secretary addressed to the Press Council shortly afterwards. "The Queen and the Duchess of Kent were seriously disturbed by these incidents," Commander Colville wrote, "and Her Majesty considers that it is not too much to ask that she and other members of the Royal Family should receive the same privacy in their homes as is enjoyed by others. On the occasion in question their privacy was not only invaded in an improper manner, but the methods by which this was achieved bordered on deceit..."

It may be that the affair had fuller repercussions than were generally realised, and that this was the final straw of many incidents that drove the Court into deeper reticence on private facts. But there was a brighter side and the public image of the Duke of Kent henceforth was noticeably in softer focus.

V

Exercising the prerogative of a Christmas child, Princess Alexandra twice celebrated her own coming-of-age, first in privacy on Christmas Day under the Queen's roof at Sandringham and then with "a small dance", as her mother phrased it on the invitation cards, on January 6th at Kensington Palace. The smallness was relative, for two hundred invitations were issued. Once again a family dinner party was held beforehand, and the Duchess of Kent's butler, Bysouth, as he moved around the great dining table, must have found it a twin of the Duke's celebration fifteen months earlier. The Queen and Prince Philip specially travelled up from Sandringham, but once again, Princess Margaret was an absentee, to her exasperation, miserably confined to her room at Sandringham with a chill.

The Queen Mother attended the dance though not the dinner, and once again there were Prince and Princess Paul of Yugoslavia and their daughter, Elisabeth, and the contingent of cousins and aunts and uncles. But curiously enough, as at the Duke of Kent's party there were symptoms of disaster two days beforehand. When the thick carpets were rolled back in the salon they revealed that the heating pipes under the floor had caused the parquet blocks to rise in a jagged fissure across the room, direly threatening the dance plans.

Princess Alexandra received a pleasant tribute to her popularity when workmen arrived before dawn and energetically hammered, sand-blasted and polished until soon after dark, the floor was perfected and ready. Doors were also taken off their hinges so that there could be an unimpeded samba line, in and out of the salon and through the private sitting-rooms. The Sid Phillips' band had their cue of the *Dark Town Strutters' Ball* for 10.30 p.m. and the problem of the first dance was solved by precedence — first the birthday girl with the Duke of Edinburgh, and Princess Marina with the Duke of Kent. Friends of whom we have already heard were there in strength, Hamiltons and O'Neils, Hambledens and Douglas-Homes, Abel-Smiths, Baileys, Bowaters and d'Erlangers.

149

Somewhere along the line, when the night was still young, Alexandra danced with Angus Ogilvy and it may have been observed that the Duke of Kent, on leave from Catterick, danced with an attractive blonde whose name was Katharine Worsley. She had not been at the Duke's coming-of-age party, and both Edward and Katharine were unaware as yet that their royal wedding in York Minster lay only three years distant.

One might add that, for good measure, Princess Alexandra also had a third birthday party, for the old people of Iver had each steadfastly saved a halfpenny a week for four months to pay her the compliment of a celebration tea-party. (The proposal had originally been 1s. a head but the Princess indicated that this was extravagant.) And so there was the cake at the old folks' club, and with it their gifts: a silver paperknife and an Italian cut-glass gum pot. The Princess played up superbly, making a pretence of cutting the cake with the paperknife and demonstrating that it was stuck in the icing. She made a fuss of the real birthday girl among the club members that Saturday, an old dear of eighty, and she explained how useful the gum pot would be for sticking stamps. Now that she was twenty-one, indeed, she would be buying her own stamps. Members of the Royal Family on the official Civil List enjoy the useful perquisite of franking their envelopes "official paid". The Kents are all required by a grateful nation to buy their own.

FUGUE

"A musical movement in which a definite number of parts or voices combine in stating and developing a single theme... Two parts or voices at least are necessary, so that one may contrast with the other."

— *Grove's Dictionary of Music*

7: THE NURSE, THE COLONEL AND THE TRAVELLER

Two months before her coming-of-age, Princess Alexandra reached a compromise in the unforgotten ambition, which had held anchorage in her thoughts for five years, that she should become a hospital nurse.

On the encouragement of her grandmama, Princess Nicholas, she had been given a "finishing" in Paris, and no one had foreseen that this would involve Alexandra's fascination with the hospital training of Isabelle of Orleans. Yet the seeds had been implanted long before, perhaps in the child's Red Cross costume and certainly in glimpses of her mother in nursing uniform when the Duchess worked as Nurse Kay at University College Hospital.

The adult world had tried in vain to stress that the duties of a princess in peacetime were by no means the same as in war. Probably Princess Alexandra's best argument — that a nurse tangibly easing pain and sickness was a better example than a royalty merely seen to be supporting good causes — was never fully resolved. Scarcely less persuasive were the plans for her young brother Michael to enter the Royal Naval College at Dartmouth as a gateway to a career in the Navy as soon as he left Eton. At the invitation of Commander David Loram, Michael had already spent a week on board an anti-submarine frigate, while on exercise off Portland, and had returned full of excitement. If a prince could combine a career with royal duties, why not a princess? "There are misgivings that the Princess does not know her own mind," wrote a family friend.

"But you know her determination. We must hope they find a way round it."

The way was found when the Princess enrolled for a course in child welfare at the Hospital for Sick Children in Great Ormond Street, London. Columnists leapt eagerly to the conclusion that Princess Alexandra would immediately be introduced to "the intricacies of diaper changing and would work a thirteen-hour day on the wards". In reality, her studies were to resemble the postgraduate course sponsored by the Institute of Child Health, though with skilful amendment to allow for her public engagements. But the Princess meant to work hard: she arrived the first day with the morning milk and it was dismaying to find that the Matron greeted her with a small cellophane-wrapped bouquet while students, ward-maids and cameramen crowded the pavement. Once the introductions were over, however, Matron Kirby said briskly "And now I suppose you would like to begin?" and in the nurse's changing room the Princess was shown her locker and presently Nurse Kent, in pink uniform and starched apron, was piloted to the lecture room.

The dream had begun, the press had been indulged with a glimpse, and the trainee student settled into the hospital routine. She took home the standard textbooks on the growth and development of children, attended the usual demonstrations of bathing and dressing a baby from the earliest age and assisted in a ward kitchen making up artificial feeds. She took her inconspicuous place in the cluster of pink-clad nurses touring the wards in the wake of a doctor-lecturer, making her notes with the rest on the problems of children having feeding and sleeping troubles. She was soon capably taking and charting temperatures, coping with colic, able to write her five hundred words on enuresis. And as at Heathfield ten years earlier she had to overcome the diffidence of her colleagues, doubtful and even suspicious as they were of the readiness and capabilities of a "royal".

The barriers dissolved fastest in the canteen, where she noticeably seemed to get on best with the overseas students and "certainly was a promising nurse" as one said "in simply having no sense of a colour bar". Four years later, in visiting the Kwetu social centre in London, she was delighted to recognise two of the East African nurses who had trained with her.

Presently she worked in the out-patients department with mothers more concerned with their ailing babies than with the identity of the well-scrubbed, sympathetic and anonymous assistant nurse whose white cap proclaimed her an unqualified beginner. One of the student nurses working with Nurse Kent could sense her difficulties in combining two roles in one. Alexandra, though technically on a three-day-a-week rota, sometimes unexpectedly had to devote afternoons or mornings to "engagements".

Her Christmas break was prolonged by her necessary presence at Sandringham in the New Year with the Queen. Her birthday party was timed not to conflict with hospital hours, but a wedding invitation was less readily foreseen, and the Princess unfalteringly made excuses to the bride's family. She was "on duty" at the hospital one day, and royally visiting another London hospital the next. One of the Coppins maids chanced to undergo an operation in another hospital and the Princess visited her with a practised bedside manner, squeezing the last juice from the lemon indeed. It afforded family fun that her first private patient was her brother. The Duke of Kent had commenced an Army riding instruction course at Aldershot and returned to Kensington Palace one weekend with his face lacerated by an encounter with the branches of a tree, brushing past at full gallop. The cuts and scars did not necessitate a doctor but were sufficient for Alexandra's jokes and sympathy and her newly expert attention.

Without missing lectures, she travelled to Durham by night train one weekend to review her regiment, the Durham Light Infantry, for the first time as its Colonel-in-Chief and the press noticed the inspired touch — made, I believe, at her own suggestion — that both the driver and fireman of the train had formerly served in the D.L.I. The Princess had been bandaging a baby's foot twenty-four hours earlier and now was followed by a sergeant with a ceremonial umbrella in the regimental colours of red, black and green. Nurse to colonel, Princess Alexandra was royally opening an exhibition when a woman near her tripped and fell heavily on the marble pavement. It was the nurse who left the official group to help the woman to her feet and, "run a professional eye over her". Touring a school science laboratory, it was satisfying to peep into a microscope and demonstrate that she knew how to handle it. Dovetailing her time with the dexterity of all her family, she sat for hours one afternoon with the magistrates of a London juvenile court. It was a characteristic royal visit which also happened to comply with a child delinquency section of her programmed studies.

As a Princess, touring the Royal Portsmouth Hospital, the press noted, "Her Royal Highness saw two cleaners hiding behind a counter and went over and spoke to them." As a student-nurse, the cleaners at the Great Ormond Street hospital knew her exceptional tidiness. Visiting Sheffield, that home of fine cutlery, the Princess had been presented with no fewer than seven pairs of scissors. Two at least were of the fine order of special mementoes, but her hospital colleagues benefited from the flush of scissors some time later. In June, 1957, Alexandra was with the Royal Family at the Horse Guards Parade to watch the ceremony of Trooping the Colour and she appeared on the balcony of Buckingham Palace afterwards. But behind the scenes there was a rush to allow her to be on time for the hospital.

From time to time, the newspapers enquired at the hospital to learn whether she was continuing with her studies. With the chameleon trick known to every working girl, the Princess left the hospital one evening and was officially at a B.B.C. studio with the Duke of Kent only twenty minutes later. Time, too, was found for the regular incognito cinema visits with her mother, and neither her music nor her friendships suffered. One scarcely noticed that Lady Moyra Hamilton had more time free of lady-in-waiting duties. The press meanwhile devoted more column inches to the Princess at dances than to her study course. By successfully deploying her time, the evening before she was off-duty, she could sit at the top committee table at a charity dance until midnight and then join her younger friends at a table near the floor, dancing till four a.m. There were the usual weekends, beloved of the columnists, with the Hamiltons, Mr. and Mrs. David Butters, Mr. and Mrs. Michael Hornby, and other friends. She had been spending the weekend with the Herberts in Wiltshire, for instance, when the young and congenial Mr. David Bailey drove her back to London in his Sunbeam Talbot on the occasion that brought two light-fingered gentry a dire surprise. The fact was unremarked by the romantic copywriters that Mr. Bailey is a great-grandson of that pivot of friendships, Mabell, Lady Airlie, whom we have long since met. It was the most natural thing in the world for the Princess to drop in for coffee at his parents' house in Notting Hill; and for Mr. Bailey to leave his car unlocked in his courteous haste. When they returned to the car the Princess's two monogrammed suitcases had disappeared.

Luckily, the police recovered them within twenty-four hours, from the left luggage office at London Bridge where one of the thieves had deposited them, and a trap was quickly set. "If I had known whom the cases belonged to, I wouldn't have touched them," one of the miscreants confessed. "I knew every policeman in England would be looking for me." But the court proceedings inevitably satisfied public curiosity on what a princess might regard as weekend luggage. Besides clothing there had been a manicure set, a radio, a photograph frame, two evening bags, a gold wrist watch, three bracelets, two bangles, a brooch clip, earrings and necklace in their jewel case and, less foreseeable, a Russian ikon, a prayer-book and a Bible. Most of the booty was recovered, and the Princess did not have to appear in court. But she worried over the fate of the offenders and must have been relieved to hear that from their point of view the six-month sentence was light.

II

The hazards of the nursing profession are well known, but a new note was introduced into Palace atmosphere in March, 1958, when Princess Alexandra fell ill with glandular fever. The attack was mild, and the Princess had shown her susceptibility by having twice had mumps. But her elders could now advance the persuasive argument of the risks that might be carried into the royal circle, and they perceived with some relief that the Princess herself was growing more steadfast in her sense of a true royal vocation.

At the time of her illness, her mother had been about to leave on a short private visit to Athens. This had to be postponed, with adjustments accordingly to other royal schedules as far away as Hellas. The Princess did not sit for any nursing exams, apart from the informal written questions-and-answers of the welfare course. She had immeasurably reduced her sense of clumsiness: she was equipped now, she felt, with reasonable knowledge and experience to cope with the problems of a nursery, and felt that she might escape the clashes that some of her friends experienced in dealing with nursemaids. She had also learned by experience, that personal experience so essential to the early twenties, that even a princess is not accepted as readily within nursing as a prince in his Army career. The relinquishment of that dream career was gradual through the early summer until at length the August holidays brought the final break.

The Duchess of Kent's private visit to Athens had concerned, among other business, the final settlement of her mother's estate. Princess Nicholas of Greece had died intestate in March, 1957, at the age of seventy-five. At all events a will was never found, and the Duchess of Kent and her sister, Princess Olga, were appointed co-administrators. A lesser difficulty lay in the disposal of Princess Nicholas's minor court of a dozen dogs and some sixty cats, a few of whom had enjoyed the privileges of her home at Psychiko while the rest were housed in a colony nearby. Marina and Olga also faced the sadness of dividing her jewellery, in part among the three granddaughters, Alexandra, Elisabeth of Yugoslavia and Helene of Austria *née* Toerring. (These mementoes included, one remembers, the residue of the Czarist collection of the Grand Duchess Vladimir, rescued from Bolshevik Russia.) Neither Marina nor Olga made a decision without the other. In their fifties, the two sisters realised they had inseparably grown together, enmeshed amid the thorns and tendrils and enjoyments of each other's families. As the summer of 1958 drew on, both also jointly faced the perplexities of another problem.

This time, the consultations concerned Edward. As Alexandra's urgent interest in nursing waned, her elder brother's interest elsewhere waxed and strengthened. The young Duke of Kent was now assistant adjutant in his Royal Scots Greys and his sense of personal crisis arose from the Army decision to transfer the regiment to Germany, apparently a posting abroad of at least two years. He was still only twenty-two, and the looming transfer heightened his ardent eagerness to become engaged to Miss Katharine Worsley. Love's young dream rarely takes the pattern anticipated by parents, and Princess Marina was uneasily aware, it must be said, not only that her son had hardly known the young lady a year but also that Katharine was two and a half years the elder. Princess Alexandra, on the other hand, contributed to the development of the romance with her usual unfettered enthusiasm, showering boundless affection on a friend of Edward's who shared, she discovered, her own deep enthusiasms: music, tennis, travel, even child welfare and her love of the byways of old Kensington.

It warmed the exchanges of early acquaintance to learn that they both often bought their records at the same shop in the neighbourhood and that Katharine had worked as a kindergarten teacher in Lady Eden's school only just down the road from Kensington Palace. Like Alexandra, the fair Katharine was the only daughter in a family of brothers and the Princess could not hear enough of her experiences at St. Stephen's — a children's home founded by the Worsley family in York — where Kate for a time had been one of a staff of three or four, looking after a score of little girls.

159

But the friendship had begun almost before they met, in Edward's letters, snapshots and confidences, and in his readiness to spend weekend leave passes in Yorkshire when he would ordinarily have preferred to come home. His romance, as things were, provided Alexandra with an example of the unexpected speed with which new avenues could open in her large and yet confined social circle, suddenly changing the royal course that always appeared so set and established. The friendship had come about when Edward was transferred with the Greys to Catterick Camp, which has the reputation of being the bleakest barracks in Britain. As Lord-Lieutenant of the North Riding, traditionally the county host of royalty, it was incumbent upon Sir William Worsley to open the doors of the neighbourhood to the Queen's cousin, and he began by inviting the Duke of Kent to lunch at his own home at Hovingham Hall.

When they looked radiantly back at that luncheon party, Edward and Katharine came to agree that it was love at first sight. Only a few days later I noted that the Duke was with the Worsley group at the coming-of-age party of Sir Leonard Ropner's daughter, Merle, and soon Katharine and the Duke "were meeting, as if by accident", ran my memo of the time "at point-to-points, dances and house-parties... People have noticed their visits to the tiny cinema in Malton. Once, when his sports car was in garage for overhaul, the Duke made the circuitous two-hour journey to Hovingham by bus rather than miss Katharine's company." That great Yorkshireman, Sir Linton Andrews, also considered it quickly obvious "that the friendship was no ordinary one... The Duke of Kent was enchanted by her appearance as a Dresden shepherdess at a fancy dress ball at Bolton Castle. He, like a grandee of Tudor days, wore red doublet and pantaloons, with an ostrich feather twirled round his tilted hat. Both were good dancers. Their interest in each other quickly grew..." We have noted, indeed, that Miss Worsley was not present at the Duke of Kent's coming-of-age party but she was very much in evidence at Princess Alexandra's twenty-first birthday party fifteen months later.

Alexandra took her brother's part in the ensuing family discussions at Kensington Palace that followed his determined announcement of his wish to get married. The well-worn phrases that the boy was too young to know his own mind, that he still needed time for advancement in his career, fell for a while on stubbornly determined though not inconsiderate ears. In August the family gathered for a final council at Princess Olga's home near Pratolino, the Villa Demidoff, in the Tuscan hills. Events were marshalled as Edward would have wished, for Katharine was also cruising in the Mediterrean on Lord Astor's yacht *Delandeira* and, with her friends the Myddletons, she planned to come ashore at Naples. Princess Alexandra could visualise the fun of whisking her to the villa, the private excitement, the celebration... But this was in 1958, we must remember, when young couples were expected to submit to the royal protocol, which insisted that they should give themselves time to decide, and should even endure a measure of separation before taking the all but irretrievable steps to the altar. The Duke could plead the obvious point that Prince Albert had been very young indeed when he married Queen Victoria, but his own grandfather, George V, had been twenty-eight when he married Queen Mary and his own father had not married until he was nearly thirty-two. Accompanied by Princess Maria Pia, Prince Alexander of Yugoslavia also arrived at the villa to add a man's point of view and the counsel of his own senior ten years, and Edward's resolution was perhaps a little shaken.

The more mature considerations prevailed, as we know, and the Duke of Kent realised that it would be better not to consider marriage before he had served his two years in Germany. Katharine Worsley had independently come to the same decision aboard the *Delandeira* after talking it out with the sensible Duchess of Devonshire. The slight difference in age, it should be added, troubled no one. To some of the older people, nevertheless, the capricious fates presented a decidedly vexing issue. Edward readily fell in love with someone two and a half years his senior, while to Alexandra the three and a half years between herself and Crown Prince Constantine, now eighteen, still seemed to make him a mere boy, out of all reckoning. Yet officially he had now come royally of age and family opinion may have decided that the time was perhaps ripe for the two cousins — second cousins — to get to know one another a little better.

III

In the autumn of 1958, it was announced that Princess Marina, the Duchess of Kent, would pay a fourteen-day goodwill visit to Chile and Brazil in the following March. Shortly before Christmas, Mr. Henry Hankey of the American department of the Foreign Office heard that Princess Alexandra would like to accompany her mother and the proposed visit rapidly escalated into a five-week Latin-America tour which would include Mexico and Peru. The two royal ladies and their party were to see the modern wonders of Mexico City, the ancient ruins of Yucatan, the beauty and gaiety of Lima, the fantastic contrasts of the Andes, the surprising skyscrapers of Santiago and, as a climax, the beaches and sugar-loaf hills of Rio de Janeiro itself.

The tour was primarily one of cultural relations; to Marina a sequel to the tour her husband had made in 1931 in company with the then Prince of Wales. In accompanying her mother, Alexandra realised she was being prepared for another journey she was to undertake five months later: her first solo tour, to be made in Australia. This was a journey to which she had eagerly agreed in prospect, but now began to dread as the reality drew nearer. But was there something more? Was there privately to be an apparently casual encounter with Crown Prince Constantine in the schedule of airliners and motorcades?

For the student of modern royal history the choice between affirmations and denials may be difficult. Tino — to give his family name — suddenly seemed to have grown up, improving into an agreeable, dark-eyed and decidedly handsome young man. By what was probably sheer coincidence rather than romantic conspiracy, he happened to be moving unobtrusively across the United States that February as a guest of the U.S. Defence Department. In the middle of the month he was visiting Hollywood and Los Angeles, an hour's plane hop from Mexico City. There he disappears from our view... Yet admittedly it would have been difficult for a wandering Crown Prince to have become invisible in Mexico City. A mêlée of hundreds of newspaper men stampeded across the airport to greet the Kents and dogged them through nearly every hour of each waking day thereafter.

Arduous as it may be, a royal overseas tour has become one of the last luxurious prerogatives of royalty in our modern age, and Princess Alexandra could hardly have had a more colourful, exciting and tempting introduction to her travel privileges than the banquet of impressions that Latin-America laid before her. From the moment when the Princess followed her mother aboard the Bristol Britannia and found the interior transformed into a semi-circular lounge, a dining-room, and a sleeping cabin with divans for herself and the Duchess, she knew that the expedition was going to be fun. The interior decor of the aircraft was mint-new, in a colour scheme of deep blue, pale grey and aquamarine, and there were pleasant overtones and reminders of the earlier journey to Canada. As on that other trip, Lady Rachel Davidson and Philip Hay were in attendance; Mr. Hankey of the Foreign Office and Sir John Taylor, a foremost expert on South America, were both congenial companions, and they were all friends together.

Princess Alexandra felt herself part of an important diplomatic mission as well as a joyrider in that swift translation from the February murk of London to the hot sunlight of Mexico City, and the others were put on their mettle by her youthful high spirits. "Take it easy now," she was cautioned, as she stepped from the plane at the airport. "You're 7,500 feet up!" "But we *have* landed, haven't we?" she responded, with mock terror.

The travellers were greeted by Senor Manuel Tello, the Mexican Foreign Minister, and as in Canada there was a procession of super-long cars. But from the first fugitive glimpse of a barrow piled with pineapples to the breathless "swoop of a journey" through the miles of smooth white suburban houses, Mexico was itself. "This place makes me gasp," the Princess said, "and it isn't only the altitude." The sight of the brilliant new university buildings, and the walking entailed in touring them, is indeed breathtaking. The reality of skyscrapers and modernist factories, broad flowered avenues and parks, invariably startles visitors after thinking in terms of pueblos and peons.

The royal ladies stayed at the British Embassy in the lavish Cuauhtémoc colony and their first active errand was, of course, the ceremonial call upon President Mateos at the National Palace. After the exchange of orders and decorations, the irrepressible Alexandra was able to write home and inform Prince Michael that she had become a member of the Order of the Aztec Eagle. Later they drove along the broad Avenida Reforma to place a wreath on the monument to the heroes of independence, and the day was crowded with an official luncheon, an Embassy garden party, the almost compulsory visit to the American-British hospital, and so forth. But the details of royal duty inevitably become tedious, and the reality is that Alexandra herself awoke each day to a fresh and vivid new travel experience. On the Saturday morning, she found her early tray piled high with mysterious envelopes. The romantic Mexicans had not forgotten it was Valentine's Day.

That evening saw a ball at the lush El Prado hotel. The Princess's hosts, the executives of a charity for the blind, had foreseen a too fervent crush of partners, but an impeccable young law student of Alexandra's own age kept most rivals at bay and she danced gaily till two a.m. Earlier she had shuddered at a three-star Baedeker sight of Mexico City, the Aztec altars of human sacrifice in the Anthropology Museum, and the royal ladies had driven out to the celebrated Basilica of Guadalupe, unnoticed among the ecstatic pilgrims, many of whom shuffle upon their knees towards the shrines.

On Sunday, after attendance at the Episcopal Church, the Duchess and the Princess watched a charreada or bloodless rodeo in the enormous new bullring, its highlight undoubtedly the moving moment when the bullfight brass band played "God Save the Queen" and the sea of one hundred thousand spectators then turned towards the royal box with deafening roars of "Viva!" While her mother rested that evening, Alexandra with unabated energy was whisked on a separate hundred-mile side-trip to the floating gardens of Cuernavaca, where a flower-laden punt propels the sightseer through a mesh of canals and islands vivid with the hues of giant pansies, petunias and violets. Another day, mother and daughter drove through orchards — where the parrot is a predatory menace — to the dead city of Teotihuacan, where they scaled the Pyramid of the Sun and explored the horrific and impressive ruins of the ancient temple of the Plumed Serpent.

After eight days of Mexico's exotic, breath-taking and unwavering hospitality, the travellers found it difficult to believe, when they left by air for Peru, that the southern hemisphere could outvie the thrills of this Mexican prelude. Their aircraft flew south over the Pacific through the star-spangled night and they crossed the equator as they slept and touched down at Lima to find a city of a million people in a fiesta mood of welcome. Royal visits to the "City of Kings" have not been numerous, and Senor Porras, the Foreign Minister, had overlooked no courtesy, from the smart guard of honour to the crash of military bands. Alexandra had chosen a blue flowered dress and a blue straw hat for the drive to the presidential palace, unaware that the light of the palm arcades would deepen the blue, creating such a charming effect that the happy crowds clapped and cried out with redoubled pleasure.

An arrival in a strange city necessarily is seldom as sharp in impressions to the waving, responsive royalty than to the average traveller with time to stare from his taxi. The Duchess and the Princess had to adapt swiftly from the tumult of the streets to the composure of the reception by President Prado, who honoured them by presenting them both with the Grand

Cross of Diamonds of the Order of the Sun, the oldest Peruvian order.

In due course, rested and acclimatised, Alexandra found herself in a city where baroque beauty jostled American commerce. Publicly the visitors were involved with a round of orphanages, model outskirt townships, colleges and cultural organisations of all kinds. Privately the British ambassador, Sir Berkeley Gage, and his family took the guests visiting through a series of rambling palacios where the grilled windows, harem balconies and flower-decked patios of old Spain were but a prelude to fine collections of antique Spanish furniture and tapestries adorning a salon where tea or coffee were offered by some charming dark-eyed aristocratic chatelaine who knew the cosmopolitan world.

There were drives past the dazzling Pacific beaches to the fashionable resort of Anton, where the Kents joined a cheerful luncheon party on board a private yacht and cruised through a sunlit afternoon. A day or two later they visited the Inca ruins of Pachacamac, where Alexandra with that unerring news sense of hers preferred sightseeing hand in hand with a shy barefooted Indian girl, and the resulting photographs appeared in nearly every illustrated magazine of the South American continent and far beyond. Peru provided only one disappointment. The Princess had hoped to visit the incredible Inca stronghold of Cuzco, 11,000 feet above sea level, where the cyclopean ruins challenge the backdrop of the Andes in impressive grandeur. As luck had it, a railway strike had closed the zigzag ascending line and so, instead, an official deputation flew to Lima, to present the Duchess with a large carved mace of Indian silver and to offer to Alexandra the splendour of a set of hand-embroidered robes such as an Inca princess would have worn — a headdress of scarlet and blue, a blanket of green, and a blouse of puce, all enriched with embroidery of blue and yellow, pink and white.

The Princess tried it all on over her cotton frock "with obvious enthusiasm". Perhaps one day, she said, she would yet see Cuzco. *Hasta la vista!* And as a token, on the eleventh and last day in Lima, the Duchess and Princess Alexandra were presented with the silver keys of the city: a gift of hand-wrought precious metal as an eternal talisman to the city of Pizarro, a symbolic gesture indeed.

On March 3rd the travellers again flew south, reaching Santiago in the early evening for their semi-state visit to Chile. Once again Philip Hay selected the correct letter from the Queen to the Head of State, and brought out a leather presentation box with the insignia of the G.C.M.G. The royal party all wondered what new surprises Chile would have in store. The itinerary scheduled visits to a paper mill, a review of naval cadets at Valparaiso, and admittedly sounded unpromising. Alexandra religiously read her *aide memoire* which reminded her that Chile had been the first South American country to adopt old age security and universal suffrage. But one never could tell. That evening, the royal visitors had expected a comparatively quiet interlude, dining with the British Ambassador. They imagined that the shouting and noise in the street outside was perhaps the rejoicing of some national occasion. Instead, they found the street packed with people who were cheering for them. As the Ambassador, Mr. Ivor Pink, explained, "You've had a wonderful press!" The next day, at the Moneda Palace, President Alessandri almost mischievously ushered them on to a balcony where the dimmed sounds of the city suddenly became a roar from thousands of throats in a square packed with excited people.

Even at the charreada in Mexico City, Princess Alexandra had never before found herself so directly a recipient of such a volume of cheering, and she tried to behave as she knew her cousin Elizabeth would. She felt in fact that the cheering was not for her but was a symbol of the popularity of Britain and, glittering in her mother's eyes, she saw the responsive tears that, she knew, were a reflection of her own inward emotion.

It enhanced her pleasure all the more to drive through the plaza later on, when the red and white pavements were full of strolling people, and the flower-sellers, the booths under the arcades, the bustle of cars and trams, all seemed part of an Italian opera. All the long, straight streets of Santiago seemed to present a vista of the snowy ranges of the Cordilleras, and Marina and Alexandra went by jeep one afternoon to see the immense Andes view from the 9,000-feet Cerro Colorado peak. The next day they were at sea-level for the visit to the naval school at Valparaiso. Back in Santiago, a young Embassy attaché remembered an unexpectedly serious conversation with Alexandra on the categoric value of a goodwill mission. The discussion was unresolved at the time. Chile's exports to the United Kingdom at that time were then four times higher than her U.K. imports ... but a year or two after the royal visit her British imports had more than doubled.

So much for value. On March 10th the royal ladies again met their aircraft commander, Captain Doug Cracknell, this time for the flight to Rio de Janeiro, north-east now over the immense backbone of the Andes and the Argentine pampas, to accomplish within hours, as Marina may have reflected, the journey that had taken her husband three days of train travel. But to Alexandra it was surely as if Brazil had rolled up all the resources, progress and excitement of South America into a grand farewell package deal.

She was so vividly occupied and the social welcome of Rio proved so intense that her letters home faltered. As she had hoped, Princess Alexandra rode around the splendid curving avenue of Copacabana Beach, a panorama rendered even more exciting with the shrilling sirens of a police escort and people waving from every balcony of every block of flats... This experience in turn was to have been capped by a flight to the new city of Brasilia, but the paralysing humidity combined with paw-paw for breakfast had the undignified effect of confining the Princess to her bed with enteritis, and the Duchess of Kent and her entourage inspected the emergent dream of Brasilia without her. On March 15th, Princess Alexandra was thinner and still "slightly shaky". Britain's exports to Brazil stood at only £13,000,000 in 1959. The definitive statistics of a royal mission are not readily assessed but the figures stood at nearly £19,000,000 within four years.

<h2 style="text-align:center">IV</h2>

Princess Alexandra returned from South America with increased self-confidence. She had discovered that protocol was a proscenium arch framing a stage on which she was free to be herself: the very illusion of royalty was itself a cause that heightened her newly assured sense of vocation. She felt eased, and freed from the need to be mindful of the ever-watching eyes that surrounded her both on and off duty. Going to Goodwood that Easter to watch the motor-racing with Edward and her cousin Elisabeth, it no longer mattered if the wandering cameramen caught her with tousled hair. Shopping for shoes in Beauchamp Place, she could shrug when some press-minded young man saw her park her car and rushed off, evidently to the nearest phone, to scoop a guinea or two by reporting her presence. One of her mother's aides had always observed the formula of alerting the house manager whenever a theatre visit was pending. Alexandra preferred strolling in so casually that she often passed through the foyer undetected. On one occasion an actor fluffed his lines when he realised the identity of the "dazzlingly beautiful girl" in the stalls.

She had often passed through London airport as a V.I.P. ... with no opportunity to sightsee before being whisked into the exclusive deep-carpeted private lounge of the Queen's Building. Now, when seeing off Elisabeth of Yugoslavia and Count Toerring one day with time to spare, she strolled around the main concourse, riding the escalators with something of a child's glee, peeping into the shop windows, until she alertly caught the first signs of a gathering crowd, and knew it was time to seek privileged shelter.

She no longer worried about any falsity of her public image, or felt concern when a journalist chose to put into quotes some remark of hers that he alone had invented or perhaps polished oft-told anecdotes till they were quite untrue. She had once been bothered lest the Queen disliked some of the wilder stories. "You might as well suppose," one relative had comforted her, "that the Queen doesn't know the difference between paste and diamonds." She was always readily amused at mishaps in public — the cake-cutting knife that broke against sugar-frosting, the curtains that bunched at an unveiling — but quick *to laugh away* the discomforture of others.

A year or so earlier, in launching the frigate *Jaguar* she had faced a chapter of accidents, hurling a champagne bottle that failed to break, and pressing a launching key that refused to respond. "That was for me a moment of despair," she comically wrote afterwards. "My ship displayed a not unnatural reluctance to enter the water... The agonising situation seemed a lifetime, but was I am told only a matter of seconds." At the crucial moment a workman shouted "Give her a shove!" and she launched the ship only by pretending to push. Yet she could recall the situation, smiling, in a luncheon speech after smoothly launching the liner *Oriana* in 1959. "*No stir in the air, no stir in the sea… The ship was still as she could be,*" she quoted. "You can have some idea of my relief when I saw *Oriana* begin to move so surely and so gracefully down the slipway." She was now writing the majority of her own speeches.

She had not yet sat upon the celebrated top hat of the Governor of Queensland, and yet the stories around her had already hardened into the royal apocrypha that, as Prince Philip has said, "have gained the acceptance and authority of holy writ". She is supposed to have blushed crimson when a mayor at an art gallery paid her the compliment, "Beauty is always welcome at our gallery." The truth is that she responded to his witticism with a smile. The gentlemen of the press never saw her take the parachute jump they had long anticipated in imagination, but the flow of anecdotes seemed inexhaustible.

"Goats are tricky," she once said when refusing to approach the horns of a famous ram at a farm show for the cameras. "They look innocent — but you never know." On an over-glamorous soft-focus photograph of herself, she supposedly commented, "Everyone thought I'd had my nose fixed by plastic surgery." On a notable occasion in a television studio, the comedian Bob Monkhouse claimed to mistake her for a fan who had got past the commissionaires. "Hello, darling," he said. "You shouldn't be in here, you know."

His account goes on, "She smiled back warmly and replied, 'I must be getting back, the people I've come with will be missing me.' I said. 'All right sweetheart. If you want a ticket to see the show, ask for me at the stage door.'

"'Oh, *thank* you.'"

The story, at least, is essentially true. Within all the varied perspectives of the Princess was the certainty that she was good-natured, cheerful, willing, loquacious, venturesome and that she could be counted on to say the first thing that came into her head, unorthodox as any Princess could reasonably be expected to be.

V

Through the early summer of 1959 the librarian at Australia House looked out six to ten books every week for Kensington Palace. Among other subjects Princess Alexandra read up the history of Queensland for more than the past hundred years, and an account of all the strange mammals of the continent. Her first lone royal tour she was determined, should be "as useful" as every preliminary could ensure. There is some evidence that she never foresaw the journey as "successful", and the adjective was not one she would have used. She viewed the project with timidity, and then devoted all her energies to the quickening tempo of preparation with growing excitement. Yet the Australian tour was to prove the climacteric of her years as a royal trainee, a culminating triumph that sealed her popularity in every shade of public opinion.

Alexandra is probably the only royalty who ever packed the music of Vivaldi and Fauré in her tour luggage, modestly hoping to find time to practise. She was, as we know, the first princess to stock a tour wardrobe with basic off-the-peg outfits, and the Australian collection included no fewer than eighteen such designs by the young and versatile Mr. Leslie Kaye. His client had one of these made up in wattle-yellow as her arrival dress, a subtle compliment to the land of wattle not lost on the Australian press. All royal ladies are noted for their appreciation of the designers who contribute to their confidence, and the promise of some is warmer than others. Through Lady Moyra Hamilton, Princess Alexandra not only sent Mr. Kaye a letter of thanks on the success of his clothes but also mailed him a batch of Australian newspaper clippings to prove it.

Victor Stiebel, on the other hand, was asked to design several couturier evening gowns, and the Princess herself contributed such a rapid spate of suggestions that Mr. Stiebel had at one time to confess himself utterly bewildered. Her ideas, he says, "flashed past like the carriages of an express train". On her homeward run, the Princess was to visit Siam and India and she hit on the happy thought of having a sari made as an evening dress. But did Mr. Stiebel know where she might buy a sari? The couturier suggested Liberty's. "How kind of you," said the Princess. "I'll go there straight away." Then she added, with a diffidence that made Stiebel smile, "And would you mind very much if I mentioned your name?"

The tour had its growing pains. Simultaneously one Australian editor protested that a schedule of ninety-eight official functions in five weeks was "punishing ... sheer murder" while another clamoured for more evening engagements. The Princess poured oil on the troubled waters by suggesting that she might give a press conference, an idea to which the Queen gave ready assent. The corps of twenty-four Australian news correspondents in London expected a starchy function and were completely won over when it turned out to be, as Pearson Phillips said, "a sparkling get-together, during which the Princess plunged into high-spirited conversation and fun-making", all of which, to general chagrin, was decreed off the record. Probably this precaution was unnecessary, though wit is apt to stale with the passing of time. One exchange might be quoted:

"Princess, why are you taking two swimsuits?"

"It's just in case the other gets wet. Besides, I can't tear both at once on the Great Barrier Reef."

"Have you been warned the warmer seawater may shrink the material?"

"Oh, will it? In that case, I shall have to do some slimming, as well as swimming."

In more serious vein, the Princess reminded her listeners, "The tour is mainly connected with the Queensland Centenary celebrations; so I mustn't play the giddy goat." The resulting despatches home were ecstatic, and all the acrimonious undercurrents were swirled away long before the Princess's arrival.

With Lady Moyra Hamilton, Philip Hay, and an R.A.F. medical officer, Wing-Commander Brian Kelly, as her entourage, Princess Alexandra flew out on August 8th, 1959, in a Comet IV, a leisurely flight with a weekend stopover in Vancouver and touchdowns in Fiji and Hawaii. A delightful week of Pacific sightseeing, in fact, preceded the six-weeks official tour. Then, on her first night in Canberra, she slept in the Government House of Yarralumla, in the bedroom which her parents had thought would be theirs twenty years earlier and among furniture which they themselves had selected.

Having cynically noted that she had shaken fifty-three official hands at the airport, Australians wondered how "the unconventional Princess" could demonstrate her talents within the usual official formula. They got the message when she decided to explore beyond the estate boundary and led the photographers and reporters on a two-mile walk along the river pastures, shooing her way through grazing cows, waving at farmworkers and pausing to take photographs for herself.

"She's a beaut!" summed up local opinion, and the Australian welcome warmed up. "She's a winner!" was the cry after the first government banquet when, despite a chilly wintery night, she repeatedly came on to the balcony in response to the crowd and returned again and again, though obviously shivering in her light organza dress. Three days later when she flew in to Brisbane to begin her scheduled three weeks of visiting twenty-two towns and cities, the crowd was overawed and silent, and indeed, rather remote behind the inevitable cordons. Presently the Princess of her own accord began walking towards them waving and smiling, and someone shouted, "Welcome to Queensland!" And then someone else took up the cry and a strange thing happened. The first shouts became a delighted roar. Thousands were already silently lining the eight-mile route from the airport to the City Hall and each crowd, each cluster, took up the cry as if spread by bush telegraph. "Welcome to Queensland! Welcome to Queensland!" The barriers were down from that moment.

The Princess shrewdly introduced into an early speech the reminder that but for the war she would have spent her childhood in Australia. Next day, at the centenary agricultural show, cheered from the moment she entered the grounds, she made a point of leaving the official party to walk round almost alone, stopping to talk to young people, trying to behave much as she would at a village fete at Iver. The public are quick to reciprocate such gestures, but this one was not altogether a success. People pressed forward, kicking up rising dust that hid the Princess from view, and the crowd became almost uncontrollable. Lady Moyra became separated from her in the mêlée and though women and children were knocked down, it was a near-miracle that no one was hurt. A happier experiment was attempted two days later when the Princess returned to the exhibition, unheralded and in a closed car entering by a back gate. Spectators of the wood-chopping contest only gradually became aware that she was sitting among them, and then gave her a spontaneous ovation at the interval.

The famous top hat incident came about when the Princess attended morning service in Brisbane Cathedral with Sir Henry Abel Smith, the Governor of Queensland, and strolled away from the red carpet, on leaving, to talk to a group of choirgirls. Walking into the road to wave with both hands to the crowd, as she often did, she got into the car by the wrong off-side door — and sat on the hat. The incident might have passed unnoticed if she had not laughed and wildly waved the crushed topper in delight at the onlookers and continued waving it to acknowledge their own laughter and cheers.

With her flair for public relations, she dubbed her contingent of news-and-cameramen "Alexandra's Ragtime Band" and usually made a point of going to talk to new members, making plain that she regarded them all as a team in which she was a unit. Hearing that another of her group — the drivers, baggage men and transport organisers — were staging a party in Brisbane, she joined them and stayed till after midnight; and waved or smiled afterwards to any one of the party-givers whenever she recognised them.

Young dance partners were an occasional problem. In Canberra Alexandra prompted Mr. Hay to suggest that six young farmers whom she had met at a reception should be invited to the ball that night. On another occasion, she suggested that four of the personable young men who had formed her R.A.A.F. guard of honour should come to the ball, and she danced with them all. In one town, two theology students flourished a blackboard that read "See you in Maryborough". When the royal motorcade reached

Maryborough the pair were conspicuous with their blackboard reading "Here we are". "They deserve a medal", said the Princess, and at her suggestion an official got their names and invited them to the ball that evening. What was more, Princess Alexandra remembered to look out for them and danced with them.

Such were the gestures, then, that memorably endeared her through Australia. As the tour swung around Queensland she stopped at every crossing track were there were people, twenty-five times in one morning on the fifty miles between townships, and at Warwick, one evening in the dusk, when the cavalcade of cars was hurrying to make up for lost time, she stopped at a cross-track to talk to a solitary child who had come to see her pass.

One can recognise the royal technique, in the larger cities, when she always walked towards any group of disabled children or went to talk to youngsters and old folk in the crowd. But her personal naturalness seemed to Australians phenomenal, as when she cuddled and made kissing noises to a couple of koala bears, and sighed at last "I could stay here all night with them." No one who saw her will forget her enjoyment at the wheel of a motor-launch on the Brisbane river, zig-zagging from side to side, and joyously answering the acclaiming ship's sirens toot for toot on the launch hooter.

In Sydney she "did a Salote". London has never forgotten how Queen Salote of Tonga rode in an open carriage in pouring rain in the Coronation procession, behaving precisely as if in radiant sunshine. The Sydney airport was similarly swept with drenching rain but Princess Alexandra heard of the extraordinary crowds lining the procession route and changed to an open car so that they could see her, though she had neither coat nor umbrella. A few days later, downtown

Melbourne gave her an artificial snowstorm welcome, with streamers and confetti swirling down from the office blocks. When she drove for the last time through the city, and clamouring avenues of humanity took up the cry "Come back, Alex! Come back!" the pull on her emotions grew unbearable and she made no attempt to hide her tears.

"I must come back," she said, repeatedly. "I have loved it all."

Her more personal experiences had included a weekend on Lindeman Island, on the Great Barrier Reef, which had entailed a rough crossing on the destroyer *Warramunga*. There indeed she found an old upright piano for music practice but she also went waterskiing, searched the rocks for oysters, made a sightseeing trip over the coral shallows in a glass-bottomed boat and went sailing in a catamaran. A weekend at Rison was spent on a cattle-station, riding, and rising soon after dawn to trail a herd of kangaroos in a Land Rover. Yet even her so-called hours "at leisure" were spent re-drafting speeches that had been prepared for her. "I can't possibly say that," she would complain, working over some tortuous phrase. As one Australian summed up the tour, "The battered top-hat was the least of it." The suggestion was made that Princess Alexandra should be dubbed the Duchess of Australia and one cannot but think that the Queen's advisers missed a trick in ignoring this opinion.

The goodwill tour did not conclude with the final take-off from Darwin later in September. The young King Bhumibol of Thailand had invited her to stop over on a five-day visit which was similarly to be linked with another five days as the guest of the King of Cambodia. If portents ever worried her, they could hardly have been worse than when she landed in a heavy rainstorm at Bangkok, for the rain had caused the dye of the red carpet to run and her shoes were stained as if with blood. Only three weeks earlier a secretary of the royal Cambodian household had been killed by a bomb in a parcel addressed to King Norodom Suramarit, and the Foreign Office in London were naturally concerned for the Princess's security. But Southeast Asia regards red as a festive rather than an ominous colour. Alexandra could jubilantly report of her first evening in Bangkok that she had dined with Dick Whittington, otherwise Sir Richard Whittington, the British Ambassador.

In London, she could not have imagined, when she saw the film *The Bridge On the River Kwai* that she would one day stand on the very bridge — sixty miles from Bangkok — laying wreaths in tribute to the prisoners-of-war who had died there. Floating through the water gardens of Mexico, she had not foreseen that within six months she would enjoy an almost identical scene on the canals of Thailand. One fruit-seller was so overcome at being visited by a live Princess that he offered her his entire sampan-load of fruit. She was advised to take him seriously, and accept, and the fruit was transferred to a hospital. The famed dragon-prowed golden royal barges, manned by sixty oarsmen, were brought out in her honour. For her share in the exotic picture, Princess Alexandra wore her sari at a Court banquet, and was presented with other saris by members of King Bhumibol and Queen Sirikit's family, cementing friendships begun in London.

Cambodia, it was true, greeted her with intensive security. To her amusement, the Princess found herself accompanied to the so-called Temple of Love at Angkor Wat by nine truckloads of troops, nine Army jeeps, and a complement of accompanying radio vans, breakdown vans and ambulances. Finding the joss-sticks of prayer burning in those strangely carved fantastic temples, she was told that the local women came to pray to be blessed with children and, as one commentator noted, she made a point of standing before the altar.

It is given to few to see the Aztec pyramids, the Incas cities and the ruins of Angkor within the same year. Princess Alexandra heightened this record with her day in Delhi on the way home, when Mrs. Indira Nehru helped her to buy souvenirs and gifts, and with a flying visit to Agra to see the Taj Mahal. The final leg of the homeward journey was in a Comet IV commanded by Captain James Hengle, and here perhaps was the strangest tale of all. Twenty-five years earlier, the Princess discovered, Captain Hengle had been a young policeman posted on crowd-control outside Buckingham Palace on the very day that Princess Marina had driven from the Palace to her wedding. The policeman's story was not least of all the things she had to tell when — too excited to have tea in the plane — she landed at London airport and found her mother and Prince Michael eagerly awaiting her in the October dusk.

8: THE WHIRLPOOL OF THE HEART

The year 1960 was of course early to become hallmarked in
royal annals by the announcement from Clarence House of the
betrothal of the Princess Margaret to Mr. Antony Armstrong-
Jones. The earlier private phase of betrothal dated from
August, 1959, observing the usual royal protocol of delay, and
Princess Alexandra wrote her congratulations from Australia.
In November, when the Queen gave a "welcome home"
dinner and dance at Buckingham Palace in Princess
Alexandra's honour, Mr. Armstrong-Jones was among the
guests. The Duke of Kent was also there, on Army leave from
Germany, and so was Katharine Worsley, bright with the
certitude of future happiness after her long stay in Toronto "to
think everything out". Then there were scores of Alexandra's
friends and kinsfolk, among them the Hamiltons and Herberts
and Nevills and Toerrings and Beresfords. There was the
young Marquess of Hamilton and Lord O'Neil, David Bailey
and Angus and James Ogilvy. It was a wonderfully happy
evening.

A week or two later, the Duke of Kent took his seat in the
House of Lords, a symbol of investiture in public duty, and in
February, 1960, Princess Alexandra reached a further landmark
of her own royal career when she made her first speech in the
Guildhall. The occasion was one of the luncheons traditionally
given by the Lord Mayor of London to members of the Royal
Family on their return from official tours abroad. The event
was however exceptional in that the guests of honour were
Prince Philip, Princess Alexandra and the Duke and Duchess

of Gloucester, all of whom had recently returned from overseas duty. As Prince Philip said, "How many Lord Mayors have had the experience of killing by kindness four Royal Highnesses at one bang?"

One of the guests noted that Princess Alexandra particularly "performed her part without fault ... and made a confident little speech" but during the presentations City protocol itself was found at fault... "Some of the hosts unaccountably failed to take the proffered hand of the Princess. They withdrew awkwardly, after the fashion of amateur actors looking for a hole in the scenery." It was left to Prince Philip to lean over and exchange some private consolatory remarks with his cousin.

Yet to the Princess it was, after all, like conquering the last peak of Everest in civic ritual. The accompanying plate of cold beef was also readily dated in memory by the birth of the Queen's son, Prince Andrew, the following day, on February 19th. At his christening Princess Alexandra was the chief godparent, giving the names "Andrew Albert Christian Edward", the third name perhaps a reflection of her own "Christabel". Meanwhile, Princess Margaret's engagement was publicly announced on February 26th and, amid the rejoicing and excitement, Alexandra herself may have felt a tacit emphasis renewed among some of her relatives that she might well be next and that the time to make up her own mind was drawing near. The Princess was not disposed to be co-operative with the match-makers. "When I marry, it will be for love," she had always said. Yet Princess Margaret's happiness seemed to have loosed a flood of romantic impulse.

Early in March Alexandra spent a few days with the Toerrings in Munich and then flew on, with her brother, Edward, and her Toerring cousin, Hans, to join in the renowned weekend in Stockholm when King Gustaf of Sweden gave a ball for his three eldest granddaughters, the Princesses Margaretha, Birgitta and Desiree. As it turned out, all three were to be married within the next four years but, so far as I know, none of the future husbands were among their dance partners that night. With more than a dozen bachelor princes to match an equivalent hand of princesses, the world however indulged in a poker game of marital pairing and, amid the sparkle of the ball, the scrutiny of the older though not necessarily wiser eyes did not lack the glitter of hopeful speculation.

On the strength of a photograph or two of them together, the press were inclined to link Alexandra with Crown Prince Harald of Norway, the young prince whose birth, we may remember, had conflicted with the arrangements for Princess Alexandra's christening when she was six weeks old. But Queen Frederika of Greece confronted a cooler reality as she watched the Princess dancing with her son, Prince Constantine. "Tino" was now nearly twenty to Alexandra's just twenty-three, good-looking and personable, and his travels and naval training had deepened and matured his character. But through the affectionate, mocking eyes of cousinhood, he no doubt appeared almost as juvenile as young Prince Michael, who was still at Eton.

We must assess the situation as best we can, for it was never defined. Princess Marina wished only for her daughter's happiness and was as perplexed by the whirlpool of the young heart as any mother. She had always tried to ensure the widest possible ambience for her daughter's future choice, and of late a summer had rarely passed without a holiday in Athens or Florence. Aunt Olga's hospitality at the Villa Demidoff seldom included her cousins, King Paul and Queen Frederika, when the Kents were visiting, but this vagary of chance meant nothing in the frequent interchange of family visits between Florence and Tatoi or even between Corfu and Coppins. Long familiarity gave Princess Alexandra reason to regard the Greek Royal Family as an extension of her own domestic circle; and Tino and his sisters, the Princesses Sophie and Irene, were old cronies of many shared amusements and adventures. King Gustav's party, then, was a cordial family reunion, with dynastic undertones insistent as the rhythm of the band. Knowing what was expected of them, Tino and Alexandra danced their obligatory quicksteps together and then conveniently found other partners.

If their elders perceived a recognisable situation, both the young people equally regarded the idea as absurd. Looking through an album of photographs of the royal ball, one factor becomes vivid in the bright floodlight of time. When the principal guests were invited to pose for a group picture, Alexandra sat far to the right with Sophie of Greece, while Tino stood far to the left, immediately behind Margrethe of Denmark. She was his precise equal in years, the eldest sister of the sweet Anne-Marie of Denmark, then only thirteen years old, who four years later was to become his Queen.

As Princess Alexandra's own uncertainties gradually clarified, one noticed indications that she was tempted to avoid Tino. In the autumn she had occasion to make short stay with her cousin Helene of Austria, *née* Toerring, in Paris and, incidentally to pay a compassionate visit to the Comte and Comtesse de Paris in their grief for the loss of their son François in the battle zone of Algiers. On the day of her return to England, Queen Frederika, Princess Sophie and Prince Constantine were also due to arrive in London, and an incautious official of the Royal Greek Embassy strangely made

185

it known that the Prince was "especially looking forward to meeting Princess Alexandra". Instead, Alexandra flew in to London Airport but was content to talk to her mother in the Commandant's suite in the Queen's Building and then immediately flew on to Belfast to spend a few days at Baronscourt with the Hamiltons. The Duchess of Kent then welcomed the Greek royals, whose appropriate choice of entertainment that night was the long-running play *The Mousetrap*. Princess Alexandra did not return home until a week later, when Tino had already left London. But there followed another week for congenial family meetings while Queen Frederika and Princess Sophie stayed on at Claridge's.

The motives behind these events can hardly be more explicit. To the press, however, Alexandra's visit to the Duke and Duchess of Abercorn at Baronscourt was not so much a friendly stay with the daughter of the house, Lady Moyra Hamilton, as an indication of continued romance with Lord Hamilton's friend, Lord O'Neill. One writer cited among supporting facts that O'Neill was a lieutenant in the North Irish Horse Territorials, a regiment of which Alexandra was an honorary colonel. In reality, it was more to the point that his sister, Fionn O'Neill, had been with the Princess at Heathfield. But Ray O'Neill was a good friend, who did not mind the rumours and would even add fuel to them if it served to distract attention from Princess Alexandra's closer interests.

A minor circumstance also mistakenly caused some elements to suppose that an announcement on Alexandra's marriage could not be long delayed. This was the announcement by the auction firm of Sotheby in 1960 that they were to sell a collection of Fabergé and other objets d'art by order of H.R.H. the Duchess of Kent, precisely the move that a fond mama might be expected to make when preparing for the expenses of a wedding.

II

In the social conventions of everyday life curiosity into financial affairs is usually considered a vulgar intrusion. We have nevertheless noted that the intractable fable of her family penury was a staple element in Princess Alexandra's popularity, at least until her marriage. Since the Kents received no specific Consolidated List annuity similar to those approved by Parliament for other members of the Royal Family, for example, it pleased the public to suppose that Alexandra bought off-the-peg clothes from necessity. In 1960 the New York Dress Institute included the Princess for the first time in their much-publicised list of the twelve best-dressed women in the world, and devotees gained the recent impression that Alexandra contrived to out-glamour her better-recompensed cousins with dress lengths of silk picked up in Hong Kong. "It is not for nothing," said the *Sunday Express*, "that Princess Alexandra has come to be known as 'the pin-money Princess'."

When Queen Mary died, leaving a net estate of £379,864, it was widely reported that Princess Alexandra was one of the beneficiaries under her will, but I have been reliably assured on private information that this is not so. Nor, on the same authority, did the Princess benefit from the trust fund generally supposed to have been set up five years or more before her grandmother's death. Similarly, Queen Mary made no provision for a dowry for her granddaughter; and all that we know of the estate of Princess Alexandra's father is that he left £157,735, the bulk of it believed to be in trust for his son, the present Duke of Kent.

The contents of royal wills are never published. The Sovereign's estate is also entirely exempt from disclosure and from death duties, and it is therefore impossible to discover whether King George VI made provision for his brother's family or indeed whether, as some contend, the King died intestate. The public is accordingly left to balance books on the available facts, namely that the Queen Mother received an annuity of £70,000, Prince Philip £40,000, the Duke of Gloucester £35,000, Princess Margaret £15,000 ... while the Kents are allowed nothing.

The book-keeping can be over-simplified for, in 1952, Parliament in its tax-saving wisdom set aside £25,000 a year for those who "by virtue of their position near the Throne are excluded from ordinary commercial activities and must, of necessity, devote their lives to public duties". The phrase "of necessity" — from the report of the Select Committee on the Civil List — now strikes one as curious, for there is no compulsion for Alexandra or her brothers to undertake public duties save the driving psychological urge of tradition. But the Select Committee evidently had the Kents much in mind for the report went on, "...younger members will soon be reaching the age when they, too, will not only be expected to take part in public life, but by doing so will also help to bear the burden of public duties".

Since the provision is nominally at the Queen's discretion, the public has a disconcerting — and for the Kent family — an embarrassing — picture of humiliating dependence. In practice the disbursement is made by the Royal Trustees, nominally the Prime Minister and the Chancellor of the Exchequer, and it appears that the payment is limited to a proportion of outgoings shown on submitted accounts. Princess Marina and her children were thus entitled to recoup part of the office and secretarial expenses entailed by royal duty. Parliament also stipulates that the expenses must be "unavoidable", and a proportion is also allowed against income tax. But in our inflationary era we have come far from the days when Princess Marina's husband comfortably enjoyed the regular spending power of his Civil List annuity of £25,000 a year. This income ceased brutally on his sudden death and Princess Marina was supposedly left with only the pension of an Air Commodore's widow of £980 a year.

A committee of enquiry might readily elicit that this sum has never been drawn. One of the absurdities of popular illusion was similarly tested and put to flight when the Duke of Kent took his seat in the House of Lords but failed to draw his attendance allowance of three guineas a day and expenses. None the less, the inquisitive are not so easily satisfied; and Princess Marina had seemed, just after the war, to afford some insight into her financial difficulties with the five-day auction of many of her husband's art treasures at Christie's in 1947. Although this raised a total of £92,341, it should be remembered that a valuation for a large part of this sum had already been included for probate in the late Duke of Kent's estate and his widow was no more than setting her house in order.

In facing unusual financial contingencies, Princess Marina always followed her mother's precept of regarding surplus possessions as expendable rather than disturb capital. Other members of the Royal Family have been fortunate in selling furniture, silver and objects of art from time to time without arousing the same close attention. In the Duchess of Kent's 1960 sale at Sotheby's we may discern family treasures that perhaps once graced the Petit Palais: a Fabergé canteen of 222 pieces of silver, an array of Fabergé clocks and cigarette cases and photograph frames... The canteen brought in £1,400, compared with £2,800 for one of the Imperial Russian craftsman's superb miniatures of a pearl and nephrite basket of flowers, and the seventy-seven lots realised £12,426. The sum was ample for the Duchess of Kent's own expenses and gifts occasioned by her son's coming marriage to Katharine Worsley, but the commentators trotted out the usual sentiments about the widow's pension, although one point of interest has been widely overlooked.

We need not concern ourselves with the eventual settlements of the estate of Prince and Princess Nicholas nor with the finances of such eventually well-to-do but childless uncles as Prince Christopher or his nephew, King George of Greece. In December, 1939, however, an old lady of ninety-one died in Kensington Palace. She was Queen Victoria's daughter, Princess Louise, Duchess of Argyll, the same aged lady whom we have met as the oldest figure at Princess Alexandra's christening.

Louise was childless and is known to have cherished a fond attachment to the Kents. She expressed a wish that they should one day have her suite at Kensington Palace and Princess Marina is said to have been left the bulk of her fortune of £239,260. In terms of taxed investment income, and allowing for capital growth, this represented £10,000 a year, a fortune not commensurate with the wealth of an oil-well sheikh, but the daughter of such an income is not a Cinderella, forced to stay at home while her two beautiful cousins go to the ball.

If we choose to regard Princess Alexandra as our new-style Cinderella, the helicopters of the Queen's Flight provide her golden coach. It is well known, also, that a supplementary contribution to incidental expenses is made for a royal tour, either by the Commonwealth Relations Office or the Foreign Office or by other departments that act as sponsors.

In October, 1960, Princess Alexandra represented the Queen at the independence ceremonies and celebrations of the new Federation of Nigeria. The Princess admittedly did not have to pay for the charter Britannia which flew her to Lagos nor for the Heron aircraft of the Queen's Flight which enabled her to tour the different regions. Her wardrobe once again balanced the couturier creations of Victor Stiebel and John Cavanagh with the cleverly adapted ready-to-wear outfits of the firm of Susan Small and others and it would be pleasant to suppose that the Princess was not a penny out of pocket in representing the Crown. But the Cinderella angle will be found to have its limitations in real life, and even the fairy tale provides hints that Cinderella's family had at least to defray the cost of providing the pumpkin.

III

Princess Alexandra arrived in Lagos during a lull in a tropical rainstorm. The airport glistened with water, the waiting crowds were soaked and the Princess had no sooner inspected her guard of honour than the rain began once more. Reluctantly she donned a white raincoat over her pink summer dress but suggested that the hood of the ceremonial Rolls should be put down. And as she had done in Australia she sat in the rain. "That gesture spoke louder than words," commented the *Nigerian Daily Times* next day. "She seemed to be saying: 'If the schoolchildren can stand in the rain getting soaked, so can I'."

Then, at the garden party at Government House a day or two later, the rain gods were in much the same mood. The trumpeters had no sooner sounded a fanfare than it was answered by the thunder and the skies opened. A coloured umbrella was ineffectively raised above the Princess as she moved down the avenue. The grey suit of the Governor-General walking beside her grew black with water; the Princess's white shoes squelched and turned tan in the mud; her dress was drenched despite every precaution, and Alexandra's smiles for the photographers grew sympathetically wider. Her route through the churned battlefield of the garden was completed in eighteen minutes, one-third of the allotted time. But happily, after this debacle, the gods were appeased and slept throughout the rest of the tour.

The day of a national pageant at the airport was bright and hot. The Princess took the salute from the royal dais, drove past the vast and colourful crowds in a Land Rover and watched the fly-past of the R.A.F. and R.A.A.F. planes in a cloudless sky. "It's one day to zero before they haul down the Union Jack," one commentator wrote home, "but Alex has already recaptured Lagos. Her contempt of the rain put her on a pinnacle of local fame." And closely watching Alexandra as the British flag came down, wondering how she would take that moment of inevitable emotion, the journalists saw that she was much more concerned for the Governor-General, Sir James Robertson, when his self-control faltered.

Nearly five years had passed since Alexandra had first watched the filmed scenes of the Queen's visit. Now, in a new Parliament House, the Princess in turn faced a brilliant assemblage of Emirs and chieftains, Ministers and representatives, and all the concourse of the three hundred and fifty members of the Federal Parliament in the vivid colours and contrasts of their ceremonial robes. The Princess herself wore a white ballgown, shimmering with delicate pearl embroidery, and she read the Speech from the Throne with confident poise and dignity. "Her voice matched her diamonds in clarity and beauty," a Belgian diplomat put it gallantly. But a more considerable compliment was paid by the Nigerian Prime Minister, Sir Abubakar Tafawa Balewa, who noticed her skill in identifying from which corner of the vast country the various delegates came by their style of dress. "That girl has really done her homework," he said.

That same day the Princess flew north to Ibadan, a garden-party figure, now, in pale blue. The largest all-African city of the continent provided immense crowds, jumping, dancing — and again getting wet. As in Lagos, it rained on the State Drive and the Princess sat it out, though prudently beneath an umbrella on this occasion so that her appearance at later ceremonies should not be too unkempt. It was no worse, she said, than taking a warm shower. Nevertheless, "Doc" Kelly watched his ward with some anxiety. She was not strong despite her good build and vitality; she had been ill with minor infections three times earlier that year, and her medical officer distrusted the continual drenchings. Yet the Princess stood the course. As the Queen had done, she saw the magnificently manned racing canoes of Port Harcourt, the whirling tribal dancers of Enugu ... and she also inaugurated huge new sports stadiums, flew by helicopter to found new universities, stood tirelessly at march-pasts and walked the usual uncounted miles on tours of inspection.

At every point the Princess impressed others, as well as Sir Abubakar, by the thoroughness with which she did her job. A tiny example may suffice. At Enugu, returning by night to Government Lodge at the end of a full and tiring day, her car headlights picked up two people waiting at a corner. The Princess switched on the interior lights in her car, waved smiling by into the darkness and then switched the light off again.

Like the Queen, Alexandra also took her own cinefilms, reserving the longest footage for the spectacular durbar at Kano, with its almost medieval pageant of armoured riders, acrobats, snake handlers, camel riders and entertainers. The Queen could never forget the thrilling climax of Jahi and Zaria horsemen, plumed and robed, riding towards her at full gallop. The riders were so determined to excel for the new royal visitor that, on violently reining-in, one sailed over his horse's head and crashed at the Princess's feet.

Princess Alexandra returned home to be publicly honoured by the City of London at a Mansion House luncheon: "a lady, young, beautiful, exquisitely clad and always smiling," as the Lord Mayor, Sir Bernard Waley-Cohen, testified. More privately she returned to the family joke that she had travelled so far and experienced so much quite unscathed, while her brother Edward, rushing to meet Katharine Worsley at Kensington Palace, had slipped on the steps and broken a bone in his foot, and would be limping around in plaster for some weeks. Princess Alexandra was content to make her own little jokes about having a lucky mascot. But it might not surprise her maid, Marjorie Dawson, to see her tenderly replacing on her dressing-table the talisman that she had taken both to Australia and Nigeria — a miniature teddy-bear which had been given to her in fun by Angus Ogilvy and was rapidly becoming a token of an attachment deeper than friendship.

IV

Inevitably, Princess Alexandra found the marriage of her brother Edward to Katharine Worsley a touchstone of profound significance. For the first time since the loss of her father, the familiar family grouping was in flux, dissolving into new patterns like surf swirling upon the tide. For eighteen years the young Kents had been grouped around their mother and, as they grew up, the matriarchal tendrils had smoothed imperceptibly into a four-point companionship. From childhood rivalry and teenage admiration, the filaments of Alexandra's own attitude towards the youthful Duke of Kent had matured into comprehending, sympathetic equality. It was the Princess, apparently, who gave her elder brother the folding leather wallet for family photographs that stood on his bedside cabinet in his quarters in Germany; and she was no doubt one of the first to discover that a picture of Katharine had been included in the gallery.

With Prince Michael, on the other hand, nearly six years her junior, her interest was more maternal, sisterly but senior. She had spent hours pounding the piano in accompaniment while he practised the bassoon, sessions when they both often collapsed into helpless laughter. She was wary of his driving, even after he passed his test. She attempted, with a touch of her Aunt Elizabeth's precept in "talking it out", to disentangle his difficulty in making up his mind whether to adopt a career in the Navy, Army or the Air Force. She sympathised with her mother's relief when he passed the selection board for Sandhurst. But first a "Coppins conclave" was held to discuss whether he should go to France for three months to improve his French. Alexandra had no sooner returned from Nigeria than the Prince packed his kit and was off to Tours, where he was to "live in" with a professor's family. And then, while Michael was still at his studies, the conclusion of Edward's phase of duty in Germany, shortly after his twenty-fifth birthday, brought the family understanding of the Duke of Kent's betrothal.

Amid the happiness, Princess Alexandra realised that her mother shared her stressful awareness of the deep surge of change that now sprang from every decision. Princess Marina began talking of making another visit to Scotland, to Wick, to her husband's memorial on the Hill of Morven, and she was not to be dissuaded. Three weeks before the wedding, indeed, her vision of a family pilgrimage was fulfilled, with Alexandra and Edward. They all three flew to Wick and made their way on foot and by car, as before, into the hills and returned to London that evening, as if strengthened and reassured, and I believe that Alexandra made a point of telephoning Michael at Sandhurst that evening. At all events, this was one of the many days contributing to a new knowledge that she could never live far from her mother. "I'm in no hurry to marry," she had always said. "Mummy didn't marry till she was twenty-nine." But with Edward's marriage now so near, her own problems suddenly grew imminent and tangible.

The official announcement of the Duke of Kent's engagement to Miss Worsley was inevitably postponed until wedding plans could be decided in fuller detail. "I can't think of anyone nicer for a sister-in-law," Alexandra affirmed, and we have already glimpsed the instant spontaneity of their friendship. Visiting Hovingham Hall for the first time, the Princess had gathered from the daughter of the house that she would find a miniature resemblance to Kensington Palace, and she was not disappointed.

Katharine's family home was in fact designed by a Thomas Worsley who had been Surveyor-General of Works — including the royal palaces — in the year 1760 in succession to Wren and others, and the arts-loving Thomas evidently considered he could find no better model for his own home than what was then the principal residence of the King himself. The painted oval dome of the staircase at Hovingham is in the manner of Kent's painted oval ceiling at Kensington, among other features, and the dramatic vaulted entry of the Hovingham riding school — often nowadays used as a concert hall — derives in ground plan from Kensington's Clock Court. But there was more than this to intrigue Alexandra. On an early visit we hear of her lingering over the notable early harpsichord, admiring its walnut and marqueterie. Lady Worsley's drawing-room was also adorned by decorated panels only recently rescued from neglect in the family pub in the village, the Worsley Arms. Some of the set were by Cipriani, the Florentine who had painted the panels of George III's gold state coach, a pleasant ancestral rapprochement.

Both families were amused by the less harmonious note struck by the portraits of Oliver Cromwell, from whom the Worsleys are descended, and in the hint of Cavalier and Roundhead both sides half expected the press to note the parallel with Montagues and Capulets and comment on the happy ending for Edward and his Katharine. In this they were disappointed. One private suggestion was that the wedding should be fixed for May 8th, 301 years to the day since the proclamation of Charles II, but this date fell on a Monday with its obvious difficulties. It conflicted moreover with the Queen's State Visit to Italy and the Duke of Kent's announced visit to Sierra Leone, and the day was fixed for June 8th. Yet here, too, a stumbling block interposed. The Archbishop of Canterbury, Dr. Fisher, was retiring on May 31st. His successor would not be enthroned until June 27th. The inspiration of an interim wedding in York Minister dropped out of the clouds, an ideal solution, especially when it was agreed that the service could be conducted by both the Archbishop of York and the new Archbishop-designate of Canterbury, Dr. Ramsey. The only perplexity, of which most people were unaware, was the real and practical obstacle that York Minister was not licensed for weddings. One of the Canons correctly overcame this quibble by posting a cheque for £25 to the Faculty Office for a special licence, available "under special circumstances, for marriage at any place".

Although the press had so curiously overlooked the romance of a Cromwellian Romeo and Juliet, they were now quick to point out that this would be the first royal wedding in York Minster since Edward III had married his Queen Philippa in 1328. A son of that marriage was to gain immortal warrior fame as the Black Prince and, oddly enough, his bride in 1361 was a Countess of Kent.

V

Princess Alexandra wore azalea pink organdie for the Duke of Kent's wedding. The bride, now to be the new Duchess of Kent, wore an utterly lovely gown that gave an appearance of iridescent gossamer, an effect gained by some thirty layers of shining silk gauze built up from more than two hundred yards of material.

As a promising sign of the accord between Alexandra and her future sister-in-law, Katharine had gone to John Cavanagh on the Princess's suggestion. The Duke of Kent similarly consulted his sister in the dire masculine agony of deciding what he should suitably wear as bridegroom before the assembled concourse of two thousand guests and the untold millions watching by television. Few realised that the successful solution was in fact found when he applied for War Office permission to wear a uniform forty years out of date. The ceremonial uniform of the Royal Scots Greys, with scarlet jacket and tight blue trousers, with yellow stripes, had not been worn for full dress since just after the First World War, and bridegrooms seldom achieve such a romantic splendour.

Traditionists were equally happy to see the spaces of the Minster decorated with roses of York, untroubled by the reality that the roses were grown at the Blaby gardens in Leicestershire. It was said that no Yorkshire firm could grow sufficient under glass for the order.

The wedding reception at Hovingham Hall would have delighted the royalist Thomas Worsley and horrified Cromwell, for no fewer than three Queens and the heirs of six reigning houses were among the guests. Prince Michael had been a model of composure as best man, and now he was notable for his newly protective and charming attitude towards his mother. Princess Alexandra was in her element trying, however briefly, to talk to everyone she knew and to many more besides. The foreign royal guests alone can indicate to the reader the strength of her family nexus, for they included Queen Victoria Eugenie of Spain, the Duke of Gerona, the Count of Barcelona, Crown Prince Constantine and Princess Sophie of the Hellenes, Prince Harald of Norway, Princess Margrethe of Denmark, Prince Charles of Luxembourg, Princess Irene of the Netherlands, and there were also Prince and Princess George of Denmark, Prince Frederick of Prussia, Princess Ileana of Romania, the various royal Yugoslavs and the Toerring-Jettenbachs and Hohenlohes besides. Then there were Hamiltons and Ogilvys and Edens and O'Neills and Worsleys and Morrisons and Beresfords, and a dozen interesting bachelors, at least, among them. Alexandra and Tino were remembered by one guest eyeing each other like startled deer, and conversing dutifully and warily as ever. This may have been the first occasion when Alexandra ever saw Tino and Angus Ogilvy together, a challenging comparison, and for the first time she may have realised that the whirlpools of the heart had begun to course more steadily towards the predestined shore.

9: ANGUS

I

Shortly after her eighteenth birthday, Princess Alexandra designed a cypher for her notepaper of two A's entwined. The two initials owed something to the blend on her elder brother's notepaper of E and K, as well as to a device once used by Queen Alexandra, but Princess Alexandra used the two simply because they looked better than one, and it is a happy coincidence that they seem to stand for "Alexandra" and "Angus" today.

Yet Angus, as we have seen, was always there. Destiny merely set the scene in the years when his grandmother, Mabell, Lady Airlie, was Queen Mary's lady-in-waiting and one of her closest friends. Angus may have visited Badminton to see his grandmama when Alexandra was a little girl of between five and ten, hardly to be noticed by a schoolboy in his teens. His father, the twelfth Earl of Airlie, also contributed to the acquaintance, particularly in his ceremonial role of Lord Chamberlain to Elizabeth, the Queen Mother. Angus, who was born in London on September 14th, 1928, was eight years and three months older than the Princess and, during the war, he may have visited Coppins from his nearby prep school. But if the then schoolboy and the nursery child can identify any tangible memory of their first meeting, it remains too vague to be recorded.

A notable "miss" was in October, 1952, when Lord Ogilvy, the eldest of Lord Airlie's sons was married at St. Margaret's, Westminster, and Angus acted as his brother's best man. The bride was Virginia Ryan, whose American parents, as we have seen, were to entertain Princess Marina and Alexandra only two years later in New York. The Queen Mother, Princess Margaret and other royals were at the wedding and normally Princess Marina would certainly have attended it with Alexandra, permitting her to take a special day off from Heathfield School. But the then Duchess of Kent and her son were away on their Far East tour, celebrating the wedding with soft drinks in Borneo, and so Alexandra missed the festivities. She already knew the bridegroom, who indeed had visited Coppins one afternoon to give the Duchess some "inside gen" on Malaya, where he had served in the Scots Guards. She was also slightly acquainted with two of his sisters who, as officers in the Wrens, had occasionally been concerned with Service activities of the Duchess of Kent. Yet Alexandra felt closest at that time to the youngest Ogilvy, James, who had been at Eton with her brother, Eddie, and was but two years her senior, an appropriate dance partner at the Eton Beagles ball.

And then came that meeting with Angus at the August weekend party at Lady Zia Wernher's, when they played tennis and danced together and talked and discovered in one another the first sympathetic glow of friendship. Alexandra felt intensely young in comparison with Angus Ogilvy's apparently all-embracing knowledge of the world, and from the immense heights of his mid-twenties he treated her with a mixture of gentle raillery and considerate seriousness. Hearing that she was going to Canada, he affected mock concern at anyone so young travelling so far from home and, so the story goes, told her teasingly, "You're only a baby!" Just before her departure on the tour, he invited her to an impromptu cocktail party at his flat, a function she enjoyed so much that she naively asked him to invite her again when she came home. His response was to send her a mysterious bon voyage package which proved to contain a tiny teddy-bear. She took it with her to Quebec and still had it, flying over the Andes, five years later.

The complex personality, the experience, the mystery of Angus Ogilvy all intrigued her. He enjoyed bewildering her with puzzles; he had gone in for athletics at Eton, he said, "sitting down" and she was left to discover the answer that he had been in the school rowing eight and had rowed in one of the wartime Henley regattas. She knew from his grandmama that his great-grandfather had bred Aberdeen Angus cattle in Texas, but Angus's own experiences were no less surprising. He had stepped from school straight into his father's regiment, the Scots Guards, serving at first in the ranks. Then, from the Army, under the post-war rules, he had matriculated at Trinity College, Oxford, and in 1950 he passed with honours in philosophy, politics and economics. At this point, however, with one of the aberrations of adventure shown by successive Ogilvys, he resigned his commission, convinced that a more enjoyable life awaited him in the Merchant Navy.

Alexandra was incredulous when she heard that he had once been a ship's boy, and yet, as a friend said, "Knowing Angus, I expect it's true." Taking a bus to the docks, he had been interviewed by a string of equally sceptical officers until one of them signed him on as a cabin boy aboard an old freighter bound for Hamburg and ports in the Baltic. He happened to choose a time when the North Sea was lashed by the worst gales known for years. His ship rolled and creaked for over a week in the Thames Estuary, and when at last they made the crossing they had to queue for twelve days awaiting a Hamburg pilot. Throughout this storm-tossed period, Angus was continually seasick and, signed off somewhat abruptly, he returned to England convinced that the seafaring life held no personal future.

At the Savoy one night he probably astonished Alexandra by remarking that he had once worked there as a waiter. Then he explained: it was during the unofficial strike of 1946 that had divided the staff into two camps and Angus, on Army leave, had put in time as a volunteer. "But my career of promise came to a sticky end after only two days," he was to aver in public later. "I deposited an enormous omelette at the feet of an important customer." Angus was full of such tales, droll, unbelievable and yet accurate. "I was once a cattle-rancher in Rhodesia," he would claim. "Yes, it's true. I lived in a shack on porridge — one had to get up to start work at four." When Eddie was first bitten with the skiing craze, Angus, in his most mischievous tones, offered to teach him by virtue of being a qualified skiing instructor. "He can't have been," Alexandra is supposed to have said, though she, too, had now learned that whatever Angus said, though astounding, could be believed. Sure enough, the answer to this riddle was that he had qualified in Austria while with the Scots Guards. When the Princess subsequently discovered that he had commenced his career in the City as a £3 a week clerk to an insurance broker, licking stamps, she realised that it was in character.

Their friendship progressed readily, as the friendships of young people will, with no ingrained sense of direction or purpose, other than the companionship of the moment. With amusement, Angus has confessed how he first became "something in the City", something at least a step up from the office boy. Travelling by train to spend a weekend with his Uncle Bruce, he chanced to pick up and read a financial paper someone had left on the seat. At the houseparty, the redoubtable economist, Sir Roy Harrod, was a fellow guest and in the course of discussion Angus trotted out some of the arguments he had read in the train. Another of the guests,

Colonel Robert Adeane, offered him a job in the Drayton financial group at a starting salary of £600 a year and after that, Angus modestly claimed, it was all plain sailing.

It is not inappropriate that the Ogilvys should distinguish themselves in the tough battlefields of banking, insurance, property and the stock market, for they come of generations of fighting men. Gilbert, founder of the house of Ogilvy, swore fealty to the Scottish king William the Lion within a century of the Norman conquest of England and built the first towers of Airlie Castle. Four generations later, Patrick Ogilvy was the ally of Robert the Bruce, and the romantic exploits of other ancestors are to be found proudly listed by Mabell, Lady Airlie, in her memoirs. An Ogilvy led the Earl of Mar's army at the Battle of Harlaw in 1411, a Master of Ogilvy perished at Pinkie in 1547 in an epic stand against the English archers, and James, the first Earl of Airlie, received his earldom in his chivalrous if obstinate support of Charles I in 1639. His son was taken prisoner and sentenced to death, but rescued on the eve of execution when his sister visited him and they exchanged clothes. Another Ogilvy fought for the Stuart cause at Culloden, and through the centuries, there have been imprisonments, romantic elopements and battlefield deaths, even to Angus's grandfather, the tenth Earl (but for the attainder), who was killed at Diamond Hill in the Boer War. Among Scotland's premier earls, the Airlies rank close to the Strathmores, the Queen Mother's family. But Angus rarely talked of his ancestry, preferring to boast — the source of another of his eccentric though accurate anecdotes — that he was a godson of James Barrie, who was born on Airlie land at Kirriemuir.

In the early days of his friendship with Princess Alexandra, Mr. Ogilvy seems to have cast himself in a chivalrous role, a knight errant rescuing her from the dragons of solitude that are apt to menace princesses. One of his relatives remembers cinema parties of six to eight young people who went to the Odeon at Marble Arch, and afterwards the group, including Alexandra, would all go to eat fish and chips in the Lyons Corner House nearly next door. Then sometimes, if the night were young, they all trooped back with Angus to his flat for coffee.

At that time Angus had a bachelor home unique in Princess Alexandra's experience, a flat at 17 Park West, then the largest of the modern apartment blocks in the Edgware Road. No one who saw the Princess engaged in her royal duties, reviewing regiments, touring hospitals, could have guessed at the sense of liberation with which she sometimes escaped to No. 17. One can sense the pervasive magic for Alexandra in the taxi-rides from Kensington Palace in the autumn dusk or on summer evenings beneath the arching trees of the roads around Hyde Park. The third-floor windows of the flat overlooked the flowerbeds and fountains of a southern forecourt, and there would be a tang of adventure in crossing the entrance foyer and taking the little lift that opened ten paces from Angus's door.

Sometimes there would be a dozen young people in the flat, listening to Mozart records, or perhaps intent on some bubble of argument that Angus had skilfully poised for their amusement. "Arguing is to my mind one of life's most fascinating occupations," he once wrote to his grandmother, "mainly because it is perhaps the best way of formulating a wide mixture of ideas into one coherent whole. And arguing one soon learns those points of one's defence which are weakest, and then either one must strengthen those weak parts in one's philosophy of life, or abandon them for something better." Alone or in a group, Angus Ogilvy's discussions were heady stuff for the Princess, and probably for Angus, too. A neighbour noticed the young man, some evenings, eagerly opening his door every time the lift whirred. One likes to think that these were evenings when he was perhaps expecting the Princess Alexandra.

No doubt she was always eager to tell him her news, and especially to confide the comedies of royal occasions. At Shrewsbury a herd of Jerseys stampeded as her helicopter landed, and some of the cows wildly attempted to charge the visitant from space, creating an extraordinary mêlée for a royal arrival. At Walsall, a frail old lady was blown over on to the red carpet by the wind from the helicopter vanes, and the incident could be taken with light heart only because she came to no harm. Accidents were not always avoidable in the crowds. But one might mention that in Australia a woman was knocked off a makeshift trestle by the royal pilot car and later died of a fractured skull, and only a consoling letter from Angus, I believe, alleviated Alexandra's shocked distress.

In May, 1961, Her Royal Highness was appointed a Counsellor of State during the absence of the Queen and Prince Philip in Italy, empowered with another Counsellor to hold a Privy Council, give the royal assent to Acts of Parliament and sign a wide range of documents requiring routine signature. But this was a duty that the Princess regarded with the utmost seriousness and discretion, and Angus understood the need for his exclusion. On the other hand, he occasionally brought his work home and discussed it with her, especially when he sought a feminine viewpoint.

It was another symptom of his versatility that he at one time designed little houses to be built upon bomb sites; and as one of the junior members in the Harold Drayton group of companies, the conversion of old residential property into flats came under his wing. Alexandra herself rapidly became expert in reading architectural plans, and found it exciting on occasion to explore some rambling unoccupied Belgravia mansion with Angus and see it through his eyes, with rooms rejuvenated into new shapes, whole staircases replanned to save space, and attics transformed into a penthouse. More than the inexperienced Alexandra, Angus was keenly aware of their mutual attraction and gravely reviewed its implications. "If ever I get married, it will have to be someone like Alexandra," he told an old friend at about this time.

It appears probable that the young Scot was himself swayed for a while, by the Tino legend — the belief among older groups, steadily becoming more explicit, that Alexandra would marry Crown Prince Constantine and become Queen of Greece. In his early thirties, one detects the swing of the pendulum when Angus had begun to think of himself as an irretrievable, impregnable bachelor. "I'm too old for marriage," he is remembered as saying. "No girl can catch me." But meantime he could pilot the Princess around on terms of firm friendship. Indeed, after Edward Kent's wedding, the Duke's new matrimonial status increased the unbidden need among close friends of "rallying round". Both Princess Marina and her daughter naturally relinquished Coppins, which was henceforth to be the new Duke and Duchess's home. The Hamiltons promptly swept Alexandra off to Northern Ireland. Queen Juliana and Prince Bernhard invited her to Soestdijk, ensuring that agreeable male companionship was also at hand in the person of Prince Karl of Hesse. While Princess Marina similarly embarked on a programme of weekend visits, Alexandra also stayed with various of her old Heathfield friends and their husbands, including Captain and Mrs. Thomas Dunne, at Gatley Park.

Lord O'Neill was also among the house-party guests at the Dunnes and when, later on, he was also a fellow guest with Alexandra at the invitation of the Charles Morrisons on their island of Islay in the Hebrides, the press bayed at his heels. O'Neill had entered the picture at Eton with Edward, and occasionally enjoyed playing up to the reporters who wished him to "confirm or deny" the "rumours of an engagement". One may suspect that at Islay and elsewhere Angus was in the background. Earlier in the year all the Kents were conspicuous in the winter-sports group with the young King and Queen of Thailand at Gstaad, and Alexandra privately extended her holiday at St. Anton. Although his difficult knee precluded skiing, Angus was also, I think, at St. Anton that year. Not that his every absence from London was for Alexandra. Their companionship was frequently interrupted by his business trips to Spain and Portugal, New York and West Africa. For her part, Princess Alexandra was a guest on the royal yacht *Britannia* at Cowes and took sailing lessons to help maintain parity with Prince Michael, who raced the yacht *Coweslip* that year. She shared the fun of the royal party aboard *Britannia* on the cruise round the North of Scotland to Balmoral, and yet also found time to visit her Aunt Olga in Florence as well as her Toerring cousins in Munich and Sophie of Greece and other friends in Athens. And all this, in turn, was but the prelude to another royal tour... Princess Alexandra's conquest of the Far East.

II

It is tempting to suppose that Princess Alexandra had hoped to travel around the world before she "settled down". In the spring of 1961 it was announced that the Princess would visit Hong Kong in the autumn but by the time she embarked in her royally fitted-up Britannia airliner at the end of October a dozen extra invitations had lengthened her itinerary. Ahead now lay a 27,000-mile flying route via Vancouver to Hong Kong, then to Tokyo, Bangkok, Rangoon, Aden and Tripoli, and so back to London in time for her mother's birthday.

The esteem in which she was held by the King and Queen of Thailand had impressed Buckingham Palace, and I understand that royal advisers entertained no mental reservations on Princess Alexandra's visit to the Emperor Hirohito, the first approach of a member of the British Royal Family to the Japanese Royal Family since the war. Alexandra read up Japan all through the late summer. The signs were propitious, she learned, for in Shinto symbolism she was in the freshness of her third twelve-year cycle while the Emperor had begun his sixth such term and the date of his accession coincided, moreover, with the date of her birthday. Such portents were significant to her hosts. In Hong Kong similarly, facing a diverse and crowded programme, she arrived fully primed with knowledge of the stepladder streets, the sampan shops of Aberdeen, the trams and ferries. She had been forewarned that many of the Chinese in the streets might not know who she was, so swift is the influx of population, and she knew from her brother that the seaward views from Victoria rank among the finest in the world.

"I can't wait to look!" she exclaimed to the Governor's wife, Lady Black, immediately on arrival. And, drinking in the spectacular panorama from the tower balcony of Government House, she uttered the very words that ensure popularity for every Hong Kong visitor, "It looks like a picture postcard come true!" Before her first public engagement, the Princess held a press conference. She had come a long way from her first nervous wisecracking with the Australians. Many of the newspapermen were from Communist China; and though royal visits are usually ignored across the frontier in Kwantung, the activities of the Princess Elegant and Beautiful — Ngar Lai Sun Kwun Tzu — made the Communist front pages for the next ten days. When she first arrived, it was merely noted that "the children cheered her". Within three days, driving through North Kowloon, her car was mobbed by eager, applauding Chinese crowds, giving no hint of the riots six years later.

Much of her sightseeing was necessarily scheduled and prearranged: a visit to the fish market with its vintage purple-jelly eggs and pickled snakes, tea with a Chinese housewife in her one-room skyscraper flat in a housing development, dinner on one of the more sumptuous floating restaurants at Aberdeen. Chopsticks were attempted and laughingly abandoned for a toothpick. After church on Sunday morning, there was even an afternoon interlude of waterskiing. Receiving a Doctor of Laws degree at the University, she clowned a little when the floppy academic cap fell over her eyes, blindfolding her. "I've longed to see Hong Kong," she told the students, with an upward glance at her cap. "I've heard all about it from my mother and my brother."

As she got to know her way around, and took to nipping out of Government House with Moyra Hamilton for the shopping undertaken by every tourist, her detective grew concerned lest she should be engulfed in an over-enthusiastic crowd. Her fervent sincerity at every turn was, no doubt, the main factor that endeared her to the Asiatic people. Every royal lady wishes to seem herself but Princess Alexandra demonstrates this gift of self-portrayal in extremely human and everyday terms.

Near the Communist border at Lak Ma Chau, she walked up to the news cameramen and borrowed a long telephoto lens so that she might take her own pictures across the Sham Chun River of the paddy fields of Red China. She took a tram ride in Victoria for the sake of the harbour view, her sightseeing interrupted somewhat by the breezy camaraderie of five American sailors. Crossing the waters around the island, she had the use of the Commodore's launch with a naval escort. But after a morning reception at Kowloon she changed her chiffon hat for a coloured scarf and travelled back on the ferry with her party, little noticed among the lunchtime crowds, buying the tickets herself at the turnstile. And within forty-eight hours of this plebeian cruise she was engaged on the opening event of her State Visit to Japan, driving to the Imperial Palace in mid-morning in a horse-drawn state coach, wearing a satin evening dress of palest gold and a diamond tiara.

Angus probably did not miss the opportunity of teasing her on reading that her arrival in Tokyo had coincided with a slight earth tremor. Here, too, the press cascaded with welcome, stressing the importance of her visit in post-war Anglo-Japanese relations. On an evening visit to a theatre, where the audience applauded her, it was noticed that she did not omit to wave acknowledgment to the topmost gallery, and so the smallest of her gestures was hailed with the headline "The Pearl Princess Greets the Poorest". East and West do not always meet with such warmth and there was only one gulf that the Princess perhaps found embarrassing. At the weekend, the Crown Prince engaged her in the exclusive — but popularly resented — sport of netting wild duck. The birds are led to the hunters by domestic decoys; the hunters then trap the ducks in nets resembling lacrosse sticks and the flapping terrified birds are fortunate if they fail to break their wings before being killed. Unable to pretend that this was enjoyable, Alexandra released one of her birds and, prudently, would not pose for the cameras with the other.

Yet it would give a false impression to stress this single incident in a happy week. The crowds on the neon-lit Ginza cheered her cordially; the pearl-fishers of Toba kissed her hand, and the climax of this rather touching welcome brought a glint of tears to her eyes when Mr. Mikimoto — of the celebrated pearl company — presented her unexpectedly with a double string of cultured pearls.

The Princess had travelled to the pearl basins on the famous Kinsei express train and she then made a three-day tour of western Japan, with a weekend spent at the Emperor's country residence at Kyoto. Her itinerary ranged over industrial factories and Buddhist temples, modern medical centres and the seventeenth-century palaces and gardens that reveal the classic age of Japanese landscaping and architecture. Back in Tokyo, avenues were cleared for her through the enormous Mitsukoshi department store. The royal visitor's Christmas shopping, the curious noted, included kimonos, an 8mm cine-camera, three transistor radios ... and a toy bear. She went to a puppet theatre and one fancies she may have felt a kinship with the performers. As Eve Perrick, a traveller with her press group, summed up, "She must have been dead on her feet — but still came smiling through. She was subjected every day to a scrimmage of photographers seemingly thousands strong," and she moved everywhere "in a group composed of equal numbers from the British Embassy and the Japanese Ministry." Somewhere behind this mêlée was the true Japan.

Then, with the pleasure of a mission accomplished, she flew on to Bangkok. King Bhumibol and Queen Sirikit, now old friends, had completed an air-conditioned guest annexe to their palace in time for her, and understood her need for relaxation that would nevertheless furnish no lack of enjoyable memories. Two days were spent in the privacy of their seaside home at Hoa Hin, a day on a picnic in the coolness beside the Krachern rapids, and on a warm delightful evening they entertained her with the charming water festival of Loy Krathong, supping on the royal launch under a full moon, afloat on a mantle of drifting flowers while thousands of rafts of tiny candles gently sailed past them downstream.

This idyllic lull thoroughly refreshed the Princess for her State Visit to Burma, which was offered all the tokens of success from the enchanting and unusual greeting when her plane landed at Rangoon and small boys in the traditional dress of Burmese warriors dashed like squirrels among the welcoming officials. Next morning she was up before seven in order to visit and enjoy the beauty of the celebrated Shwe Dagon pagoda while the day was still cool. Later President U Win Maung gave a garden party in her honour and Princess Alexandra wore the wonderful ruby necklace he had given her, part of a set that included bracelet, brooch, earrings and rings. Her letters home confessed that she had caught a cold in Bangkok, but as my private memo noted, "Not one of her engagements was cancelled. She went to the huge war cemeteries of the Burma campaign, walking tirelessly up and down the paths... Returning from up-country, down the Irrawaddy, she was eaten alive by mosquitoes. 'They like me because I'm sweet,' she said... A ride to the pagodas in a decorated bullock cart must surely be mixed up in her mind by now with a visit by canoe to one of the stilt villages. She will soon have travelled round the world in 44 days, and she has shaken hands with about 30,000 people on the journey to date."

But Alexandra repeatedly told her hosts, "I will be back!", with a consistence explicable only in 1967 when she returned there with Angus. Looking back, one sees that she may have felt like a Somerset Maugham character, trying to decide her emotional problems in her own mind on the road to Mandalay. And I feel sure the answer became irretrievably known to her heart on the plane somewhere between Rangoon and Aden when, rummaging in her day luggage, she discovered that her lucky mascot had gone astray. Protocol was quite abandoned in her pleas back to the British Embassy in Burma to help her retrieve the teddy-bear which she last remembered seeing on the Irrawaddy river boat *Emerald Water*.

Lost or kidnapped, it was never found. The Princess allotted it no superstitious importance but was dismayed at losing something Angus had given her. Its loss seemed to reflect the desert landscape on the flight to Tripoli, but the aircraft also touched down at Wadi Haifa to allow time for a steamer trip down the Nile to see the temples north of the Aswan Dam, and she was soon her ebullient self. Then, at Tripoli airport, she had the fun of a rendezvous with Prince Michael who had a suntan equal to her own, gained on a Sandhurst training exercise in the mountains of Cyprus, and they chatted excitedly all the way home.

At Kensington Palace, Edward Heath, "Rab" Butler, Lord Perth, the Duke of Devonshire and other members of the Government were waiting to thank her for diplomatic services superbly rendered. Later, Angus was at the private family dinner party. This was surely the moment of truth that soon made her uncle, Prince Paul, hint unguardedly that he could not imagine Alexandra marrying anyone but a Britisher "and preferably a Scot". But Angus, who had only recently set up a new bachelor establishment by leasing a house in Culross Street, Mayfair, had not yet foreseen his date with destiny. And the Princess was due to fly off again almost immediately on another family reunion in Greece.

Her departure for Athens with her mother, less than forty-eight hours after returning from the Far East, in fact, considerably puzzled public opinion. Her aunt Olga awaited them both at the Villa Herodes Atticus, a mansion near the Palace used for Greek royal hospitality. Ostensibly this was a double celebration, a family reunion both for King Paul's sixtieth birthday and for the engagement of his eldest daughter, Princess Sophie, to Prince Juan Carlos of Spain. Princes and princesses converged on Athens from all sides. Moreover, in London and Greece, there swirled ripples of undercurrent rumour that the betrothal of Alexandra and Tino would be announced.

Whether by design or otherwise, King Paul contributed to this impression when he personally went to meet Princess Marina and her daughter at the airport. As if preparing public opinion, one Greek newspaper described the Court ball and singled out Alexandra as "the most beautiful there". With hardly less reticence, another journal asserted "If Paris — who stole Helen of Troy and was judge in a beauty contest among goddesses — were alive, he would have awarded the prize of beauty and elegance to Princess Marina, after having hesitated for a long time in favour of her daughter, Princess Alexandra." The well-informed were clearly aware that, on her impending twenty-fifth birthday, Alexandra would be free to wed whom she pleased without the previous consent of her cousin, the Queen of England. But Alexandra and her mother stayed in Athens only long enough for Tino to learn — probably much to his relief — that his cousin's thoughts were definitely elsewhere and, indeed, the travellers were back in Kensington Palace after only three nights' absence.

Glancing forward, it may be convenient to mention here that Alexandra's engagement to Angus Ogilvy was announced on November 29th, 1962. Seven weeks later, on January 23rd, 1963, the King and Queen of Denmark announced the engagement of their sixteen-year-old daughter, Princess Anne-Marie, to Crown Prince Constantine and we may notice the swift felicity of events. Tino and his Anne-Marie had first met at a dance given by King Frederick for his daughters in January, 1962, and the probability of their engagement was "leaked" in London just before Princess Alexandra's own betrothal was announced. "Our engagement was not planned beforehand by our parents," said Tino significantly. "It was the first time in my life that I took a decision without asking my parents."

III

The wedding of Princess Sophie of Greece and Prince Juan Carlos of Spain was anticipated as 1962's romantic royal event of the year, and Princess Alexandra sought permission of her cousin, the Queen, to become a bridesmaid. The bridegroom was Catholic, the bride Greek Orthodox, and Cupid with a sense of irony had fired his dart during the Duke of Kent's Protestant wedding in York Minster. Princess Sophie had accepted the invitation to Yorkshire, it seems, only at the last moment. Jean Dessès, her Paris couturier, was hastily asked by telephone for two dresses, the style and colour to be left entirely to his judgment, provided the order was ready within a week. But M. Dessès recalls that Queen Frederika warned him on the telephone, "If she's not the prettiest princess there, I'll kill you!", a well-intended threat putting him on his mettle. Protocol and the plots of Cupid did the rest by seating Sophie and Juan Carlos next to each other in the Minster. They had often met before, but Juan looked with fresh eyes at his companion and was won.

King Paul and Queen Frederika checked in at Claridge's with their daughters, Sophie and Irene, early in February and lunched at Buckingham Palace next day. The other bridesmaids were to include the Protestant or Lutheran princesses, Irene of the Netherlands and Benedikte and Anne-Marie of Denmark. Did the King and Queen fondly hint for the last time that Alexandra could readily be a bride in Athens as well as a bridesmaid?

The Dessès team came to London to fit Princess Alexandra for her dress. In ensemble with the other bridesmaids, this was to be in white with a high-waisted accordion pleated skirt and a wide palest yellow cummerbund with a plaited headband to match, while Irene and Anne-Marie wore cummerbunds of blue and pink. But if Alexandra had been the bride herself that May she could hardly have been more occupied in the busy gala atmosphere that mantled the courts of Europe. Queen Juliana and Prince Bernhard of the Netherlands literally opened the ball on May 1st with their silver wedding celebrations — deferred from January — when they took over the whole of Amsterdam's Amstel Hotel to house their guests. Queen Elizabeth and Prince Philip found themselves booked into a suite on the first floor next door to the Shah of Persia and his Queen, while King Frederik and Queen Ingrid of Denmark and King Baudouin of Belgium were just along the corridor, and Princess Marina and Princess Alexandra were allotted a suite on the floor above, close to King Olav of Norway, Princess Margaretha of Sweden and many others.

Indeed, after the opening dinner, a leading Dutch photographer could hardly retreat back far enough to focus all the hundred royalties posed for a group photograph.

Princess Alexandra was not responsible for the precedence that saw her escorted into dinner by Prince Karl of Hesse but, two weeks later in Athens, the Princess had her own reasons for not dissuading hints of romance, and the Reuter news service announced as from a palace source that at the royal ball Princess Alexandra and Prince Karl danced together "most of the time". On this occasion, in Athens, all the Kents, including Prince Michael, were booked into the King George Hotel which shared with the adjoining Grande Bretagne an unrivalled guest list of four kings, seven queens, thirty-two princes and forty-five princesses, not to mention the eminent lesser guests. Princess Alexandra found it fun to look from her balcony at the ovation given to Princess Grace of Monaco nearly next door, and seems to have thought that she was herself unobserved. But at the Catholic wedding it was Alexandra who noticed that the bride's train had become awkwardly tangled and was among the first to unravel it. And at the long, exhausting Greek Orthodox ceremonial — a superb spectacle in a cathedral decorated by thirty-five thousand roses — the professional observers agreed that Alexandra looked the coolest one there.

But we must hurry on from the wedding festivities, that royal jamboree of dancing and glamour and gossip, and record that, barely a week later, events placed Alexandra in another setting. Her duties took her to Sweden as part of the promotion of the British Exhibition in Stockholm and now, instead of the Aegean bathing party at the Asteria Club beach, Alexandra found herself with the King and Queen of Sweden in a receiving line for stolid Scandinavian businessmen, and instead of bridal toasts there were trade speeches in the Stockholm Town Hall. (The Princess had an alarming moment when she discovered that she had mislaid her brooch, Granny's brooch, a gift from Queen Mary, which was happily retrieved later by the major-domo.) And once again her personal popularity was explosive. "The most successful export Britain has sent to Stockholm has been Princess Alexandra," the *Daily Telegraph* reported. "The sombre, formal Swedes, who boast they can take royalty or leave it, think she is absolutely wonderful." But personally one need mention only one tiny incident contributing to this triumphant over-all effect. Outside a church, a small girl plucked at Alexandra's skirt and offered her a solitary columbine. The Princess accepted it as if it had been a State bouquet, inhaled its perfume and carried it for the rest of the morning.

Shortly after her return from Sweden, Princess Alexandra went into King Edward VII Hospital to have her tonsils removed, the answer to the recurrent throat infections that had troubled her for years. The flowers sent to the hospital included bouquets from Tino, who came to London at that time, and a certain "A", at whose identity we may guess if it were not proclaimed by the replacement teddy-bear that graced the dressing-table. The Princess then went to recuperate with her Aunt Olga in Italy, and from the Villa Demidoff she moved on, at Queen Frederika's earnest invitation, to join the Greek Royal Family in the summer sunshine at Mon Repos.

IV

It is hard to tell whether Alexandra was a superb strategist or whether sheer chance contributed to the final happy outcome of her heart's desire. Angus Ogilvy direly missed her whenever she was away that summer. One detects an inkling fear that his proposal, if refused, might spoil a perfect friendship. Family and friends are able to assess the truth only by after-events but apparently Alexandra had long hoped he would speak, and as the summer of 1962 turned to autumn his reserve *on the one point that mattered* grew miserably tantalising.

In October, Angus and Alexandra were both guests of the Queen Mother during a house-party at Birkhall, and their hostess probably divined the situation and ensured that the young people were left a good deal together. During a walk on the moors, it is said that Angus at last attempted, as calmly as he could, to put his problem into words. As one family chronicler has recorded, "he told her of the longing and indecision and to his delighted astonishment learned that it had been worse for Alexandra than for him!"

Bubbling with their secret, they drove to Princess Marina at Alt-na-Guithasach to tell her the news, and went on that same afternoon to see the Queen at Balmoral. Then Angus had to return to business in London, determinedly "beginning as he meant to go on". Apart from the Queen and Princess Marina, they still kept their betrothal to themselves, although they now wished to marry as soon as possible. The following weekend Angus arranged with his parents, Lord and Lady Airlie, that Princess Marina and Alexandra should be invited to Airlie Castle for lunch. Until that moment he had said nothing even to his own brothers but his happiness was self-evident in talking to his father and mother on the telephone. The small Georgian dining-table at Airlie is normally decked with five regimental Dresden figures — an officer of the 10th Royal Hussars, a Scots Guard, a Royal Archer and other statuettes, representing different stages in the Earl of Airlie's career — but now his mother saw to it that it was adorned with late roses.

"Angus is so much more thoughtful than other people," his old grandmama had once said, and now he characteristically asked permission of his parents before he produced the engagement ring, a large and lustrous sapphire flanked with diamonds, which for a time was still to be worn only in privacy. Typical of her own sweetness of character, Alexandra decided that the engagement should be publicly announced on November 29th, the anniversary of her mother's wedding day, thus once more bringing the grace of happiness to a day so long cloaked for Princess Marina only with poignant remembrances.

With his usual meticulous precision, Angus also had worked out a list of kinsfolk — aunts and uncles, cousins and the closest friends — whom he wished to alert ahead of the official announcement. "I'm calling because there's something I want to tell you," he telephoned his aunt, Lady Helen Nutting. "I'm engaged and I didn't want you to hear it casually. I can't give you her name over the phone but it will be announced on the six o'clock news tonight. We're terribly happy about it." He spent the morning conveying these hints from a room in Kensington Palace while Alexandra sat beside him, phoning her news in the same way, with a longish booked list of continental calls. And then, that evening, there came the announcement, "It is with the greatest pleasure that Princess Marina, Duchess of Kent, announces the betrothal of her daughter Princess Alexandra to Angus Ogilvy, second son of the Earl and Countess of Airlie, to which the Queen has gladly given her consent."

The phrasing was notable for its lack of "Highnessing" and the nation received it in their homes with precisely the same delight, enhanced by surprise, as the bulletin on Alexandra's birth nearly twenty-six years earlier. The Duke and Duchess of

Kent had meanwhile received the happy news in Hong Kong, and Prince Michael heard from his sister while he was again in Cyprus. Lord and Lady Airlie were already Princess Marina's guests at Kensington Palace, and that evening all their children joined Marina's dinner party — Lord and Lady Ogilvy, Mr. and Mrs. James Ogilvy and Angus's sisters and brothers-in-law: Lord and Lady Lloyd and Captain Iain and Lady Margaret Tennant.

It was widely noted that Princess Alexandra had driven her own Mini car to Buckingham Palace "to tell the Queen", which as we know was but an outward form to the already established family understanding. The Queen, in fact, gave her formal consent at a Privy Council meeting on December 19th. By then, in keeping with the eccentricity of events that have so often underscored her life, the Princess had again been in hospital, this time for a dental operation, and was once more back at home. Only a week or two before the engagement, an American writer had published a paperback in London under the title *The Secret Heart of Princess Alexandra*, romantically woven around all the young men whose names had been linked with the Princess in the gossip columns. But it had failed completely to mention Mr. Angus Ogilvy, and Angus could not resist the humorous impulse to carry it conspicuously, his fingers as if marking the pages, when he went to visit his fiancée in hospital.

V

Until the engagement, the public had of course never heard of the Honourable James Bruce Ogilvy, "34-year-old... Eton, Guards, Oxford, the City", as the *Daily Express* summed up succinctly. "Rugged" immediately became the best-favoured adjective for his handsome good looks; and it was made to seem apposite that Alexandra that December presented the prizes at the Royal Smithfield Show to a champion Angus named Black Bob. It was bewildering to those unaccustomed to City practice to discover that so young a man was director of twenty-nine companies, with interests ranging from tin to television, from Brazil to the Transvaal, through the gamut of property, electricity, garages, Anglo-Portuguese oil and Ashanti goldfields. It could be explained that Mr. Ogilvy was one of the "bright young executives" of Mr. Harold Drayton who, as in a fable, had commenced his career in a tobacconist's shop in Streatham and yet was now head of one of the largest groups of investment trusts in the City of London. Like Angus, he had begun at the bottom of the ladder and had succeeded in business by really trying ... rather as Alexandra had done in her royal career.

Perhaps, in public esteem, Angus was shadowed at first by the antibodies of popularity in his record: it was probably a handicap to favour that his father was a director of Barclay's Bank, that Lord Ogilvy was a managing director of the banking firm of Schroder Wagg and that his close business mentor, Sir Robert Adeane, was cousin of Sir Michael Adeane, the Queen's Private Secretary. The British caste system persists in erecting its own barriers of pompousness and circumstance; although it must be said that Angus seemed to be as blithely unaware of these hindrances as Princess Alexandra herself. In the New Year, for instance, he took the Princess along to the office staff party where, in the Paul Jones, she found herself dancing with the man whose firm supplied the office towelling and a young accounts clerk who irresistibly told her that *he* was getting married next day. To the delight of the press, she also met the office liftman who confessed, "Well, really I shouldn't be here — because I retired yesterday." To Fleet Street Angus also had the engaging American attribute of appearing to be available on the telephone. The curious quickly gathered at his office door in Broad Street, and he had replies to well-wishers and a disarming line in repartee. Moreover, it contributed to favourable public impressions that he seldom wore a bowler-hat in the City, but naturally wore the kilt at home in Scotland.

If one may say that the legends of the Glamis ghosts have contributed their mite of popularity to the Queen Mother's public following, we may note that Angus also had a background of Scottish folklore. There had been, for example, the Airlie drummer, beating his ghostly tattoo to herald the death of the head of the family. The fatal drumbeats were heard an hour or two before the tenth Earl died in Colorado, allowing for the difference in transatlantic time, and again in South Africa when all the sergeants' mess heard the beating of a non-existent drum the day before the eleventh Earl, Angus's grandfather, was killed in battle. Then, in addition, to strengthen the family ghosts, there was the "thing" in the Airlie Den...

Angus and Alexandra went up to Scotland a few days before Christmas to pose at Airlie Castle for a series of colour photographs, and the sun obligingly shone for them. The family home was now a very different establishment to the decrepit draughty house that had given the Ryans such pleasure and which Alexandra had first seen with her mother. When Mabell, Lady Airlie, died in 1956, the roof-timbers had been about to collapse and the main wall of the old castle was crumbling to ruin for lack of repointing. The new Countess of Airlie turned to her son for advice, and Angus drew on his architectural experience in helping her with its restoration into a comfortable family home.

Princess Alexandra in her visits shared vicariously in the flights of imagination that seemed to make all things possible. Leaning from the old dining-room window and glancing six feet down to the daisy-studded lawn, it may have been difficult to visualise Angus's proposal that this should be the new front door. In reality, it took no more than two short flights of steps to make it possible, and the old dining-room was transformed into a spacious entrance hall, while the old dark coved kitchen became a delightful new dining-room, enjoying the extra light of a window created in a former blank wall.

The purpose of every room had been challenged in this way before renovation, and now the young couple looked at the little castle with fresh eyes, keenly discussing what might be possible in some other house, that undiscovered dream house somewhere, when they created a home of their own. For the second time, betrothed and proclaimed, they went on their long walks, down the wide paths (created for a visit of Queen Victoria that never occurred) through the yew gardens where the clipped trees stand in the battle formation of Waterloo and, by another route, down to the little bridge across the River Meldrum by the thicket that from time immemorial has been called the Den.

That other Airlie ghost, that intangible "thing" manifests itself in an inexplicable sense of terror lurking in the Den, a sudden fear that has made dogs bristle and compelled grown men to turn and run. Old Lady Airlie described such an occasion in her memoirs when, walking there in the early evening, the haunting hour, her dog refused to go any farther and she herself was seized with a sense of unseen evil that made her rush away in panic. John Colville, a former secretary to the present Queen, has testified to being overwhelmed with terror "impossible to describe" and Princess Mary, without knowing the legend, was once seized with an inexplicable fear and horror of which she refused to speak for days. And yet, to round off the story, Princess Alexandra and Mr. Ogilvy often wandered there without being troubled, and that's as it should be, for the "thing" is said to be powerless against people in love.

Angus was also a guest at Sandringham for Princess Alexandra's twenty-seventh birthday anniversary and the last Christmas of his bachelor life. The Queen delighted in hearing them shape their marriage plans and, indeed, contributed a few ideas of her own. She wished the glass coach, for instance, to be romantically drawn by four royal greys, though only a pair had drawn the coach at the weddings of the Queen and her sister. The Princess proposed making a bride's list of appreciated gifts available at Harrods, and the Queen evidently thought it a good idea although, royally, it was an innovation. (When ultimately drawn up the list comprised a green Celadon-pattern Wedgwood dinner service, contemporary Chinese lamps, white garden furniture, a roulette set, bathroom scales, even an ironing board and heat-proof oven dishes.) But above all the Queen contributed her ideas for the entertainment of the wedding guests and mentioned to Alexandra that she would like to give a dance at Windsor. As Her Majesty's enthusiasm seized hold, the plan developed into a State Ball, the night before the wedding eve, which proved to be the largest party held at Windsor Castle for more than a century.

Anyone who saw it will never forget the sumptuous effect of the Waterloo Chamber with its portraits bowered in flowers, and the brilliant and beautiful oval of guests around the gleaming floor, looking indeed like the splendid throng depicted in a watercolour of an early Victorian ball in that very room. The dancing was preceded by a family dinner party and a reception; there were the alternating bands of Joe Loss and the Life Guards' strings — with pipers of the Scots Guards for the Scottish dancing. Princess Alexandra wore a gown of snow-white, and most of the two thousand guests did not disperse until nearly four in the morning.

The Court Circular next day glittered with a rare list of the names of the royalties and others who had arrived at the Castle: "The King of Norway, the Queen of the Hellenes, the Queen of Denmark, the Queen of Sweden, Queen Victoria Eugenie of Spain, Queen Helen of Romania, the Crown Prince of the Hellenes, the Crown Prince of Norway, Princess Irene of the Hellenes, Princess Anne-Marie of Denmark, Princess Irene of the Netherlands, Princess Margriet of the Netherlands, the Princess Hohenlohe-Langenburg, the Prince and Princess of the Asturias, the Margrave and Margravine of Baden..." and many more. The day before the wedding, the Queen and Prince Philip kept this illustrious household amused by piling them all into two motor-coaches, the kings and queens, princes and princesses, and sweeping them all off on a sightseeing tour around Windsor and along the Thames Valley to an exuberantly merry luncheon party at the Hinds Head at Bray.

That night Angus dined with his parents and his best man, Mr. Peregrine Fairfax, at Claridge's, while Alexandra quietly stayed at home with her mother, although her chief bridesmaid, Princess Anne, came to tea. On that last unmarried evening in Kensington Palace, Princess Alexandra had cause to review the happiness that rippled all around her. Her sister-in-law, Katharine, now had a little son of ten months, the apple of Alexandra's eye as well as his mother's, and both Edward and Katharine had flown home from Hong Kong, where the Duke was posted, so that her brother might give her away. It was only a month since young Prince Michael, too, had been gazetted, as he hoped to be, into the Royal Armoured Corps Regiment, the 11th Hussars, and Alexandra planned to return from her honeymoon in time for his coming-of-age. To turn in thought to her Aunt Olga's family, her cousin, Elisabeth had married an American and had two baby girls, the second barely four months old. Her cousin, Prince Alexander, was equally the proud father of twins; and the six-year-old daughter of her Toerring cousin, Ann — the little Princess Elisabeth of Austria — was to be a bridesmaid. All the family life around Princess Alexandra coalesced in new patterns, and now her own love for Angus opened the enchanted doors of the future.

10: MRS. ANGUS OGILVY

I

Princess Alexandra tenderly incorporated into her wedding dress bridal keepsakes of both her mother and grandmother. John Cavanagh was briefed to design a dress around a cherished piece of Valenciennes lace which Princess Nicholas had worn at her wedding in Imperial Russia, and he commissioned a French weaving firm to create a fabric of the same mellow tone and traditional detail, making only the length he needed for the gown and train and not an inch more. The original lace itself was used to edge the long head-dress which was in turn held by the train worn by Princess Marina as a bride. Layers of tulle, silk net and organdie created a stately yet simple effect over a slender high-necked gown, and a lace pattern of oak leaves and acorns flecked the sleeves in accordance with Princess Alexandra's wish for a touch of English symbolism. The bridesmaids' dresses were magnolia-tinted and, of course, the choice of bridesmaids and pages embodied the affections of both bride and bridegroom.

Apart from Princess Anne, her hair worn "up" for the first time, and little Princess Elisabeth of Austria, the bridesmaids included Lady Zia Wernher's granddaughter, Georgina Butter, and Angus Ogilvy's two nieces, Emma Tennant and Doune Ogilvy, Lord Ogilvy's elder daughter, while the pages were Doune's eldest brother, David, and young Simon Hay, son of Sir Philip Hay. The public read these names with acute curiosity leavened by puzzlement, perhaps discovering that despite the familiar public image they knew little in reality of the bride's private life. Yet it demonstrated the general enjoyment of her wedding that a Lyons Corner House dubbed two dishes Steak Ogilvy and Sole Alexandra, just as it was recognisably in character that the Princess visited Lyons' chief bakery to inspect her five-foot-high wedding cake and asked for miniature bagpipes to be added, modelled in icing with Ogilvy tartan ribands. And among the royals and the noble families in Westminster Abbey, the diplomats from every land the Princess had visited and the representatives of all her "organisations", the typical gesture was noted that the Princess had also invited her customary chain-store saleslady from the Marble Arch branch of Marks and Spencers.

On her wedding morning April 24th, Princess Alexandra glanced from her window at Kensington Palace to find clusters of local onlookers already gathered, and a sky darkening with hints of rain that were happily unfulfilled. Enthusiasts had camped overnight in the Mall, some bedded down with sleeping-bags, nearly all with transistor radios tuned for the weather. Those who stayed at home watching by television shared the close-up views seen on monitors by most of the two thousand Abbey guests: the royal processions from Buckingham Palace and the approach of the bride and her brother by car from Kensington, the Princess being one of the few brides ever to exercise the royal privilege of riding under the Wellington Arch. The Lord Chamberlain's office having been at some pains to indicate that this was a civil and not a State wedding, the Princess's own vicar, from St. Mary Abbots, Kensington, assisted the Archbishop of Canterbury in the ceremony, whereupon some complained that the gorgeous vestments of the Abbey clergy far outshone the morning dress of the bridegroom and the royal dukes.

The Princess promised to "obey", and instead of the hackneyed Wedding March she preferred Widor's gay Toccata in F which she had heard at her brother's wedding. Television lip-readers assert that she murmured "I love you" to her husband as they walked down the aisle. Whether this was true or not, the patient street crowds had their own ample reward when they saw the fairy-tale spectacle of the bride and groom in the glass coach, that fragile and charming vehicle, drawn by the four trotting greys, with the escorting pageantry of the Royal Horse Guards, burnished and jingling alongside.

The reception was held in the State Apartments of St. James's Palace where, owing to anxiety over the weight-bearing hazards of the old floors, a limit of five hundred guests had been fixed as the bounds of safety. A mix-up occurred with these more privileged invitations and both Angus and Alexandra had to do a great deal of telephoning and apologising before the wedding to sort out the muddle. But weddings will always go well; the royals were a little less royal when they all returned to the Palace doors in Friary Court and the white glare of the television lights fixed to enable the world to watch the "going away". The Queen of England stepped on the King of Norway's toes, Charles of Wales staged a duel of confetti and rice with Juan Carlos of Spain, and the skirl of the bagpipes tactfully blanketed the eavesdropping microphones.

Recent royal brides have presented a diversity of departures for their honeymoon, by special train, by the royal yacht gliding down the Thames, but Angus and Alexandra sped to London airport in a limousine decorated with tartan ribbon and a baby's shoe. There, where Alexandra had begun so many journeys, crowds were waiting at every entrance, craning from every public balcony and enclosure and the cheers for the wedded couple drowned the roar of the police outriders' motorbikes. A Heron aircraft of the Queen's Flight stood waiting, but at the last moment, the bride and groom received a representative of the great crowd of reporters and photographers. "Now the ordeal's over," said the Princess, "we do want to thank everyone for being so kind."

Two hours later, Queen Ena of Spain dreamily remarked to Queen Helen of Romania, "Now they will be at Birkhall!", but one might have expected Alexandra's honeymoon journey to have an unforeseen interlude. Fog diverted the plane from Aberdeen airport, close to Deeside, and they flew into Lossiemouth naval air station eighty miles away. The station commander's wife, Mrs. David Kirke, was preparing for a dinner party when her husband telephoned the startling news that the hero and heroine of the day were arriving at the airfield, and probably at her doorstep, within minutes. With Service aplomb, Mrs. Kirke turned down her cooker and was in time to join Captain Kirke on the tarmac as the Heron landed. The honeymooners almost tumbled out of the plane, delighted at this surprise development.

Captain Kirke suggested a drink at his house, perhaps dinner, and they gleefully accepted the first invitation but politely demurred at the second, and so it came about that while the Royal Family imagined them basking before the log fires at Birkhall, Alexandra and Angus were enjoying champagne and sandwiches in a little granite house at Lossiemouth, and giving the captain's arriving guests the surprise of their lives. At about half past eight someone remembered that a tele-recording of the wedding was on television, and the couple could not resist settling down to watch it, holding hands. Eventually the Princess said, "I can't bear it! It's too wonderful!" and Angus suggested, "I think we should go." By this time the news of their arrival had spread and hundreds of people lined the airfield approaches. It was nine-thirty before they left in the borrowed car and nearly midnight before they reached Birkhall.

Both in the calm of Deeside and in the sunshine of Spain, near Marbella, the newly-weds enjoyed a honeymoon free of intrusion. "It's probably the one and only time we will be able to have a private holiday for the rest of our lives," Angus had said, gloomily, in envisaging life with royalty. Only when they flew home at the end of May were the photographers waiting again, outside 10 Culross Street where the Ogilvys planned to settle in for a few weeks. The press boys are always optimistic and their vigil was not in vain. That evening smoke poured from the kitchen windows and Mayfair was disturbed by the clamour of fire engines. The fire was no more than the smoke and charring of an overheated refrigerator, and Angus and Alexandra only heard of it by telephone while they were dining with Princess Marina at Kensington Palace. But it provided an anecdote in true Alexandra style for the beginning of married life.

II

Seven miles south-west from the busy heart of London herds of fallow deer graze peacefully over the two thousand acres of Richmond Park and wild herons can still be seen patrolling the fishponds. Few cities can boast such a rural sanctuary at their gates, and Richmond Park is in fact the largest royal park in Britain. King Charles first enclosed it as a royal hunting ground in 1637, and some forty years later a lodge with a thatched roof was built as "an abiding place" for the keepers.

Mr. Angus Ogilvy originally took Thatched House Lodge in March, 1963, on a five-year lease from the Duchess of Sutherland. Despite his expertise, he and Princess Alexandra had discovered the pangs of house-hunting, during their engagement months, when they inspected houses in Mayfair, Chelsea and Berkshire. The Queen suggested a grace-and-

234

favour residence in Kensington Palace but both Angus and Alexandra favoured country air, bearing in mind future family prospects. The Princess first saw Thatched House Lodge on a wintry day when a wonderful gust of warmth greeted her in the entrance hall. She had been enticed by the rural approach road, charmed by the guardian figure of Hermes on his plinth and enchanted by the fine scrolled iron gates of the little forecourt. Then she climbed the sweeping staircase to the main bedroom and was captivated by the view from the big bay windows, reminiscent of the vista from Airlie Castle, south across the lawns to the wooded glens of the park.

Slightly to the right, to the west, in a heather-clump, there even stands an old thatch-roofed white-plastered summerhouse, not un-Scottish in effect. This is, in fact, the 240-year-old gazebo from which the main house derives its name. Though one of the oldest houses in Richmond Park, Thatched House Lodge itself is also one of the most modern. A room adjoining the entrance hall still has its seventeenth-century oak beams exposed, and may be part of the original "abiding place". Princess Alexandra knew that Queen Mary and the Queen Mother — her grandmama and her Aunt Elizabeth — had once been tenants of White Lodge barely a mile away, where Nelson had traditionally sketched the battleplan of Trafalgar with his finger, dipped in wine, on a tabletop. But Thatched House Lodge in World War II had been occupied by the American High Command, hence the admirable central heating, and some of the strategy of the Allied invasion of Europe had been sketched on a baize table there. General Eisenhower's own suite of rooms at the western end of the house, Princess Alexandra at once noted, would make a wonderful guest wing for her mother or the Airlies ... if not a superlative nursery.

Angus rightly balanced her enthusiasm with sterner considerations. If they settled into the house, it remained problematical whether they could acquire the 55-year-term of the Crown head lease. Was it perhaps too large? The house boasted six bedrooms on the first floor, four with bathrooms, and a suite of five reception rooms ran across the southern garden face of the house. To the right of the large double drawing-room lay a small sitting-room and an erstwhile conservatory room. To the left was a library in which a wall of leather-bound books, ominous histories of Greece and Rome, folded away to reveal an inviting bar. Beyond this again was the dining-room, panelled and intimate.

When Angus and Alexander first viewed, some of the Duchess of Sutherland's furnishings were still in place, including perhaps the comical life-size china piglet that long presided in the main bedroom. In addition to the bachelor furniture from Culross Street, the young couple mentally placed their wedding gifts: the circular Sheraton library table from the Durham Light Infantry, the Dutch walnut china cabinets from the Junior Red Cross, the Tai Ping carpet from Hong Kong, the Chippendale kneehole writing desk from the County of Angus, the Chippendale Gainsborough chairs from the Association of Men of Kent, the especially touching gift of a mirror from the Commonwealth Society for the Blind, and so many, many more. Everything fitted well and the lease was promptly signed.

The Princess spent hours of happiness arranging and rearranging her new possessions when they moved in that mid-summer. They debated whether the conservatory room could be converted into a patio, particularly when considering a sheltered nook, not too much in the sun, for a pram. And soon after their return from Spain the question of the baby-carriage was paramount, for the young couple knew that their happiness was to be complete, if all went well, early in 1964.

III

Princess Alexandra once disarmingly described herself and her husband as the world's two luckiest people. "Everything always goes right for us," she said. It has always seemed to me highly characteristic that whenever she takes friends on to the little balcony of the thatched summerhouse to show them the prospect over the Thames Valley, she appears oblivious of what one visitor called "a hideous sprouting of pre-fabs with corrugated-iron roofs" in the foreground. And no doubt an equal note of allegory can be found in the sheltering of other unsightly elements in the view by the growth of a young plantation, the Prince Charles spinney, which was mostly planted by the Crown Estate Commissioners in 1952, the year in which the Princess first commenced public duty.

Among the other amenities in its four acres the Lodge enjoys a small swimming pool, with a sunbathing shelter and with changing rooms conveniently near in the summerhouse, and through the summer and early autumn of 1963 this became a pleasant focus point of the newly-weds' hospitality. The Queen Mother came, keeping to herself her own daunting early-married memories of the Richmond fogs. Princess Olga of course saw the house at an early stage, amused to find there was even a family cinema, converted from a squash court by the Duchess of Sutherland: what a luxury it would have seemed to the film-minded Foxy if she had still been alive! As at Airlie, some of the finest views are from the former servants' bedrooms at roof-level, and the more intimate friends among the early house-warming visitors were invariably ushered to a vantage point up the attic stairway. The garden tour similarly always included the gazebo, for where else can one step into a summerhouse and find two rooms with rococo decorations painted, if not by Angelica Kauffmann, at least by her Venetian husband, Antonio Zucchi?

Under an earlier tenancy, in George VI's reign, thieves had broken in one night and ripped one of the glued canvas panels from the plaster. This might have served as warning that Thatched House Lodge was not then on the electronic warning system of other royal residences and such a safeguard, early on in her marriage, might have saved Princess Alexandra a fright.

On a misty November night, shortly after dinner, she chanced to go upstairs to her bedroom … and disturbed a man in the act of rifling her jewel-box near the window. It all happened in a flash, her stentorian screams, the flurry of the curtains as the man disappeared, leaping into the darkness, and her husband's terrific rush up the staircase. His first fear was that she had fallen and hurt herself and, while the staff searched the grounds, precious minutes had to be lost while Angus telephoned the police. The intruder had evidently entered the house through a bathroom window and may indeed have been concealed for a time in one of the huge wardrobes in the first-floor corridor.

The greatest distress to the Princess, however, came in ascertaining all the sentimental treasures that were missing. On their wedding day, she had given Angus a watch, inscribed "A to A" and set in a twenty-dollar American gold piece, and now it was gone. On the dressing-table before dinner, Marjorie, her maid, remembered seeing the brooch which the Princess had been wearing that day, a cabochon, ruby and diamond brooch, given her by Princess Olga and it, too, was gone. So also was the gold pencil inscribed with their wedding date, which

Alexandra had given her husband, and her mother's wedding gift to him of a set of ruby buttons and cufflinks.

Now they all had to be coldly listed and described for the police and insurance assessors: Item, One gold cigarette case inscribed "To Angus from Elizabeth and Philip"; Item, One pair of pearl and diamond cluster earrings; Item, One pearl and diamond tiepin; Item, One sapphire, diamond and gold bracelet... This last was a gift to Alexandra from her mother, and later it was found that her wonderful Mikimoto cultured pearls, two other pearl necklaces and a snap-on diamond bracelet, had also disappeared. But what worried the Princess was the thought of alien hands pawing her treasures and, worse, the thought that the intruder had been lurking undetected in the house. She felt that she could not stay there alone at night, even with the staff or with guests, listening for every unfamiliar sound, and to enhance her fears Angus was due shortly after the burglary to take a weekend business trip to Spain. Despite her six-months pregnancy the Princess decided to go with him.

This set a novel problem in protocol for B.E.A. Mr. Ogilvy had booked to fly tourist to Paris by British European Airways in a first-and-tourist class plane, and naturally the Princess was also booked to travel tourist-class with her husband. With an ingenuity worthy of a Feydeau farce, the airline got round that one by declaring the whole plane tourist, refunding the fares of the two or three "first" passengers and then by seating the touristic Ogilvys in what had been the first-class cabin. A nonchalant eye was turned on overweight baggage. Travelling home by Iberia, the Spanish airline, the 72lb excess baggage was assessed at £13 but, an official explained, the charge was made only if a plane was full and the surcharge was waived.

Meanwhile the police investigation of the robbery had concentrated on the unusual configuration of the ruby in the brooch from Princess Olga, and Princess Alexandra returned home to the welcome news that, some at least, of the jewellery had been recovered. A man was in fact found guilty of receiving the ruby at the Surrey Quarter Sessions two months later, but another five months passed before a stolen suitcase containing a few of Mr. Ogilvy's possessions was found in a clump of bushes on the South Downs and the affair seemed at last to be at an end.

A question that the young couple had not foreseen also exercised the public mind as Princess Alexandra prepared for her baby. This was the problem of whether Mr. Ogilvy should have a title, an absurd and irrelevant question to Angus, a source of both sympathy and fun to the Princess, and a possible embarrassment to the Queen. When Her Majesty conferred the dignity of an Earldom on Mr. Antony Armstrong-Jones, the announcement had been greeted with a curious mixture of pleasure and derision. One now knows that Princess Margaret's husband had been disinclined to accept ennoblement but the controversy recurred in full measure around Mr. Ogilvy.

As the younger son of an earl, he was entitled to the prefix of "Honourable" and an editor of *Debrett* worked it out that he stood in precedence above the eldest sons of baronets. But otherwise it was incontestable that no legally married princess in British history could be remembered to have had an untitled husband and it was widely suggested that Mr. Ogilvy had at the least refused a peerage. My information is that the topic was never discussed, except in deft supposition and delicate nuances.

IV

A remarkable house-party ushered in the New Year of 1964 at Sandringham. For the first time there were four pregnant royal ladies under one roof, an oddity unmatched even in the great baby race of 1818, when four of George III's daughters-in-law vied in producing a prospective heir to the throne. In that year of hope, the ultimate winner was the Duchess of Kent, mother of Queen Victoria who was known for many years as Princess Alexandrina of Kent. In 1964 our own Princess Alexandra was more advanced towards maternity, and inevitably endured more secret trepidation than the others.

The Queen was expecting her fourth child, who was born on March 10th at Buckingham Palace, the present Prince Edward. Princess Margaret was anticipating her second, the girl baby of May Day, Lady Sarah Armstrong-Jones. The Duchess of Kent equally was looking forward to her second child, who arrived on April 28th, the little Lady Helen Windsor. All these three mothers-to-be tried to reassure Alexandra, whose natural disquiet in first motherhood could not be entirely soothed by her nursing experience and careful preparation. Following her sister-in-law Katharine's example, she had attended a specialist clinic for relaxation tuition, and in the choice of her obstetrician, Mr. Ian Jackson, professional colleagues were aware of his noted skill in caesarean sections, a useful stand-by asset. Alexandra's chief anxiety was, however, disposed of at an early stage on learning that she would not be having twins. It was only a few months since Prince Alexander of Yugoslavia and his wife, Maria Pia, had jubilantly announced their second set of twins, as a vivid reminder that there was a predisposition to twins in the family.

That February, when Sister Angela Commings, the Middlesex Hospital superintendent midwife, moved into

Thatched House Lodge, she found her patient "very happy about it all". The calculated date of February 16th passed without event, and now it was the father-to-be's turn to be anxious. Angus had promised his wife that he would not leave her, that he would be there, indeed, at the bedside. "I hope I don't faint," he said. The nagging thought was unavoidable that the baby would be born thirteenth in succession to the throne, and another thirteen days passed before, in the thirteenth hour, the young parents' hopes came true.

Just after midday on February 29th, the Princess gave birth to a nine-pounds six-ounces son, and Angus was indeed at the bedhead that morning, in surgical mask and overall, to administer the inhalant mask and, above all, add his own encouragement. The announcement of this hefty baby was in time for the Saturday evening news bulletins, and the news-angle of the Leap Year's Day baby born to the Christmas Day Princess made a wonderful line for the Sunday papers. Princess Marina had driven down from Kensington in good time. Mr. Reid, the gardener and his wife, went in "to wet the baby's head" from their adjoining cottage. The photographers hoped to see Angus and he could not resist sending out the reply, "Mr. Ogilvy is resting". But characteristically and almost unnoticed next day, he quietly went to morning service at Westminster Abbey to give thanks before the altar of his marriage.

A new figure now moved into the Lodge in the person of Miss Olive Rattle, a middle-aged, sensible children's nurse who had been recommended as a nanny by Viscountess Melgund. The young mother, she found, had equipped the nursery to perfection except for a rocking chair, a shortcoming Nurse Rattle no sooner mentioned than Angus went personally to a local furniture store to buy one. Her new charge was only ten days old when the advent of Prince Edward safely removed him to the fourteenth in line of succession and, shortly afterwards, the Ogilvys announced that they had chosen the names of James Robert Bruce.

The new baby was christened on May 11th at Buckingham Palace by the Archbishop of Canterbury. Appropriately, Master James was the first infant baptised in the private chapel since the bombing, and his mother, one remembers, had been the last British princess christened there before its destruction. Now her son wore the same Honiton lace christening robe, reserved for Queen Victoria's royal descendants, before the same lily font from Windsor; and the main difference imposed by time and happiness was that the baby also wore its own dress of embroidered white lawn, a token made as a labour of love for Princess Alexandra at a hostel for disabled workers in South London.

It is on record that the infant slept through most of the ceremony, unperturbed by his unusually high quota of seven godparents. Besides the Queen, the Duchess of Kent, Prince Michael, Lord Ogilvy, Mr. Peregrine Fairfax, who had been best man at the wedding, and Lady Rowley, Angus's cousin, the then Prime Minister of Australia, Sir Robert Menzies, was a sponsor by proxy, a unique personal tribute in Commonwealth relations.

A sister for James was born on July 31st, 1966, at Thatched House Lodge, in the golden light of the summer evening. As before, Mr. Ian Jackson, Sister Commings and Mr. Ogilvy himself were in attendance, this time for a seven and a half pounds Sunday child, full of grace. The Queen was an early visitor and the first to hear that the names proposed were Marina Victoria Alexandra. Miss Marina Ogilvy was a guest at Airlie Castle when only four weeks old. The King and Queen of Thailand hovered about her cradle when she was a babe of only two months and King Constantine of Greece gave a dinner party at Claridge's in her honour on the eve of her christening: the cause of the celebration, of course, being absent and safe at home in her cot. At the christening itself, in the almost medieval setting of the Chapel Royal, St. James's Palace, her twenty-month-old brother may be regarded as the principal guest, although Princess Margaret and the Prince of Wales were among the sponsors.

The Archbishop of Canterbury officiated, noticeably handling the fragile Victorian christening robe of these occasions as tenderly as the fist-waving baby. But the venue of St. James's Palace is normally reserved for the outer circles of the Court, and so one may deduce that the Queen acceded to Princess Alexandra's desire to identify herself in a different private and personal status as the Hon. Mrs. Angus Ogilvy rather than in her strict precedence as a member of the Royal Family. One may recall that Princess Margaret's daughter, Lady Sarah Armstrong-Jones, was christened within the enclosure of the private chapel at Buckingham Palace, and that the daughter of the Duke and Duchess of Kent, Lady Helen Windsor, was received at the font at Windsor Castle. Little Miss Ogilvy, having been hatched, was thus placed as her parents wished in the same slot of prestige as their wedding reception.

11: THE BALANCED LEDGERS

In balancing the ledgers of happiness, through the fifth year of her married life to the accounting date of the present time, we may find Princess Alexandra experiencing a deep and sacramental sense of thankfulness. We may discover it "drawn up to the best of our knowledge and satisfaction" on a drowsy summer afternoon in the garden of Thatched House Lodge, when the Princess sits checking through the daily sheaf of letters, and her mother sits with her drawing board making a sketch in pastel of little Marina, while the roguish young James pores over his toy farmyard on the grass. Or the double line of contentment is explicit on an early autumn evening when Alexandra hears the arriving purr of her husband's car and greets him at the door, full of news of the children or the day's events. The couple are as eager for this exchange as when they were first married, and the Princess can detect the mischievous glint when Angus has some droll or surprising item of office news or perhaps brings home some unexpected picture of her in the latest editions of the evening papers.

We see Princess Alexandra now in her early thirties, while her husband is young enough to feel a twinge of incredulity at finding himself at the gate of his forties. For them both, this married pair, marriage has brought the serene happiness they expected, coupled with a fuller life than either had dreamed possible. Neither had anticipated that the opportunities of the royal round could be shared so equally, with such a mutual enrichment of experience. Neither had realised that they could both contribute to the royal task without loss to their private need for relaxation and the pursuit of happiness: in their case chiefly the pursuit of happiness for others.

A generation ago, a Princess of the Realm could not have walked with her children in Richmond Park, pushing a pram, without running a gauntlet of watching eyes, but now local folk politely pretend not to notice. Alexandra's grandparents, King George V and Queen Mary, could not have visualised royal patronage of a vaudeville performance held in a local cinema on a Sunday evening; but the Ogilvys needed only to know that the performance was in aid of cancer betatron equipment for a hospital, and the Princess attended with her husband without arousing a wisp of Sabbatarian animus or losing a jot of royal dignity. Far from retiring into their matrimonial status, Alexandra and Angus have formed a new widely recognised nucleus of philanthropy and enterprise. Angus takes it for granted that his now not inconsiderable private income should foot the bill for benevolent sidelines, and he has curtailed his directorships while increasing his voluntary activities. In buying a second-hand ten-year-old Rolls-Royce, it was explained that it would prove cheaper than constant car hire fees for public engagements, and probably few had realised until then how frequently Angus Ogilvy's own funds also underwrite the Princess's official functions.

If the theory is true that the monarch personifies the people, Princess Alexandra precisely demonstrates this concept in her own supporting role. She can be identified as a suburban housewife while remaining — with the Queen, the Queen Mother and Princess Margaret — in the active first four of royal duty. She still represents the Queen at a Commonwealth occasion at Westminster Abbey, or deputises cheerfully for the Queen Mother, and even Prince Philip has opted her at times for less suitable tasks, such as opening the International Boat

Show. Mr. Ogilvy has taken up a skilful, and only occasionally equivocal, attitude in defining his attendant status. As a rule, he is available to share the Princess's engagement only outside business hours, unless a discourtesy to a foreign Head of State or indeed to the Queen might be involved. The rule, though neither firm nor binding, is observed whenever possible. On one occasion the Clothworkers' Company entertained his wife, his mother-in-law and himself to luncheon in the City of London. But he was correctly back in the office soon after three.

The guiding committee at Buckingham Palace seldom considers the everyday trivialities that build the ultimate popularity of a royal figure. The prestige of Princess Alexandra was enhanced early in her married life when she was seen buying a five-shilling cookbook, *Learning to Cook* by Marguerite Patten, and when she was espied shopping for lamb chops and frozen peas in Barker's food department. Inspecting a Territorial field kitchen, she drew on her housewifely experience and chanced to comment, "I think electricity is very difficult to cook with. Now with gas you can switch it off and it goes off." The incautious critic gained only public sympathy when she was compelled to submit to the demonstration of an electric cooker in her own kitchen.

Simultaneously the Princess was inundated with what Angus called "lethal catalogues of expensive kitchen equipment", and in a speech at a catering exhibition he pretended to deprecate "this culinary exploitation". But even his occasional speech-making burnished the image, giving the impression of a married couple living at unextravagant average levels. At one of the Commonwealth-relationship receptions which Princess Alexandra so often attends, the occasion gained news value when she wandered up to the buffet chef and enquired, "Where *do* you get your sausages?"

There was a phase when American magazine editors invariably expected me to stress the domesticity of the Hon. Mrs. Angus Ogilvy "inviting her husband's business friends home to dinner, expertly able to converse on the percentages earned by angels or theatre backers or the prospects of new hotels in Sardinia". Democracy would suffer, I was instructed, by hinting that theatre angels might be an equally fascinating topic for Princess Beatrix and Claus von Arnsberg when they were entertained at Thatched House Lodge before their engagement, or in mentioning that the hotel entrepreneur was the Aga Khan. When Prince Albert and Princess Paola of the Belgians were guests one Saturday night, a French republican newspaper chose to suspect a deep-laid City-Congo plot rather than the mutually spellbinding topic of babies and child welfare.

The atmosphere of cosmopolitan hospitality long associated with Kensington Palace has taken on new vitality at Thatched House Lodge. The King and Queen of the Hellenes (Tino and his Anne-Marie), the Shah of Persia and his Queen Farah and the King and Queen of Thailand come and go. Princess Chichibu of Japan was a natural visitor when she came to Britain, warmly eager to hear honeymoon news of Lady Moyra Hamilton, who had recently married one of the Queen's naval equerries, Commander Peter Campbell. No doubt the motherly Princess Chichibu had divined Alexandra's own romance on her first visit to Japan, and Angus was all the more welcome when he visited Japan with his wife in the late summer of 1965. As at Kensington, the entertaining at Richmond has often reflected the hosts' wide-travelled interests; and amid the table-talk of Jordan, Burma, the Shan States and Cambodia, it is little wonder if Angus and Alexandra have come to be regarded as the Royal Family's Middle East and Asian social experts.

If, in addition, showbusiness and theatre management are conversational catalysts, it is because Angus is a governor of the Mermaid Theatre. As an angel he has disarmingly confessed that the first show in which he ever put money came off after one night, but he was also a reputed backer of *Lock Up Your Daughters*, the twice-revived Restoration comedy that handsomely recouped all investments.

II

On the debit side of her marriage, Princess Alexandra has had to assess the longterm effect of the tensions inseparable from public life, and especially the nervous strain on her husband in sharing royal activities. Angus was reported to have lost fourteen pounds in weight during his first year in the limelight, an indication that even a husky ex-rugger player may lack the stamina of a working princess in standing up to the adulation, fevered attention and incessant conversation showered upon the royal celebrity.

Mr. Ogilvy's predisposition to gastric troubles soon seriously worried his wife and he was slow, I think, to consult doctors. In his twenties, he had been a practising member of the Christian Science Church for a time, and its teachings lingered. Besides, every appeal and invitation that came his way was a challenge to his compulsive energetic temperament, an obligation that seemed even to involve the quality of his marriage. One realises — not without a curious sense of affront — that Princess Alexandra could have elected to retire into almost complete privacy after her wedding, and given her minor place down the scale of the succession, the precedents of earlier royal marriages suggested the probability. In that event, her son would have had his name put down for Eton when a month old, as it was; her husband might have become a Court chamberlain, like his father, and Princess Alexandra would have faded in our memories as an arch-type of the nineteen-fifties, becoming no more than a minor royalty opening very minor bazaars.

Instead, it has all been different. Instead of repudiating their share on the royal treadmill, Angus and Alexandra helped to keep it spinning, working incessantly behind the scenes with preparations for future engagements, even when the arc-lamps of public attention were switched off. Although one recognises the implicit rewards of the royal treatment, it remains apparent to everyone that the Ogilvys have convinced themselves that they could not do too much in return.

As an honorary financial adviser to Centre 42, the trades union cultural group, for example, Angus began working over the financial statements at home at night. He has equally tended the accounts of the Friends of the Poor, sponsored the top committee work of the National Association of Youth Clubs and was often inclined to retreat from the garden over the weekend, saying, 'I'd like to work for an hour". Claiming that sleeping was a waste of time, he had been known to set an alarm clock for five a.m. to enable him to get through his homework before all the business or social duties of the day. But there was a phase of nerves in the second year of his marriage when he twice dinted his Jaguar in minor traffic collisions; and after his health had much alarmed his wife one weekend, the doctors persuaded him to enter hospital for a check-up.

When this occurred, Princess Alexandra was due to fly off to Lancaster for the long-prepared ceremony of her installation as the first Chancellor of the new University, and she only had

time to visit her husband at St. Mary's Hospital and make sure
he was comfortable before going on to the airfield. (One
recalls that among the honorary degrees she handed out while
worrying about Angus was a Doctorate of Laws conferred on
Mr. Harold Wilson.) Happily the doctors found nothing
seriously wrong and prescribed only a spell home from the
office for a week. But the difficulties of his health persisted and
in January, 1965, Angus had to be peremptorily ordered to take
a long rest.

III

Mr. Angus Ogilvy's idea of a rest was a winter sports holiday at
St. Anton, in the Arlberg, but his doctor's advice also gave him
an unexpected bonus of time — time off with his wife, time
when they could do as they wished, enjoying a second
honeymoon. They had in fact planned a brief holiday some
weeks earlier, but now they cancelled their plane reservations
and took the car. In the wan January sunshine they motored
across France and into Switzerland, stopping where they
pleased, in hotels almost deserted at that time of year. At St.
Anton they booked into the Pension Haus Staffner, where as a
tyro skier Alexandra had once decorously entertained Angus to
lunch. But the carefree quality of their return was interrupted
by a telephone call, and if Angus had told his doctor that a rest
was something "easier said than done", so it proved, for the
Princess and her husband interrupted their holiday to return
home for the State Funeral of Sir Winston Churchill.

This was a mark of respect they both wished to observe
although, amid the sadness, they were to receive a sharp and
untimely reminder that the fringe annoyances of their position
could extend to kith and kin. Thieves had rightly counted on
every member of the family being at the funeral and selected a

vulnerable victim in Angus's younger brother, James, who returned home from St. Paul's to find that his house had been ransacked and cherished jewellery was missing. It surely ranked among the meanest thefts of the year.

When the "rest cure" was resumed at St. Moritz — partly to satisfy an urge Angus had to try out the improved Cresta run — the holiday again had to be interrupted for Princess Alexandra's programmed visit to Belfast to launch the New Zealand frigate *Waikato*. But this showed what was possible. They celebrated young Master James' first birthday, inevitably with the gift of a teddy-bear, and then were off again. The formula of phases of leisure alternating with high-pressure duty periods has long been observed by the Royal Family, but the Ogilvys tested and gave it a fresh interpretation for themselves.

Like many born islanders, Angus had but to cross the Channel to experience a liberating, invigorating ease of spirit, and he found that his dyspeptic symptoms did not accompany him abroad. The Ogilvys spent a short holiday in Paris (not omitting to visit the Duke and Duchess of Windsor) and they joined Princess Margaret and Lord Snowdon in Sardinia. Airline hostesses checking their flight-lists found that "Mr. and Mrs. Kent" or "Mr. and Mrs. Butler" were to be recognised as "Mr. and Mrs. Ogilvy" whenever Princess Alexandra accompanied her husband to Spain, Portugal and Genoa on business trips. Their roles in the royal set-up were however officially shared for an overseas visit in September, 1965, with the announcement that they were to fly to Tokyo to attend the British Exhibition.

This privately fulfilled the hopes Princess Alexandra had cherished since her first visit, to share the beauty, exotic novelty and ever-surprising excitement of the eastern scene with Angus. Now she could display the splendours of the

Hong Kong view as it had been stored in her memory, once again at Government House under the aegis of Sir David and Lady Trench. Her second visit to Tokyo was to see another visit to Emperor Hirohito in his extraordinary palace, and the same swaying dense swarms of sightseers, the unfailing battery of cameras, the receptions and inspections, the quality of fantasy in the walk through the shrines and temples of Kyoto. On her first visit she had preferred not to try the adventure of shooting the Hozugawa rapids, but with Angus, in a craft part-canoe, part-raft, she could squeal happily, clinging to her man, like any girl on the big dipper. And like any young married couple enjoying the thrill, both stepped ashore and exclaimed, "We will come back. What a thrill it will be for our son when he gets bigger!"

From Tokyo they flew to Teheran to be entertained by the Shah and his Queen; and from this wonderland, in October, they arrived in Amman, the capital of Jordan, to be guests of King Hussein and Princess Muna. That friendly young monarch had arranged four days of intensive sightseeing, from the holy places of Jerusalem and Bethlehem to the rose-red rock city of Petra, the extraordinary Roman ruins of Jerash, the King's beach house at Aquaba and, not least important, his own new contemporary dream house in the mountains at Hummar, nearly ready for occupation and in the last stage of furnishing.

In reviewing the shared vistas of their marriage, Alexandra and Angus look back already over all these changing scenes, still almost too close for biographical record. "Do come and see Alexia!" Queen Anne-Marie had said, in the winter of 1965, and in the New Year they were both in Athens, not only to coo over the chubby infant of whom Tino and Anne-Marie were such proud parents, but also to confide Alexandra's own new-discovered hopes of having another baby in July. Oddly enough, Princess Alexandra's absence from public life for the advent of Miss Marina Ogilvy was little noticed, so thoroughly did she fill her engagement book before and after her retirement for this happy event.

One might mention that Angus was also nearly left holding the baby in another, less secure sense when the crisis of Rhodesian oil supplies brought the elements of his private and business life into unexpected conflict. He happened to be one of the three British directors on the board of the Anglo-Portuguese firm controlling the oil pipeline from Mozambique to Rhodesia, liable to be outvoted by the five Portuguese directors but equally liable to be fined or imprisoned or both if the oil were set flowing in face of the embargo imposed by the British Government. For the public, the interest in the situation lay in considering how the Queen's cousin-in-law would behave: would he resign to avoid the risk of punishment or would he indeed go to gaol? Amid these cliff-hanging perils, Angus kept his head and his common sense until the issue was withdrawn into the care of the United Nations.

IV

Both in 1966 and 1967, the observer can discover brief periods when Princess Alexandra was undertaking more public royal engagements than anyone else. The New Year's Day of 1967, for example, fell on a Sunday. On Monday the 2nd, Mr. Ogilvy was back in his office as usual, on the 4th the Princess set out in her Rolls to visit a home for the disabled and the following evening she and Angus attended the Charles Chaplin film premiere in aid of charity. These voluntary unpaid duties were hardly onerous, and the Princess would wish to repudiate any impression that she is more readily or frequently "operational" than any other member of the Royal Family. Yet the essence of popularity is that the royalty shall be seen in action, preferably in praiseworthy activities approved by the bulk of the people; and later in the same month Princess Alexandra was seen to be fulfilling engagements in Leicester, Edinburgh and London while the guns were still barking at Sandringham.

The following month Alexandra and Angus left on their first joint overseas tour, commencing with a visit to Burma at the invitation of General Ne Win, the head of state. It was characteristic that they were received and seen off at London Airport by a great mustering of officials and yet travelled on a scheduled flight as ordinary first-class passengers. From Rangoon they flew on to Hong Kong, and then spent what was called a private visit to Australia both in Canberra and Sydney as guests of the Prime Minister, Mr. Holt.

This journey in turn was a prelude to the astonishing centennial tour of Canada in May and early June when, within a month, the Princess and Mr. Ogilvy travelled from coast to coast and north to the Arctic Circle, taking in Toronto, Victoria, Banff, Calgary, Edmonton, Whitehorse, Yellowknife, Jasper, Regina, Brandon, Winnipeg, Ottawa and Montreal. The Princess began by opening the International Trade Fair in Vancouver and ended with their visit to the wonders of Expo 67, and the tour surprisingly contrived to blend the purposive goodwill of the monarchy with the exuberant enjoyment of two likeable people.

The calm restful journey home on the *Empress of Canada* was, of course, a necessity, for in the autumn they were scheduled to set out again, this time on a journey embracing New York, Minneapolis, Dallas, Houston, Washington and the crowded events of a British week in Toronto. From every journey, moreover, the Princess has returned, effervescent and unspoiled, to plunge with little respite back into the perpetual round of hospitals and schools and old folks' homes, pressing buttons and unveiling plaques. "They'd much rather have Elizabeth Taylor or a TV star," she is supposed to have said, "but the TV people all charge fees, I hear. Ah, well, I may not be as pretty as a pop star but at least I'm free!"

Rueful, witty, self-deprecating, the remark has been widely quoted, and authentic or otherwise it sparkles with its sharp-cut facet of the honest truth. While photogenic princesses are in short supply, Princess Alexandra will continue to oblige, to the last smiling handwaves, the last packed minute on the programme, and more, continually polishing the silver legend that she thinks of as her own tiny contribution to the lustre of the Crown.

THE PATRONAGES, ETC., OF H.R.H. PRINCESS ALEXANDRA

Her Royal Highness is Patron of:
Alexandra House, Newquay
The Ernest Read Music Association
The Girls' Venture Corps
The Scottish Girls' Training Corps
The Guide Dogs for the Blind Association
The Light Infantry Club
The London Association for the Blind
The National Association of State Enrolled Nurses
The National Birthday Trust
The National Florence Nightingale Memorial Committee of Great Britain and Northern Ireland
The National Heart Hospital
Queen Alexandra's Royal Naval Nursing Service
Royal Alexandra Hospital for Sick Children, Brighton
The Companions of the Royal Commonwealth Society
The Twentieth Century Group of the Royal Overseas League
The Royal Soldiers Daughters' School, Hampstead

Her Royal Highness is Vice-Patron of:
The Young Women's Christian Association

Her Royal Highness is President of:
The Children's Country Holidays Fund
Queen Alexandra's House Association
The Royal Commonwealth Society for the Blind
The Star and Garter Home for Disabled Sailors, Soldiers and

Airmen

Her Royal Highness is:
Vice-President of the British Red Cross Society and Patron of
the British Junior Red Cross, the Canadian Junior Red Cross
and the Australian Junior Red Cross.
Royal Patron and Air Chief Commandant of Princess Mary's
Royal Air Force Nursing Service.
Colonel-in-Chief of The Durham Light Infantry and of the
Queen's Own Rifles of Canada, and Honorary Colonel of
The North Irish Horse.

Her Royal Highness is an Honorary Yellow of the
Royal College of Physicians and Surgeons of Glasgow, and of
the Faculty of Anaesthetists of the Royal College of Surgeons
of England.

Her Royal Highness holds the Honorary Degree of
Doctor of Laws of the University of Queensland, Australia,
and of the University of Hong Kong.

ACKNOWLEDGEMENTS

In a recent Mass Observation survey undertaken over a balanced cross-section of the community, Princess Alexandra of Kent was placed close behind the Queen and Prince Philip as a "favourite royal person". This book began as an enquiry into the phenomenon of her popularity, its origins and persistence, and inevitably the theme developed into a full-scale biography, so far as one may use that term in writing of a young and contemporary personality.

Former neighbours of the Kent family at Iver, Bucks, kindly devoted their time to assisting my accuracy in writing of Princess Alexandra's childhood at Coppins and I would wish to acknowledge my sense of obligation to Lady Spens, the former Miss Kathleen Dodds, in drawing on her Heathfield reminiscences. My indebtedness to a member of the Greek Royal Family for background material may be apparent and I particularly wish to express my thanks to the helpful officials of the Greek Royal Embassy in London for providing further information from Athens on points of detail. Though only briefly quoted, I must also make it clear that the copyright in material from royal journals and letters is reserved.

I also gratefully acknowledge brief incidental quotations from *Thatched With Gold* by Mabell, Countess Airlie, published by Hutchinson, *Not All Vanity* by Baroness de Stoeckl, published by John Murray, and *Crowded Life* by Lady Cynthia Colville, published by Evan Brothers. The present Viscount Simon very kindly checked through his father's diaries for me; the officials of Aslib most courteously made me welcome at 3 Belgrave Square, and I should also like to express particular thanks to

the secretariat of the High Commissioner of Canada in
London; to the library and press personnel who helped me at
Australia House, and to officials at Nigeria House and the
Hong Kong Government Office in London.

HELEN CATHCART
1967

A NOTE TO THE READER

If you have enjoyed this book enough to leave a review on **Amazon** and **Goodreads**, then we would be truly grateful.
The Estate of Helen Cathcart

Sapere Books is an exciting new publisher of brilliant fiction and popular history.

To find out more about our latest releases and our monthly bargain books visit our website:
saperebooks.com

Ingram Content Group UK Ltd.
Milton Keynes UK
UKHW020729100723
424846UK00018B/593

9 781800 555174